The Robert Burns Songbook

for Guitar and Voice

Volume 2

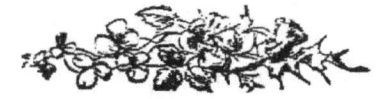

The Robert Burns Songbook
for Guitar and Voice
Volume 2

By Adrian Allan

Edited by Allan H. Jones

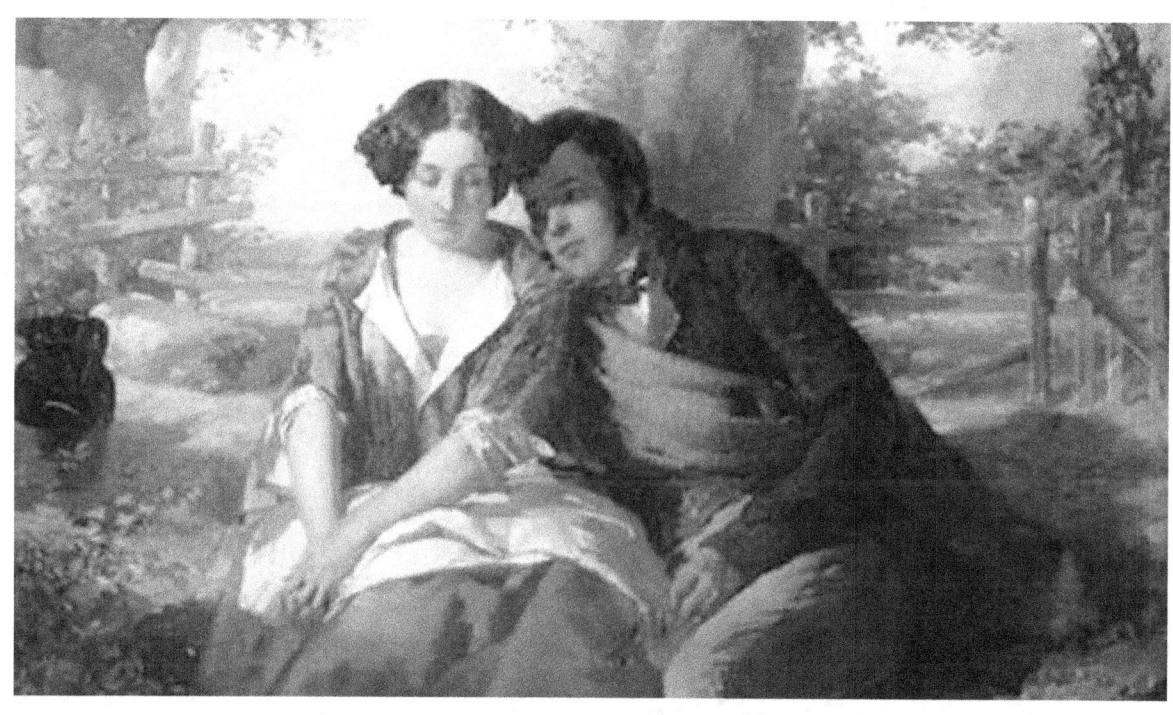

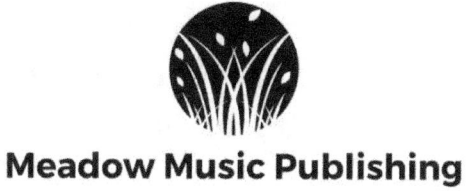

Meadow Music Publishing

First Printing: 2017

ISBN 978-0-244-00548-1

Meadow Music Publishing
23c Burford Road
Manchester, M16 8EW

Tel: 0161 881 2997

www.juliealford@btinternet.com.

www.facebook.com/meadowmusicpublishing/

Front cover illustration:
Burns and Highland Mary by Thomas Faed (1826-1900)

Other illustrations from The Songs of Burns by J.K.Lees

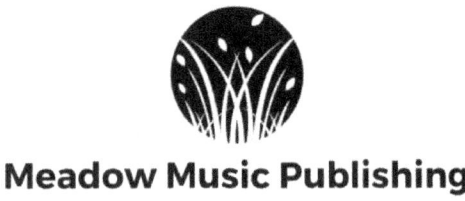

Meadow Music Publishing

Adrian Allan Website:

Meadow Music Publishing:

Dedication

This book is dedicated to Hannah, Eleanor and James

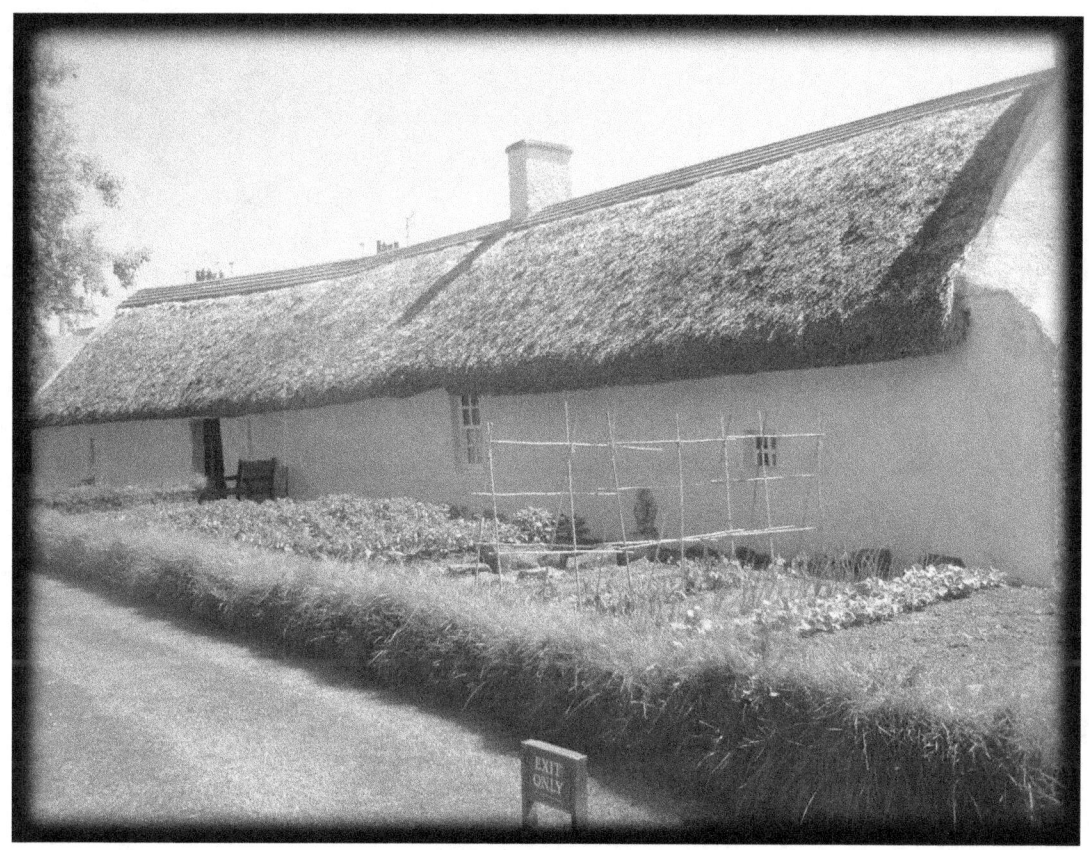

**The cottage where Robert Burns was born,
Alloway, as it stands today**

Contents

Further Information/ Reproduction of Documents

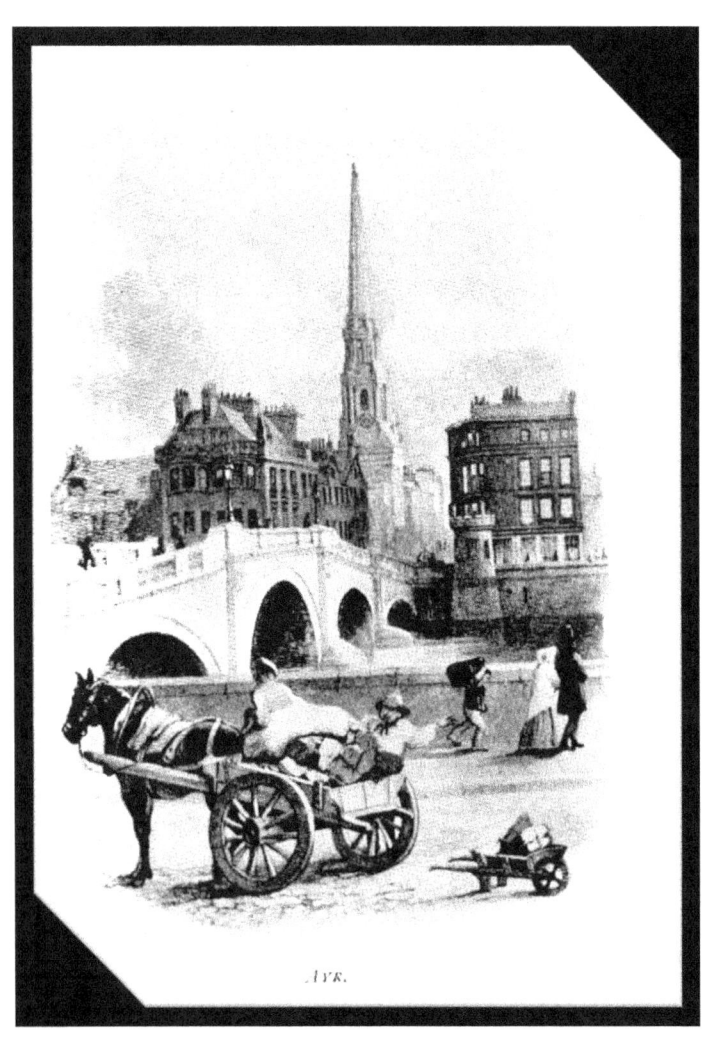

Preface

Since the release of volume one of this book in April 2016 I have been looking for Burns songs that would be worthy of inclusion in a second volume. There are perhaps forty or so songs that are still regularly performed, and hundreds more that languish in obscurity. I have included in this book a selection of popular songs and a few that are less well known but deserve to be rediscovered.

For my sources, I have used a number of piano scores from the Victorian period onwards, and have tried to reach a solution that is idiomatic for the finger style guitar. I have also consulted the Musical Museum, the six-volume collection that consolidated Burns' reputation as the foremost collector of traditional songs of his era.

What is fascinating for any researcher of folk music is how the melodies for these songs have in many cases completely changed over time. It has been a long-held belief that popular songs passed partly by the oral tradition tend to gradually change, or evolve. However, with many Burns songs, once a new melodic setting gains popularity, it tends to completely replace its predecessor as the favoured version in books and in performances.

Ae Fond Kiss, to take one example, has changed no less than three times; the melody that is currently sung is erroneously believed to be that which Burns originally used. In fact, the original version is completely different in both character and time signature. I have included two versions in this book for comparison, and perhaps the vague hope that an earlier version may regain some popularity. I have provided two versions of *There Was A Lad Who Was Born In Kyle* for the same reason.

Tablature has been used to widen the appeal of the music to guitar players who do not read conventional notation, or who need some assistance in finding the notes in the higher positions. As in the first volume, guitar chords are included, but they do not always precisely match the harmonies of the guitar accompaniment, particularly when the harmonic movement is rapid; too many strummed chord changes can sound disjointed, so a compromise has often been reached.

There is, I hope, a good balance of guitar styles and music; from rippling arpeggios, to more sedate contrapuntal accompaniment. The constant aim was to be sensitive to the mood of each song, and provide a musical background that supports the singer, but never detracts from the richness of the melodic line.

The key signatures were arrived at with a consideration for the needs of the guitar, and to accommodate the range of most singers. Some songs feature a D-tuning, shown by the symbol (6) = D. This means that string 6 is re-tuned to D, an octave below string 4. Some songs will be more of a challenge than others for vocalists, but they all lie within a reasonable range.

A quarter of the works in this book are love songs written for the women in Robert Burns' life, and between them, they certainly awakened the romantic sensibilities of the poet. It therefore seems fitting to include summaries of the lives of Jean Armour, Mary Campbell and Agnes Maclehose.

I hope that this second volume continues to renew interest in some of the most beautiful and enduring songs in Scotland's musical heritage.

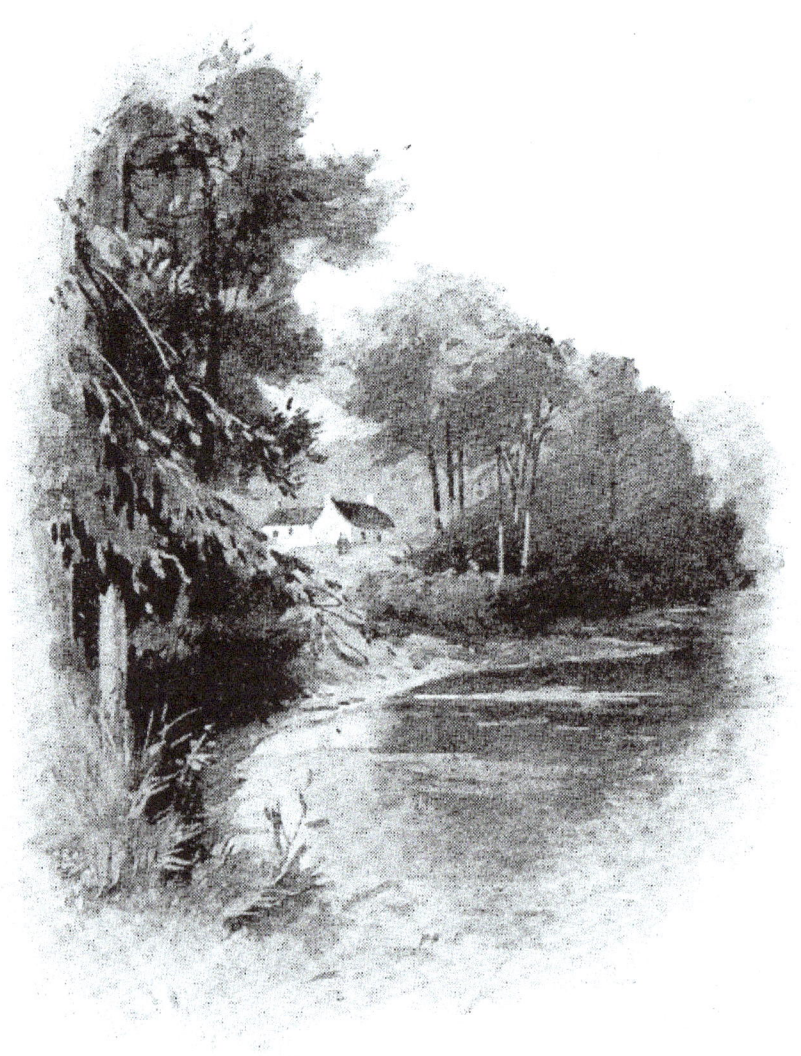

ELLISLAND.

Jean Armour

Jean was born in Mauchline, Ayrshire, and was the second oldest of eleven children. She first met Burns around 1784 on the occasion of a country dance. According to tradition, a collie dog followed burns around the dance floor and he remarked, "I wish I could find a lassie as fond of me as my dog".

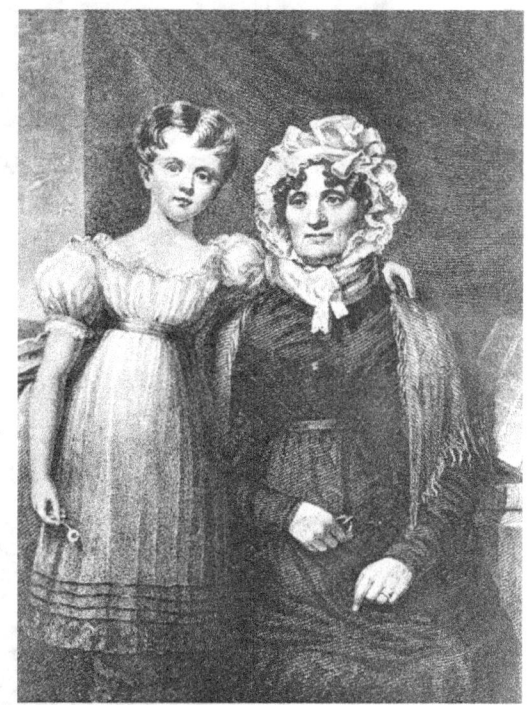

Not too long after, they met again on the village green at Mauchline and Jean asked if Robert had yet found, "a lassie to love ye as well as yer dog?" This brief exchange seemed to have marked the start of their relationship.

By 1785, Jean had fallen pregnant with Burns' child, and this was met with great disdain by Jean's father, the stonemason James Armour, to the extent that Jean was sent to Paisley to prevent local scandal. Both Jean and Robert eventually admitted to the birth of their child outside of wedlock at Mauchline Kirk.

The kirk session (which dealt with moral issues and minor offences) records:

Rev[eren]d sir I am heartily sorry that I have given and must give your session trouble on my account. I acknowledge that I am with child and Robert Burns in Mossgiel is the father. I am with great respect Your most hu[mbe]ll serv[ant] Signed Jean Armour Machline 13 June 1786.

Jean remained with her parents at Mauchline, and Robert stayed at the farm in Mossgiel. They did not live together until the birth of their twins in 1786. It was only after the success of Burns in Edinburgh that James Armour allowed his daughter to wed Burns, and their eventual marriage was registered in 1788.

Jean and Robert had nine children together, the last of whom was born on the day of his funeral in July 1796. Jean lived until 1834 (aged 68), and during that time, she saw Burns' popularity spread across the world.

In recent times, the Burns club of Dumfries started a campaign for a statue of Jean Armour. The fund reached £30, and this resulted in a statue of one and a half times the approximate life size of Jean. The design features Jean Armour as she would have appeared during the lifetime of Burns, with Bible in hand and accompanied by a small child. The statue was unveiled in September 2004, to great acclaim.

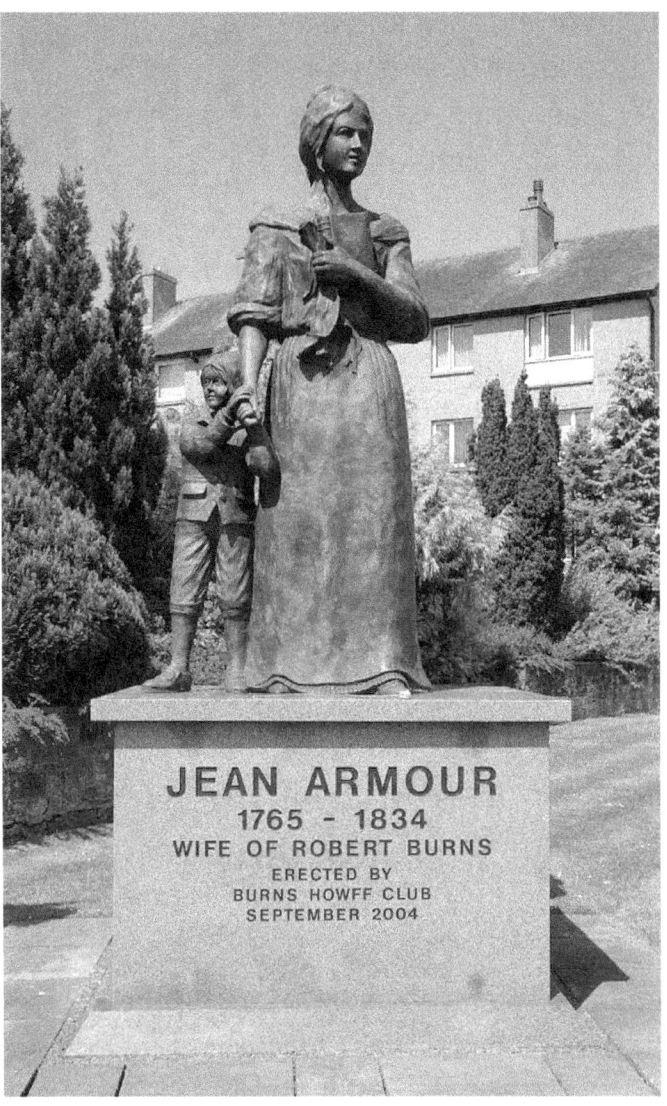

The song *O A' The Airts The Wind Can Blow* in this book is dedicated to Jean Armour by Burns.

Highland Mary – Mary Campbell

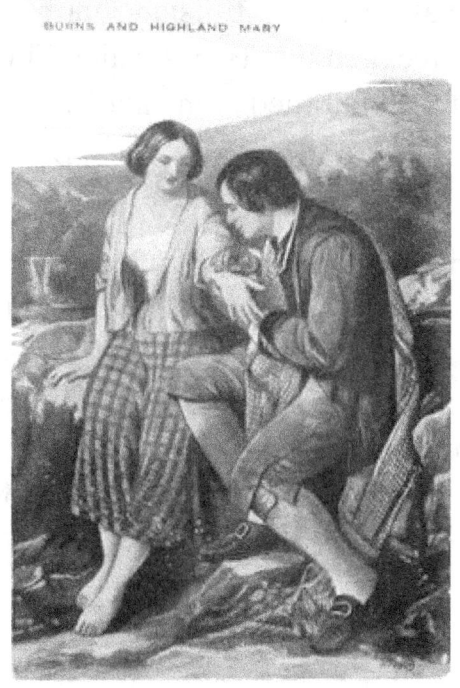

BURNS AND HIGHLAND MARY

Mary Campbell was born in 1763 to Archibald and Agnes Campbell of Dunoon, and was the eldest of four. According to accounts, Mary was "tall, fair haired with blue eyes". When Mary met Burns she was working as a dairymaid at Coilsfield, six miles from the birthplace of Robert. She had previously worked at Lochranza on Arran, and was fluent in Gaelic. She spoke English with a highland lilt, and may have earned her nickname for this reason.

Her association with Burns is rather sketchy, but we know that he dedicated the poems *The Highland Lassie, Highland Mary* and *To Mary in Heaven,* to Mary, and the latter two are included in this volume. Burns also wrote the song *Will ye go to the Indies, my Mary,* and *Leave auld Scotia's Shore?* which suggests that Burns planned to emigrate to Jamaica with Mary.

Burns first turned seriously to Mary after his wife, Jean Armour, had been despatched to Paisley in March 1786 when she fell pregnant out of wedlock. Burns and Mary took part in traditional Scottish matrimonial vows on the banks of the River Ayr, where they exchanged Bibles. Although the Bible that Mary gave to Burns has now been lost, the two-volume Bible that Burns gave Mary is now in the monument at Alloway, where the smudged names of Mary in one volume, and Mary, in the other, can be identified. The Bible also contains a lock of what is claimed to be Mary's blonde hair.

Mary died in 1786, probably as a result of typhus, contracted when nursing her brother Robert. She was buried at the old West Kirk churchyard at Greenock.

It seems that Burns was haunted by the death of Mary throughout the rest of his life. *To Mary in Heaven* was written at Ellisland farm on the third anniversary of her death. Jean Armour recalled that Burns walked in solitary contemplation around the River Nith, and then returned home and wrote the song.

In 1930, 134 years after the death of Mary, the Kirkyard at Greenock was demolished to make way for a Harland and Wolff shipyard. Mary's grave was carefully removed, and alongside the remains of two other adults, the coffin of a small child was found, which caused speculation about the nature of Burns' relationship with Mary. Mary was subsequently re-interred at Greenock cemetery under a monument that depicts the romantic couple designed by John Mossman. The monument was restored to its former glory in 2015 and re-dedicated in a ceremony. The funds had been raised by the Greenock Burns Club.

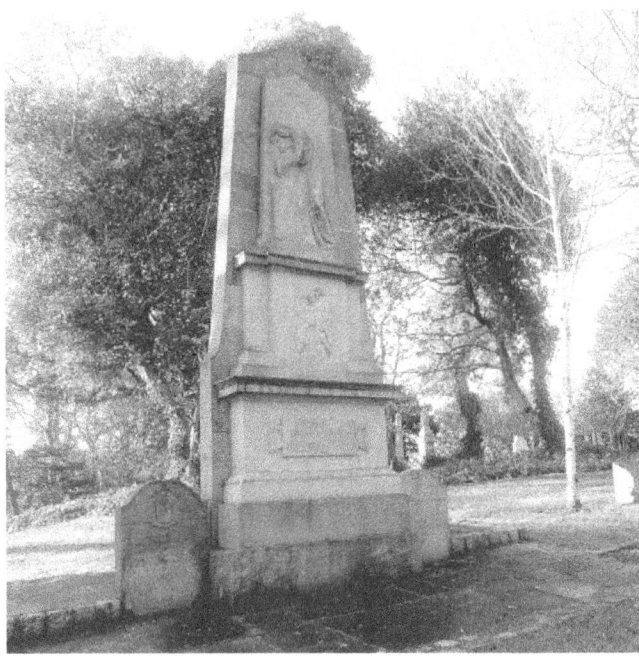

The songs *Highland Mary* and *To Mary In Heaven* in this volume are about Mary Campbell.

Agnes Maclehose

Agnes Maclehose (known as Nancy to her close friends) was born in Glasgow in 1758. She was the daughter of Christian Maclaurin and Andrew Craig, who was a prominent surgeon. At the age of eighteen, Agnes married the lawyer James Maclehose. She had four children with James, one of whom died at an early age. She left her husband shortly before the birth of her fourth child.

Robert Burns met Agnes in Edinburgh in 1787, after she had been separated from her husband for seven years. This was the start of a relationship that involved the exchange of many letters, poems and songs under the assumed names of Sylvander and Clarinder.

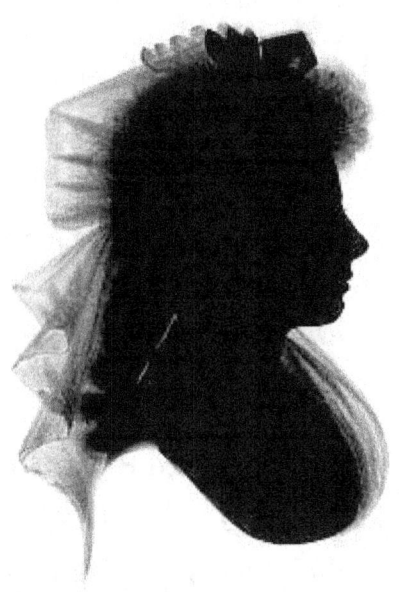

A contemporary silhouette of

Agnes Maclehose

Burns' attraction was undoubtedly due in part to Maclehose's cultured outlook. She was a regular guest at the house of Miss Nimmo, who hosted literary teas. After meeting Agnes on one such occasion, Robert / Sylvander, wrote:

I can say with truth, Madam, that I never met with a person in my life whom I more anxiously wished to meet again than yourself... I know not how to account for it. I am strangely taken with some people; nor am I often mistaken, You are a stranger to me; but I am an odd being: some yet unnamed feelings; things, not principles, but better than whims, carry me farther than boasted reason ever did a Philosopher.

Their poetic exchanges resulted in the very popular song *Ae Fond Kiss*, which was published in the Musical Museum in 1792, albeit in a totally different form from the melody normally sung today.

The letters that the pair exchanged reached an intensity that threatened to tarnish the reputation of Agnes, to the extent that she wrote:

I entertain you not to mention our correspondence to anyone on earth

In February 1788, Burns returned to Ayrshire only to discover that Jean Armour had been sent to Greenock, as a result of her pregnancy. Burns wrote to Agnes:

Now for a little news that will please you. I, this morning as I came home, called for a certain woman. I am disgusted with her; I cannot endure her! I, while my heart smote me for the prophanity, tried to compare her with my Clarinda;

Nevertheless, Burns returned to marry Jean shortly after writing the letter.

Agnes outlived Robert by 45 years and took delight in recalling her association with the Ayrshire poet into her old age. She remarked:

This day I can never forget. Parted with Burns, in the year 1791, never more to meet in this world. Oh, may we meet in Heaven!

The two versions of *Ae Fond Kiss* in this volume are love songs to Agnes Maclehose.

And the others...

Robert Burns' first child was with his family's farm servant, Elizabeth Paton in 1785. Although Burns' mother encouraged her son to marry Elizabeth, soon afterwards, Robert began a relationship with Jean Armour, but the child was welcomed into the Burns family home.

Around the time that Burns was exchanging letters with Agnes Maclehose, her maid, Jenny Clow, fell pregnant at the hands of Burns. Jenny was summarily dismissed from the household of Agnes; destitution ensued, and it is thought that both Jenny and her small boy did not live much longer.

When Robert Burns worked as an exciseman based in Dumfries he encountered a barmaid called Ann Park. She bore Burns a baby girl. It is documented that Jean Armour allowed the illegitimate offspring of Burns in her household after Ann Park died.

Notes on the Songs

Ae Fond Kiss

This is one of Robert Burns' most famous and endearing songs, but the two versions presented in this book are not the same as that which is commonly sung today. The version used today (and found in volume one of this book) is a Gaelic love song called *Hi Oro 'S Na Horo Eile*. The original version of *Ae Fond Kiss*, found in the Musical Museum, used the tune known as *Rory Dall's Port*. Rory Dall was a harpist based in Skye, and Port is another name for a Scottish air. The original melody contains a number of ornaments that are reproduced here, but may be omitted at will.

From the Victorian period, yet another version of *Ae Fond Kiss* started to gain ground, and is subsequently found in many Robert Burns collections arranged for piano and voice. I have re-arranged the accompaniment for guitar, and changed the key to suit the guitar.

Ye Jacobites By Name

This song was amended by Burns from an older song whose subject is the Jacobite Risings of 1688-1746, where the aim was to replace the Hanoverian monarchy (which ascended after the Glorious Revolution of 1688) with a Stuart dynasty, led by Charles Edward Stuart / Bonnie Prince Charlie. The original version was decidedly anti-Jacobite, but Burns' version is more generally anti-war in sentiment.

Ca' The Yowes To The Knowes

Burns first heard this song being sung by a clergyman by the name of Mr Clunie. He asked a companion to transcribe the song into notation and, with the addition of some more verses, the song was submitted to Thomson for inclusion in *The Musical Museum*. Burns wrote, "In a solitary stroll which I took to-day, I tried my hand on a few pastoral lines, following up the idea of the chorus, which I would preserve". The Clouden is a tributary of the River Nith and the "silent towers" are the ruins of Lincluden Abbey in Dumfries. Burns found inspiration walking down the river when he worked as an exciseman, and to this day, the route is known as *The Burns Walk*.

Tam Glen

Isabella Begg, Burns' youngest sister, insisted that *Tam Glen* was an older song that Burns adapted. However, there is no recorded evidence of such, and the lyrics may be completely from the pen of Burns. The melody is, however, from the traditional song known as *The Muckin' O' Geordie's Byre*.

To Mary In Heaven

Burns wrote this sentimental song, dedicated to Highland Mary, during his tenure at Ellisland in 1789. It was apparently composed after a bout of introspection during a frosty evening at the farm. It is probably true to say that Burns never overcame the grief brought on by the early death of Mary.

Musing On The Roaring Ocean

Burns wrote this song after his tour of the North Highlands, where he became acquainted with many airs. The melody is the Gaelic Air, *Druimion Druth*. The heroine of the song is apparently Mrs. Maclachlan, whose husband was an officer in the East Indies.

Logan Braes

The Logan is a river in southwest Scotland. Braes means "hills" or "hillside" and this sad song recounts the departure and eventual return of a soldier, Willie to his wife and child.

O! Willie Brew'd A Peck O' Maut

Burns himself tells of the origin of this song:

The air is Masterton's, the song mine. The occasion of it was this: Mr William Nicol, of the High School, Edinburgh, during the autumn vacation [of 1789] being at Moffat, honest Allan – who was at that time on a visit to Dawswinton – and I went to pay Nicol a visit. We had such a joyous meeting, that Mr. Masterton and I agreed, each in our way, that we should celebrate the business.

If nothing else, it is an honest celebration of the joys of inebriation.

O A' The Airts The Wind Can Blaw

This short song is a celebration of his love for his wife, Jean. The melody is taken from the *Miss Admiral Gordon's Strathspey*, a favourite of his wife. The Strathspey is a dance form named after the River Spey in North Scotland. It is in 4/4, but quite irregular in rhythm, making use of "scotch snaps". Being a love song, it is most suitably performed as a slow Strathspey. Burns wrote the song shortly before moving to Ellisland Farm.

Leezie Lindsay

This song first appeared in *The Musical Museum* in 1803. It is not clear if the words are original, or are based on an earlier song. It has been suggested that the name Lindsay is of lowland origin, so the song is a metaphor for the relationship of the highlands and the lowlands.

Highland Mary

This song is thought to have been composed on the sixth anniversary of Mary Campbell's death, and is set to the air *Katherine Ogie*. Burns writes about the song to Thomson (the editor of The Musical Museum) in 1792:

The foregoing song pleases myself; I think it is in my happiest manner: you will see at first glance that it suits the air. The subject of the song is one of the most interesting passages of my youthful days, and I own that I should be much flattered to see the verses set to air which would ensure celebrity. Perhaps, after all, 'tis the still glowing prejudice of my heart that throws a borrowed lustre over the merits of the composition.

By Yon Castle Wa'

This song, with obvious Jacobite sympathies, is also known by its refrain, *There'll Never Be Peace Till Jamie Comes Hame*. It was set to the tune of *Fee Him Father*. "Jamie" refers to Prince James Edward Stuart (1688-1766), son of the deposed King James VII of Scotland and II of England, and the leader of the unsuccessful Jacobite uprising of 1715. He was the father of Prince Charles Edward Stuart, or Bonnie Prince Charlie. It gained a new surge of popularity after this song, was included in the collection, Hogg's *Jacobite Reliques* in the Nineteenth Century.

A Rose-Bud By My Early Walk

This song was written in 1787 and dedicated to a Miss Jean Cruickshank who was the daughter of the Latin master at the High School of Edinburgh. Jean was only 12 years old when Burns wrote this, but she was an accomplished singer who also played the piano. The melody is based on the traditional tune *The Shepherd's Wife*.

My Heart Is Sair

The lyrics to this song are based on a verse by the English poet Allan Ramsay, but were elaborated by Burns. *Sair* means strong or committed. The song appears in the fifth volume of the *Musical Museum,* in the key of F Mixolydian, with a flattened seventh degree (Eb). In modern arrangements, and here, it is presented in non-modally, with a raised seventh (B, in the key of G major). Modal scales like the Mixolydian are often a feature of ancient and non-western music.

There Was A Lad Was Born In Kyle

This jovial and spirited song is obviously autobiographical in nature. It was written in 1787, and was originally set to the tune *Dainty Daisy*. This version is presented here, as well as a later setting to the tune *O Gin Ye Were Dead Guidman*. The later version is the one that is generally performed today, and it is sometimes called *Rantin, Rovin Robin* as a result of its popular refrain. The last verse (which tells of *lassies* who *lie aspar*) tends to be omitted from Victorian editions. It is always interesting to hear the song as Burns originally intended.

Scots Wha Ha'e

The lyrics in this patriotic song are in the form of an imaginary speech given by Robert the Bruce before the Battle of Bannockburn in 1314. The tune is set to the melody of *Hey Tuttie Tattie*, which, according to tradition, was played by Bruce's troops at Bannockburn. Burns sent a note to his publisher saying that he had been inspired by Bruce's "*glorious struggle for Freedom, associated with the glowing ideas of some other struggles of the same nature, not quite so ancient*", which may be a reference to the radical Thomas Muir, who encouraged the Scots to oppose the British government. The song is still used today as the anthem of the Scottish Nationalist Party, who are currently campaigning for independence from the United Kingdom with a renewed vigour.

Ay Waukin' O

It is generally accepted that this is a very old song, that Burns made only a few alterations. As ever, the version here is slightly different from that found in the Musical Museum where it was first published, and predictably, there is yet another version doing the rounds judging by the performances found on the internet. *Waukin* means waking up.

Up In The Early Morning

Burns stated that the chorus in this song was old, but the verses were his own work. In the version found in the Musical Museum, the verse seems to be in the Dorian mode, with a sharpened 6th degree, but minor seventh, but in later printed versions, the sixth is left unsharpened. I have sharpened the C in bars 4 and 8, but it might be worth trying to sing both ways before forming a preference.

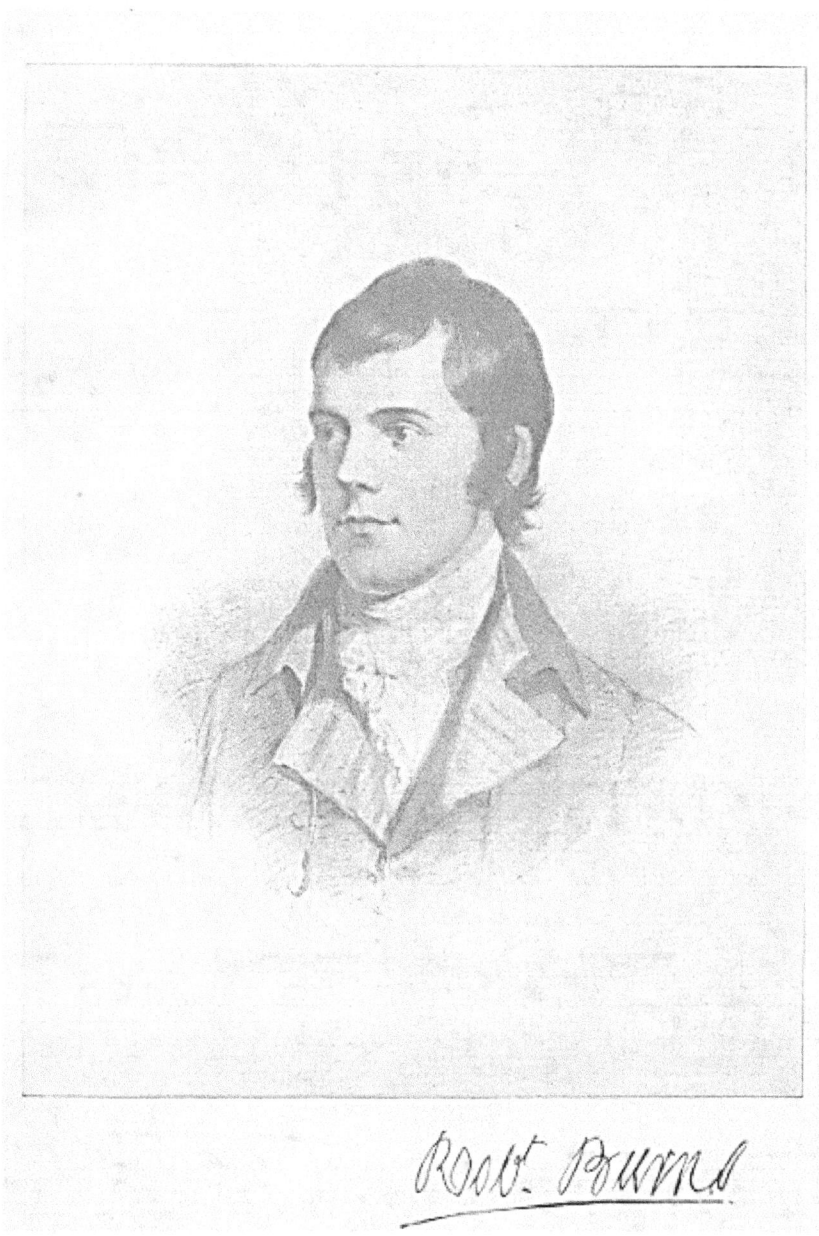

Ae Fond Kiss (Original Version)

Robert Burns

Rory Dall

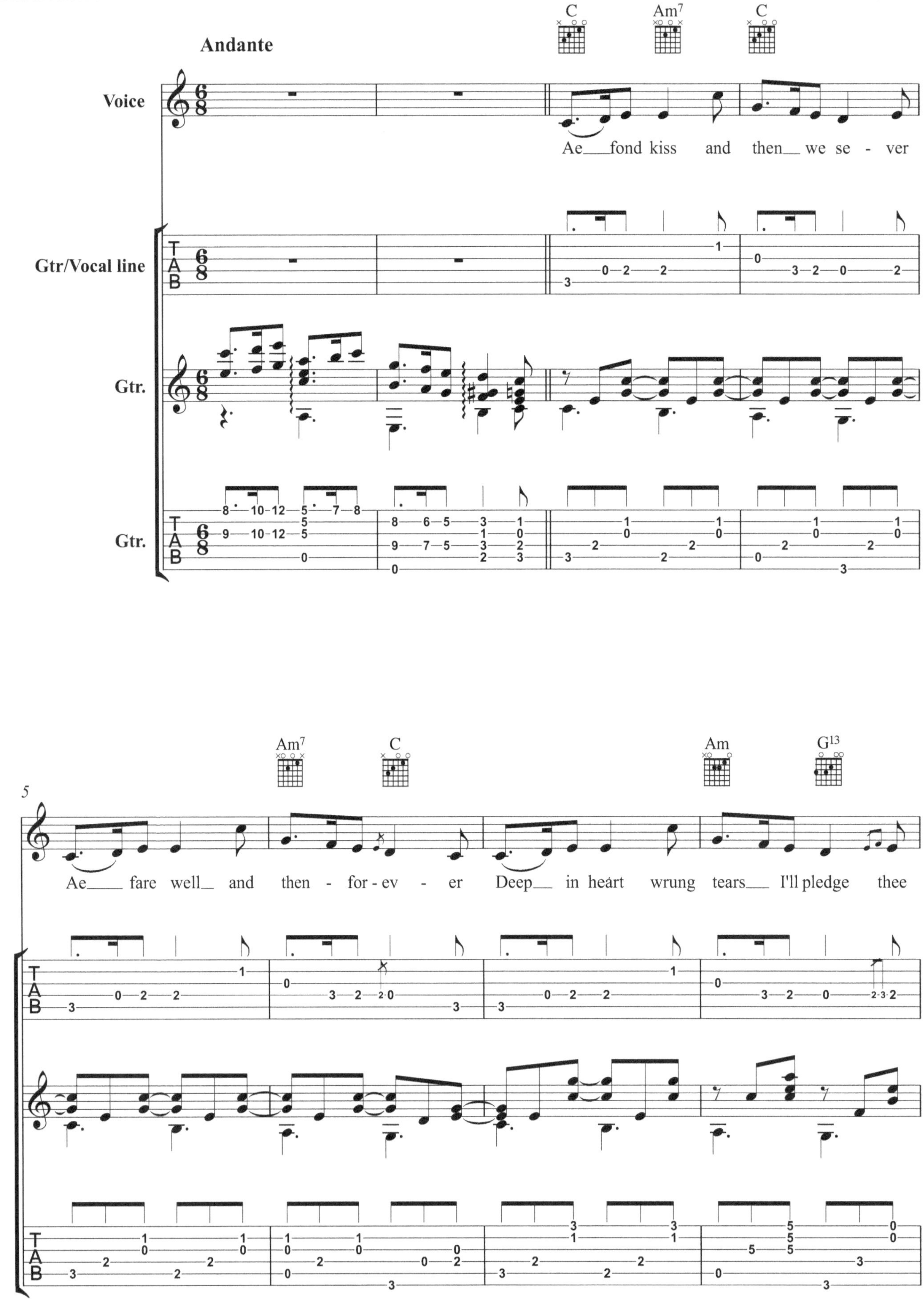

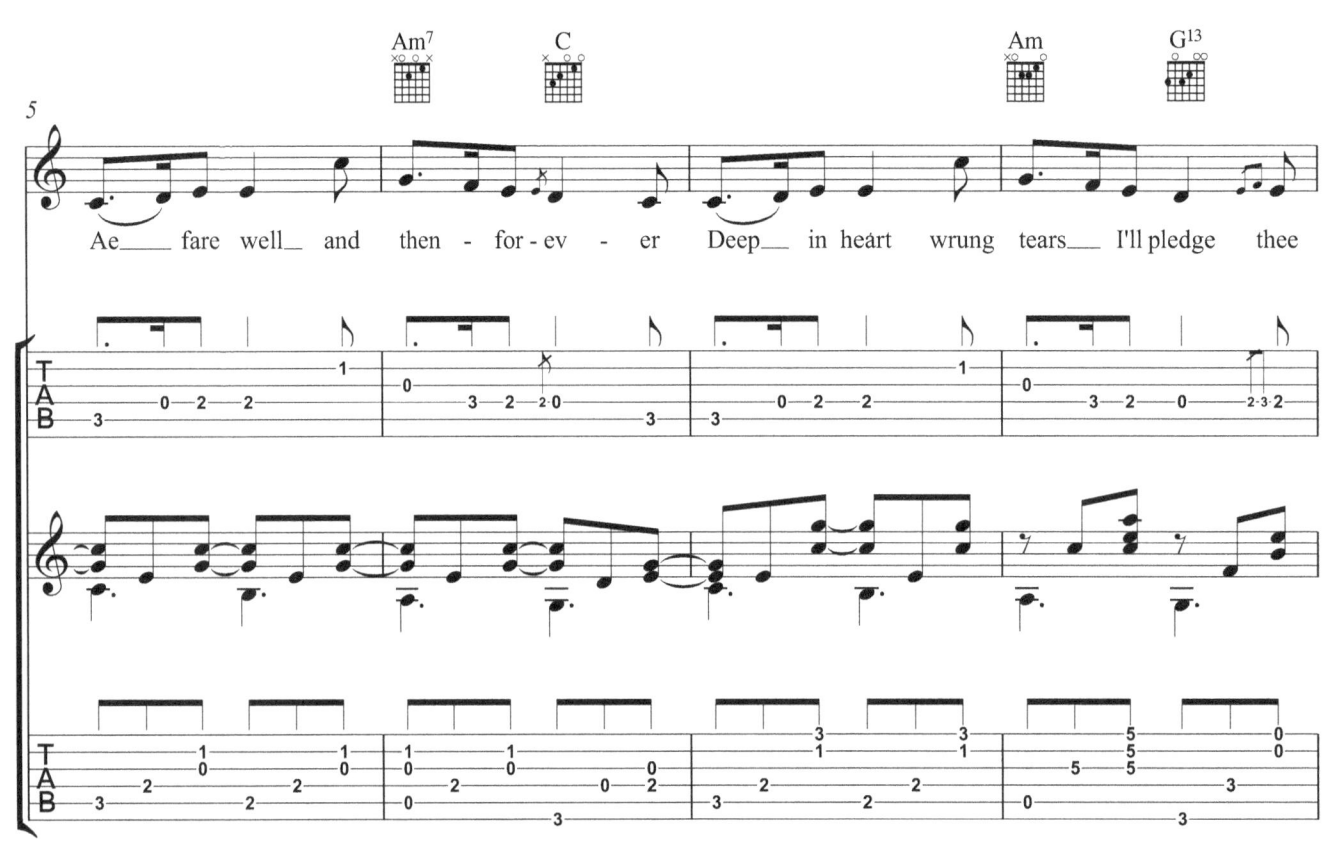

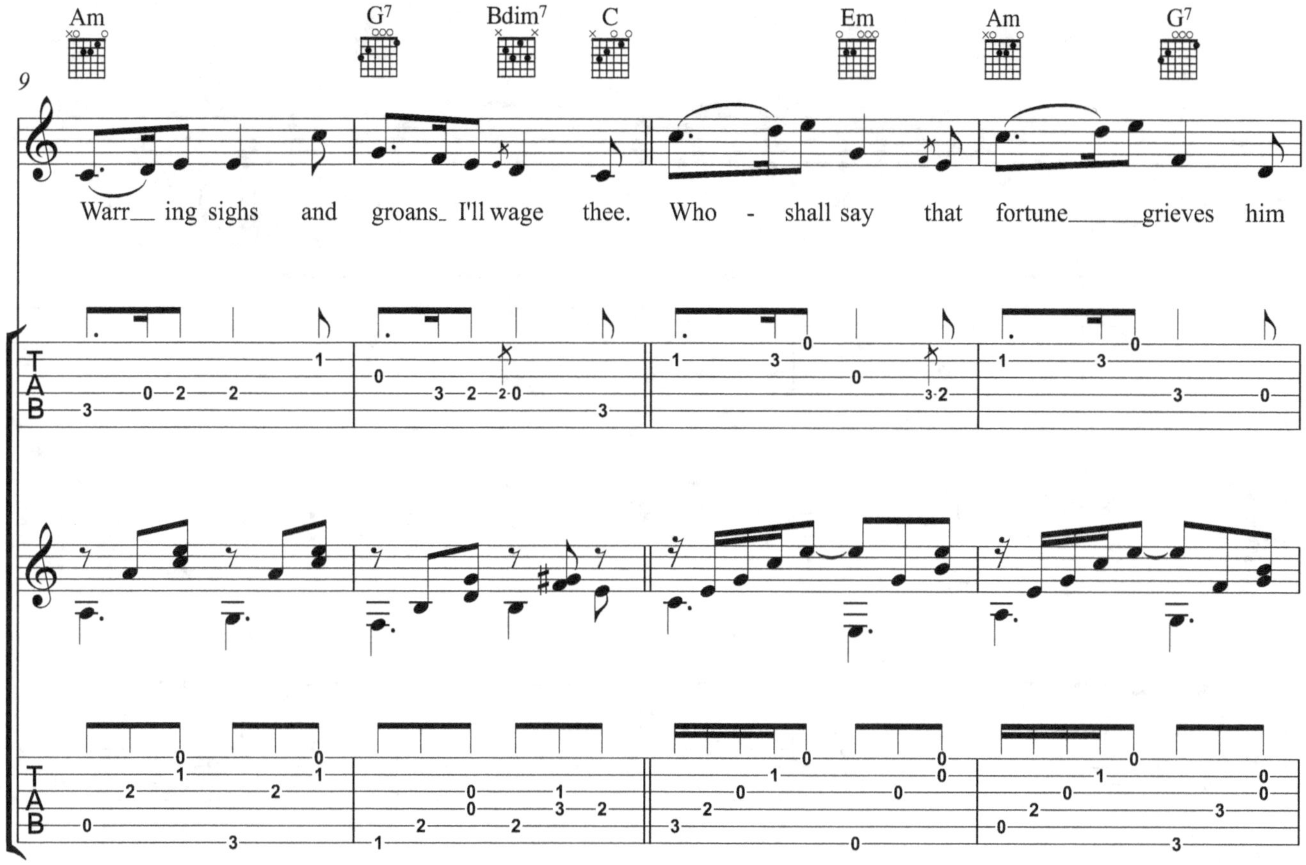

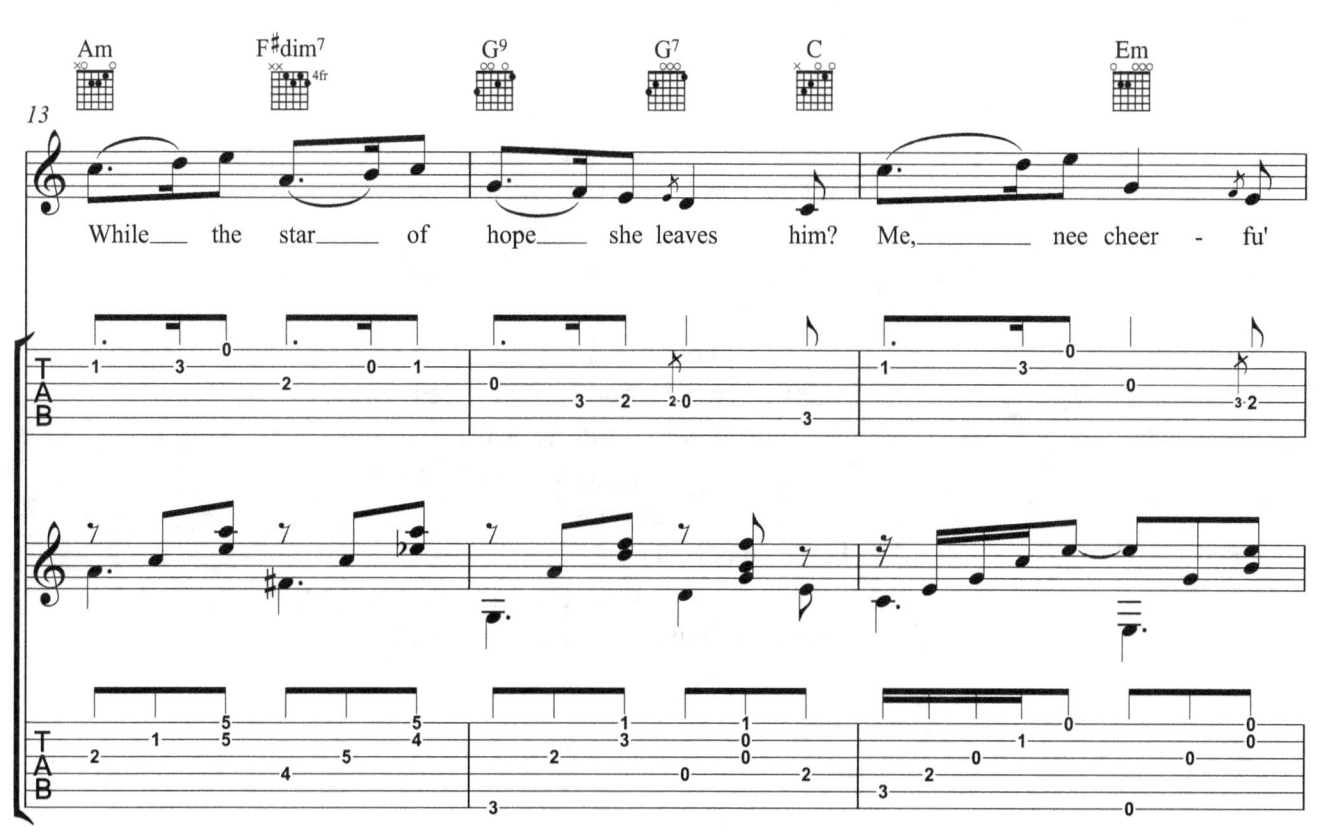

Warr__ ing sighs and groans_ I'll wage thee. Who - shall say that fortune____grieves him

While___ the star___ of hope___ she leaves him? Me,_____ nee cheer - fu'

2

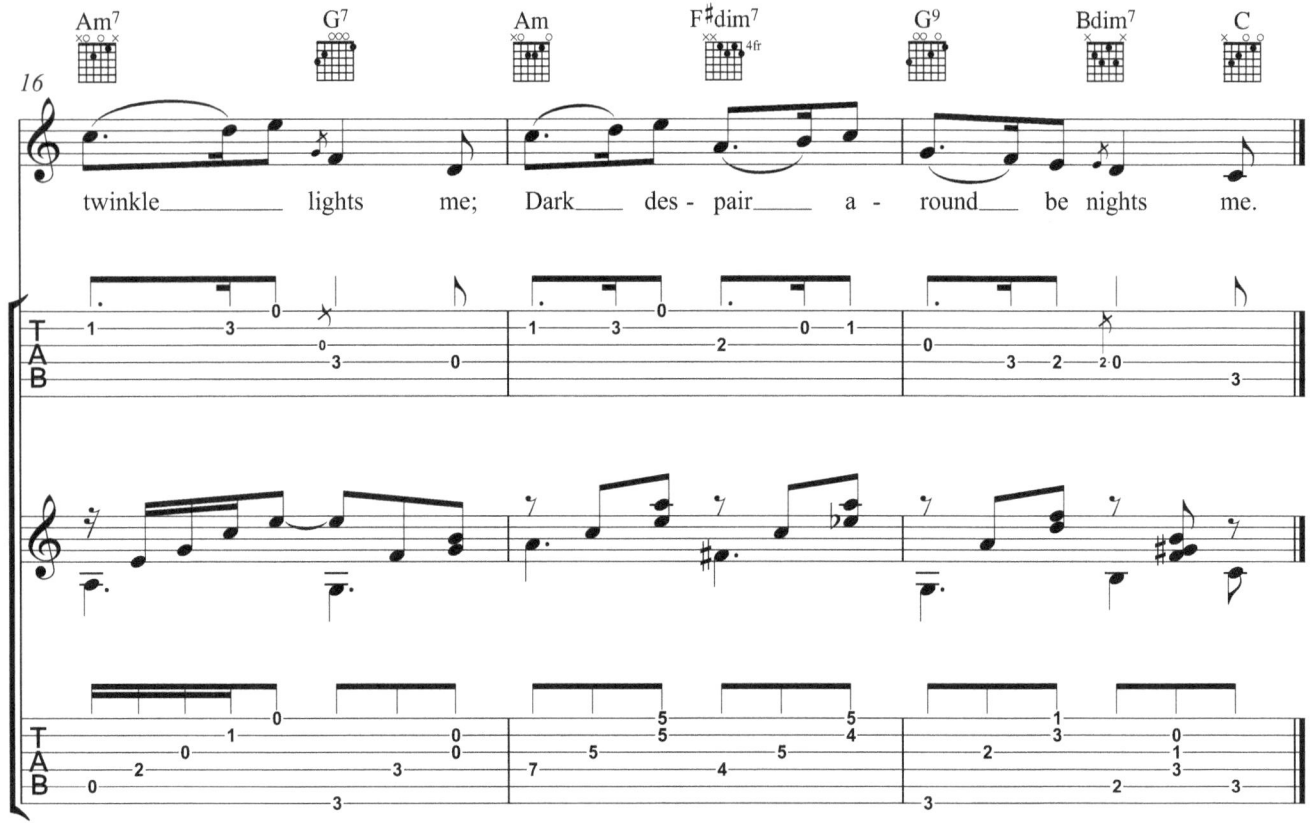

twinkle_____ lights me; Dark____ des - pair____ a - round____ be nights me.

I'll ne'er blame my partial fancy,
Naething could resist my Nancy;
But to see her was to love her;
Love but her, and love forever.
Had we never lov'd sae kindly,
Had we never lov'd sae blindly,
Never met—or never parted—
We had ne'er been broken-hearted.

Fare thee weel, thou first and fairest!
Fare thee weel, thou best and dearest!
Thine be ilka joy and treasure,
Peace, enjoyment, love, and pleasure!
Ae fond kiss, and then we sever;
Ae fareweel, alas, forever!
Deep in heart-wrung tears I'll pledge thee,
Warring sighs and groans I'll wage thee!

Ae Fond Kiss (Victorian Version)

Robert Burns

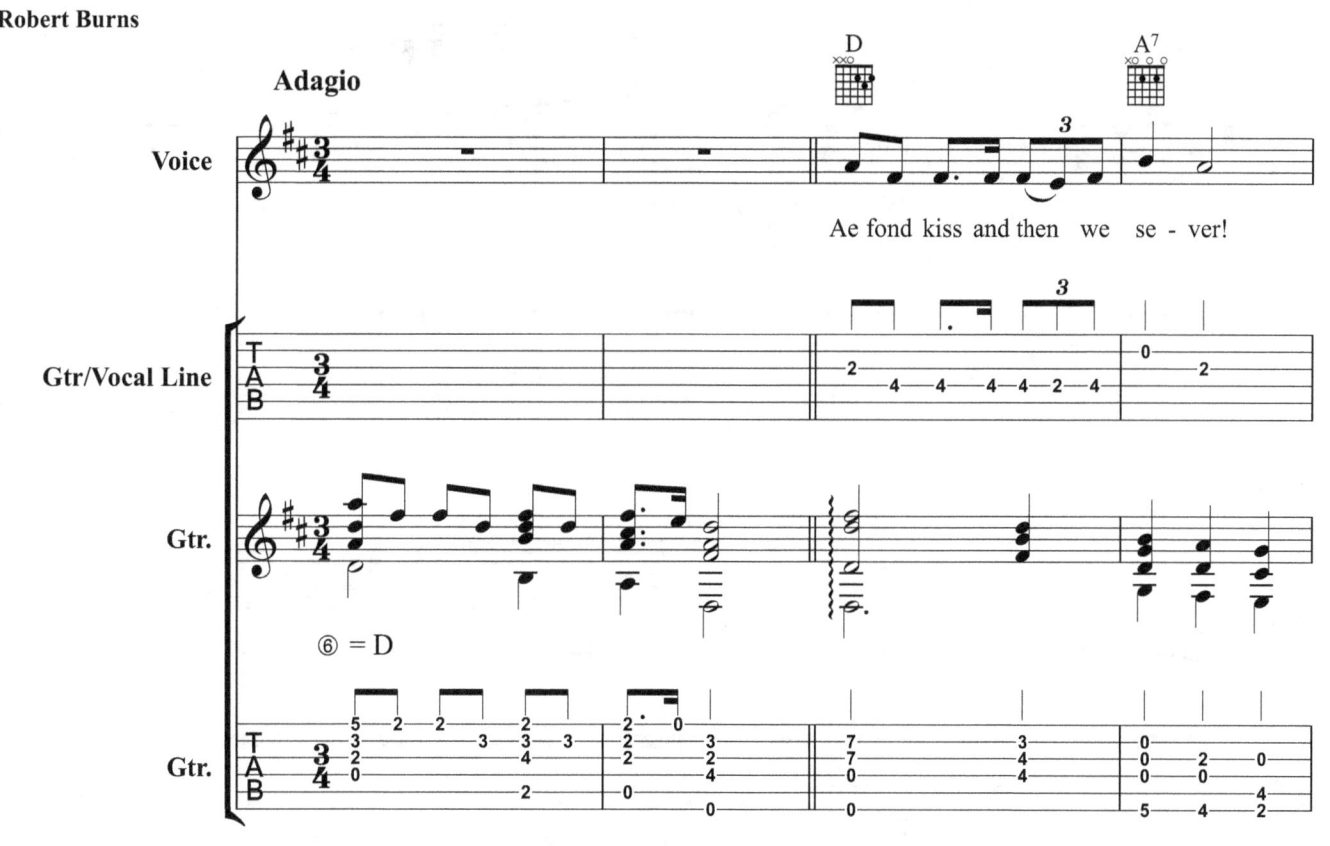

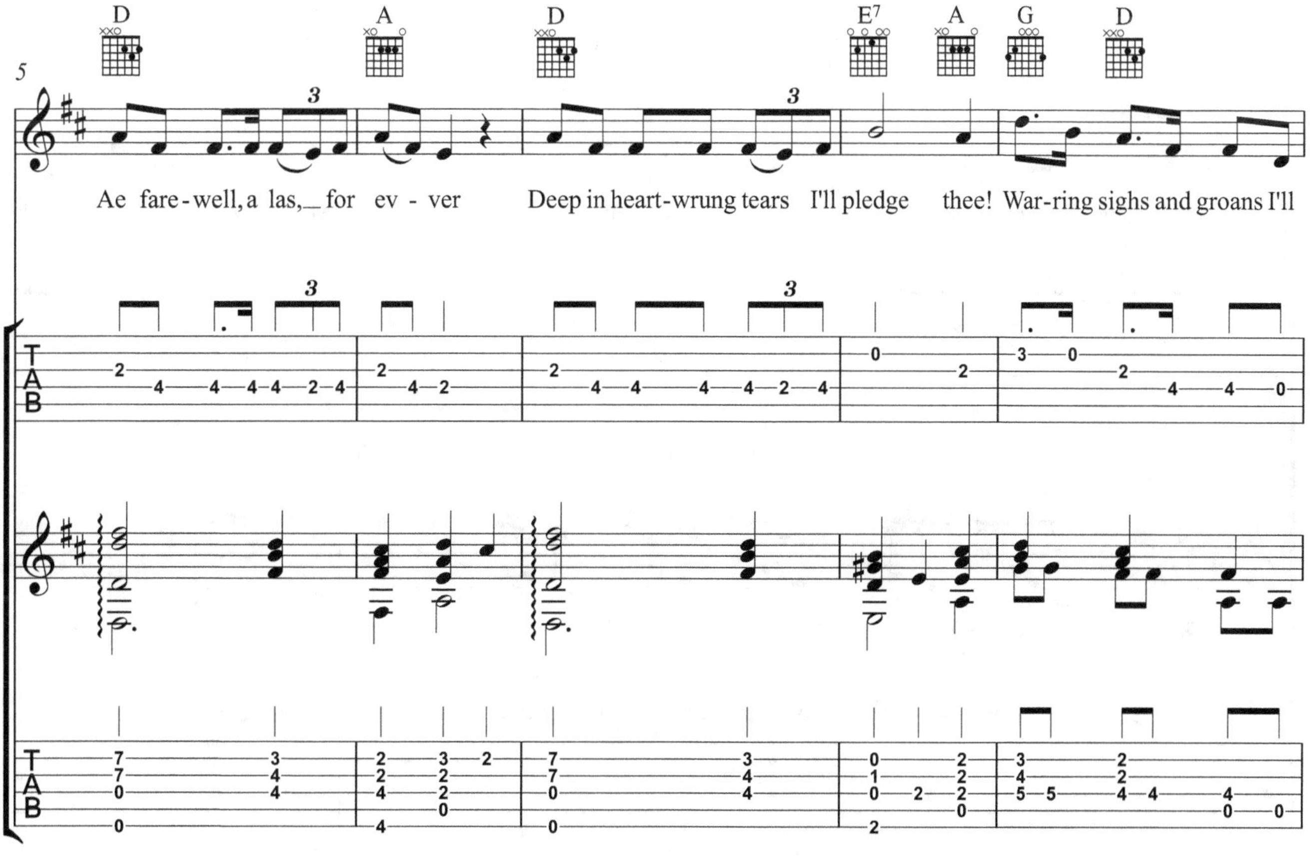

Ae fond kiss and then we se - ver!

Ae fare-well, a las,___ for ev - ver   Deep in heart-wrung tears I'll pledge   thee! War-ring sighs and groans I'll

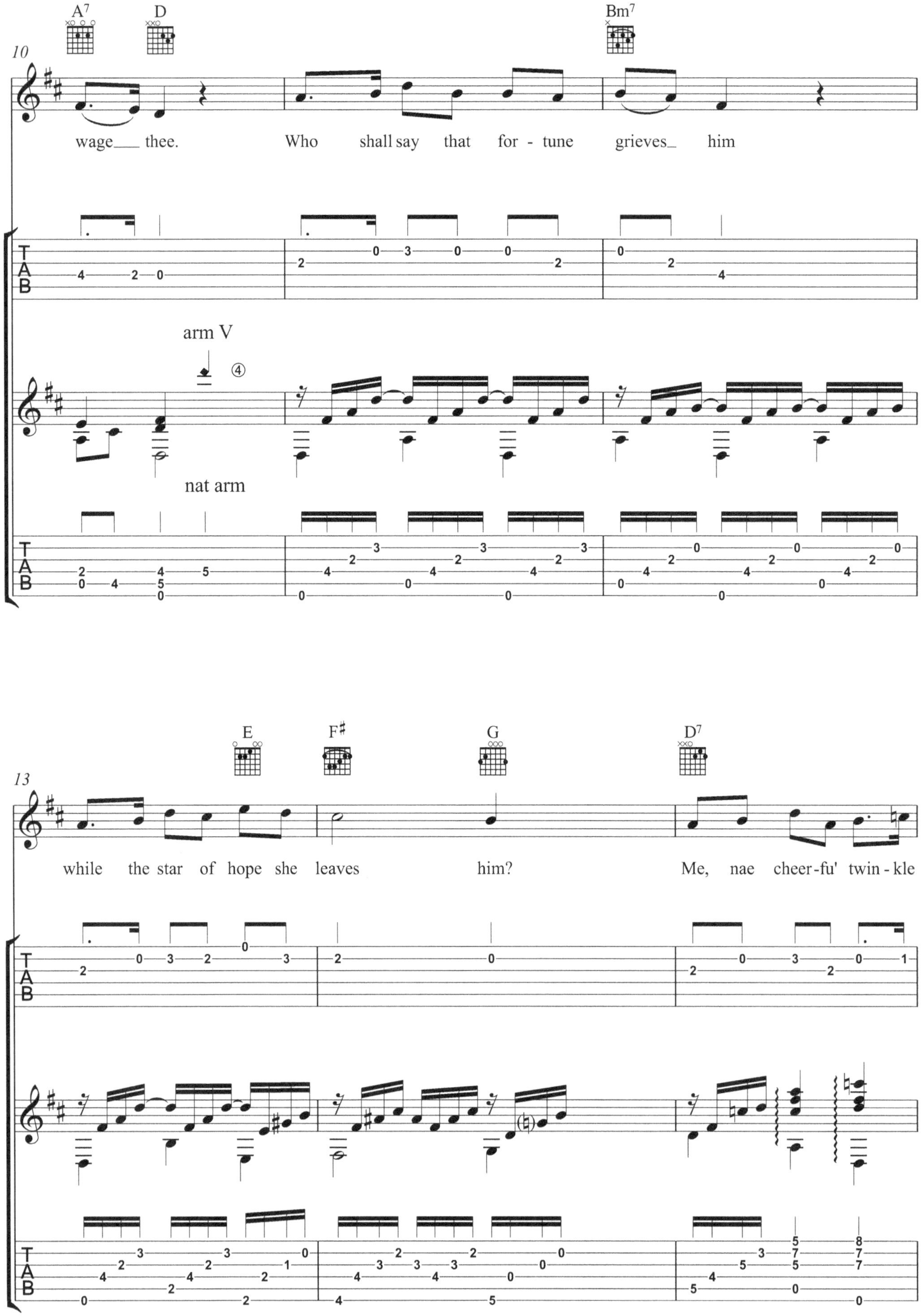

Lyrics:
wage___ thee. Who shall say that for-tune grieves___ him
while the star of hope she leaves him? Me, nae cheer-fu' twin-kle

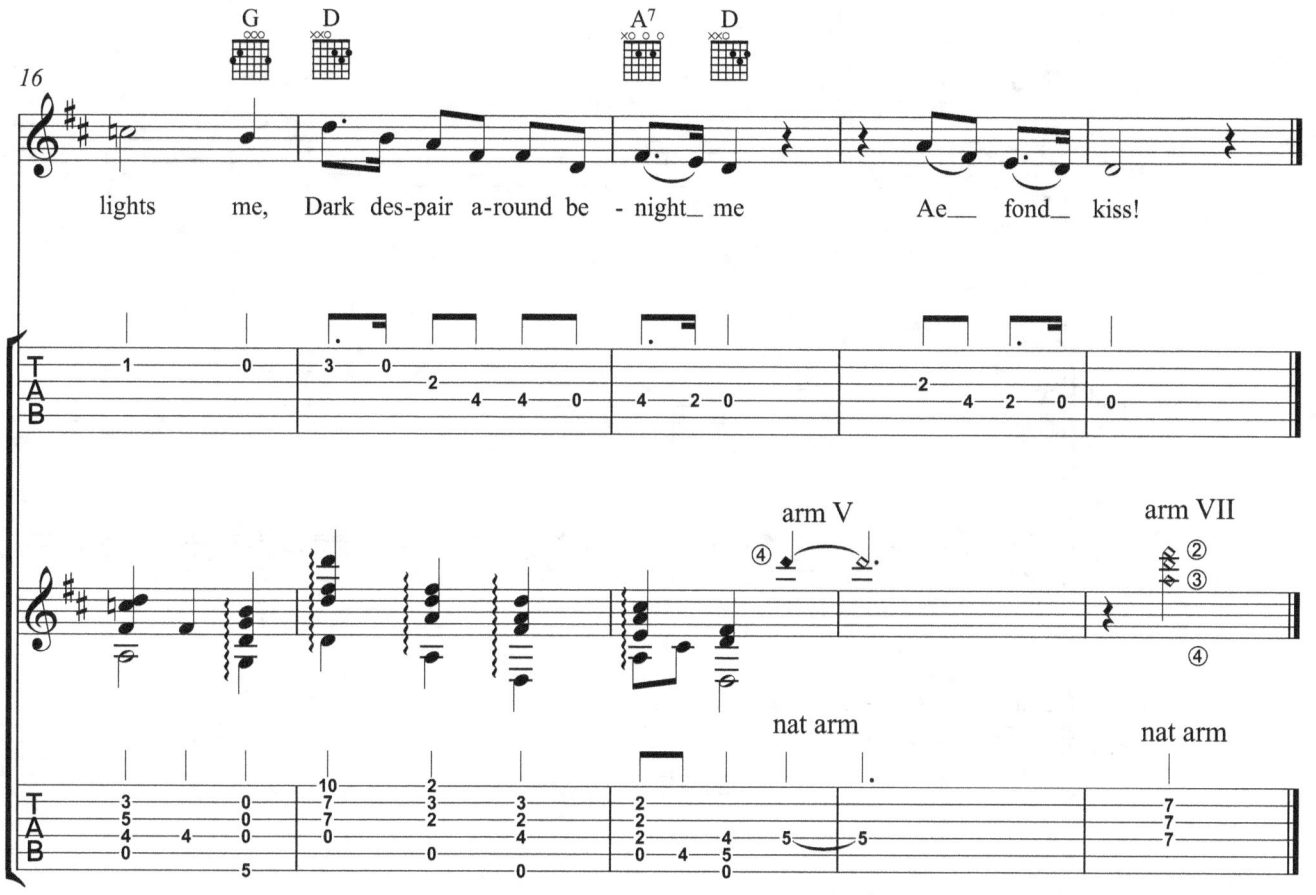

lights me, Dark des-pair a-round be - night me   Ae fond kiss!

I'll ne'er blame my partial fancy,
Naething could resist my Nancy;
But to see her was to love her;
Love but her, and love forever.
Had we never lov'd sae kindly,
Had we never lov'd sae blindly,
Never met—or never parted—
We had ne'er been broken-hearted.
Ae fond kiss!

Fare thee weel, thou first and fairest!
Fare thee weel, thou best and dearest!
Thine be ilka joy and treasure,
Peace, enjoyment, love, and pleasure!
Ae fond kiss, and then we sever;
Ae fareweel, alas, forever!
Deep in heart-wrung tears I'll pledge thee,
Warring sighs and groans I'll wage thee!
Ae fond kiss!

6

Ye Jacobites By Name

Robert Burns

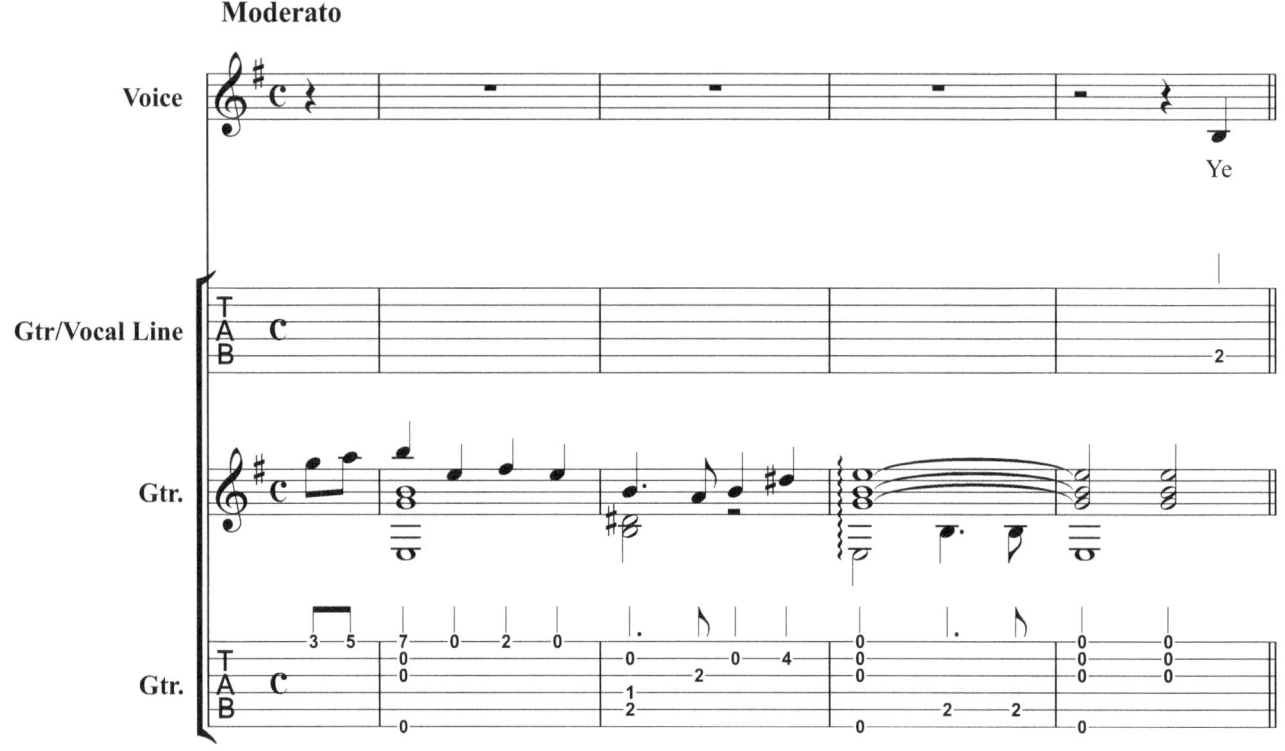

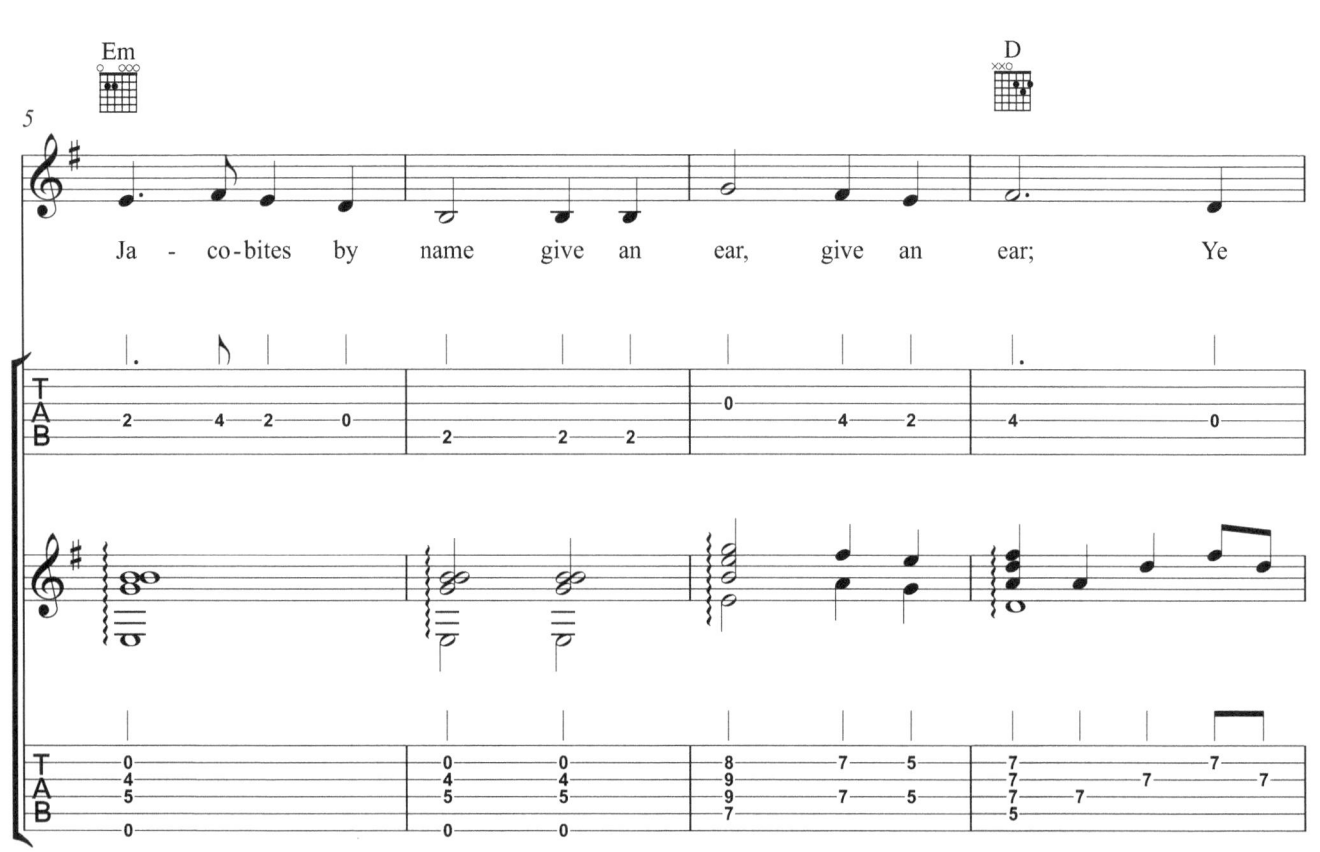

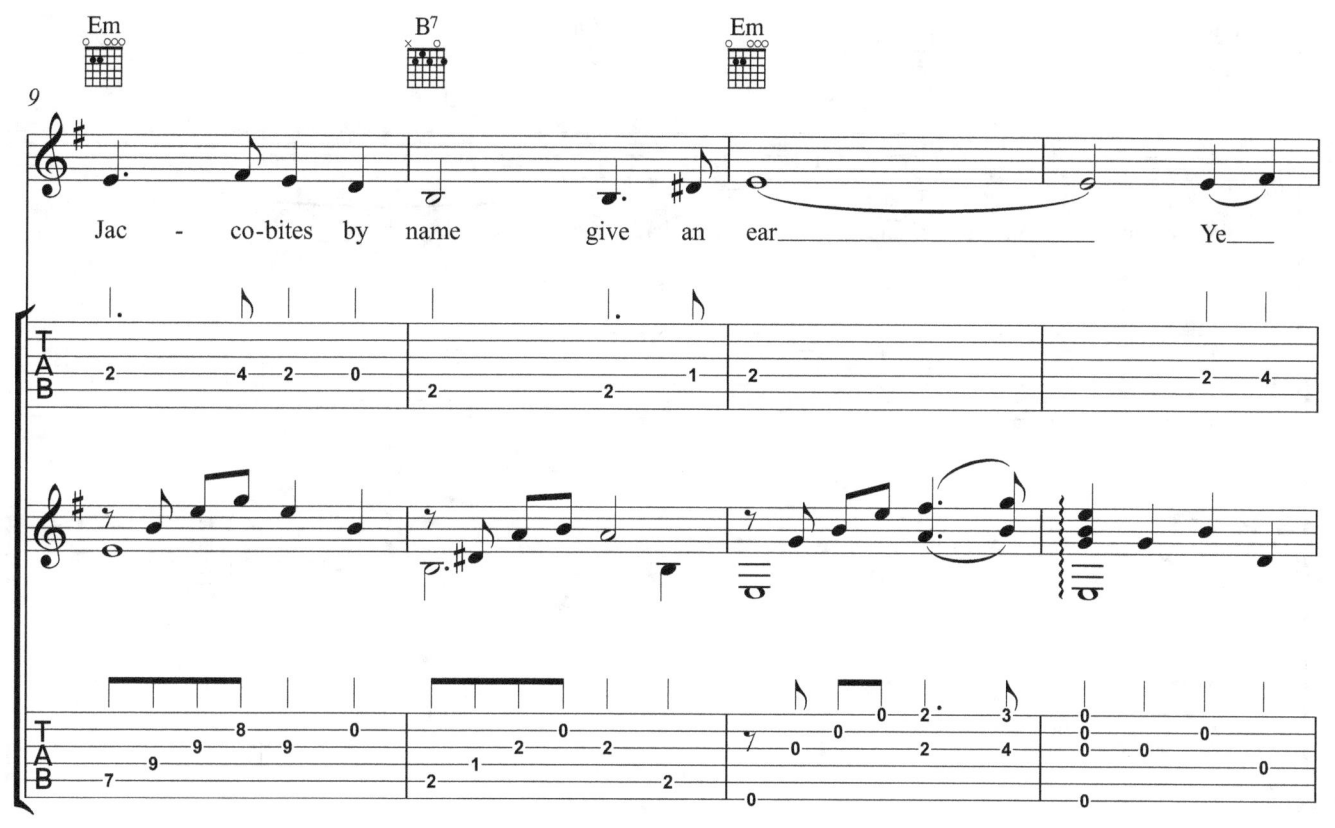

Jac - co-bites by name give an ear_____ Ye____

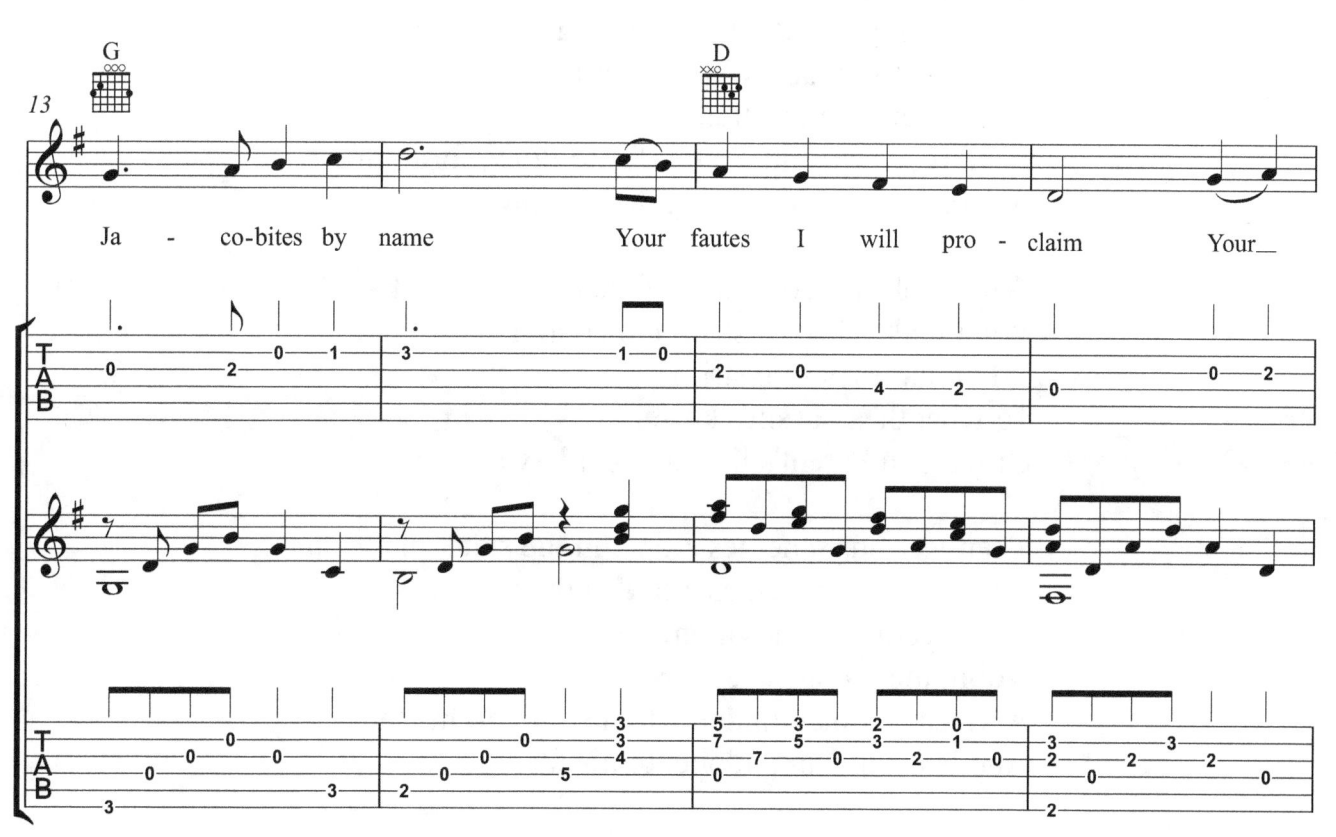

Ja - co-bites by name Your fautes I will pro - claim Your__

8

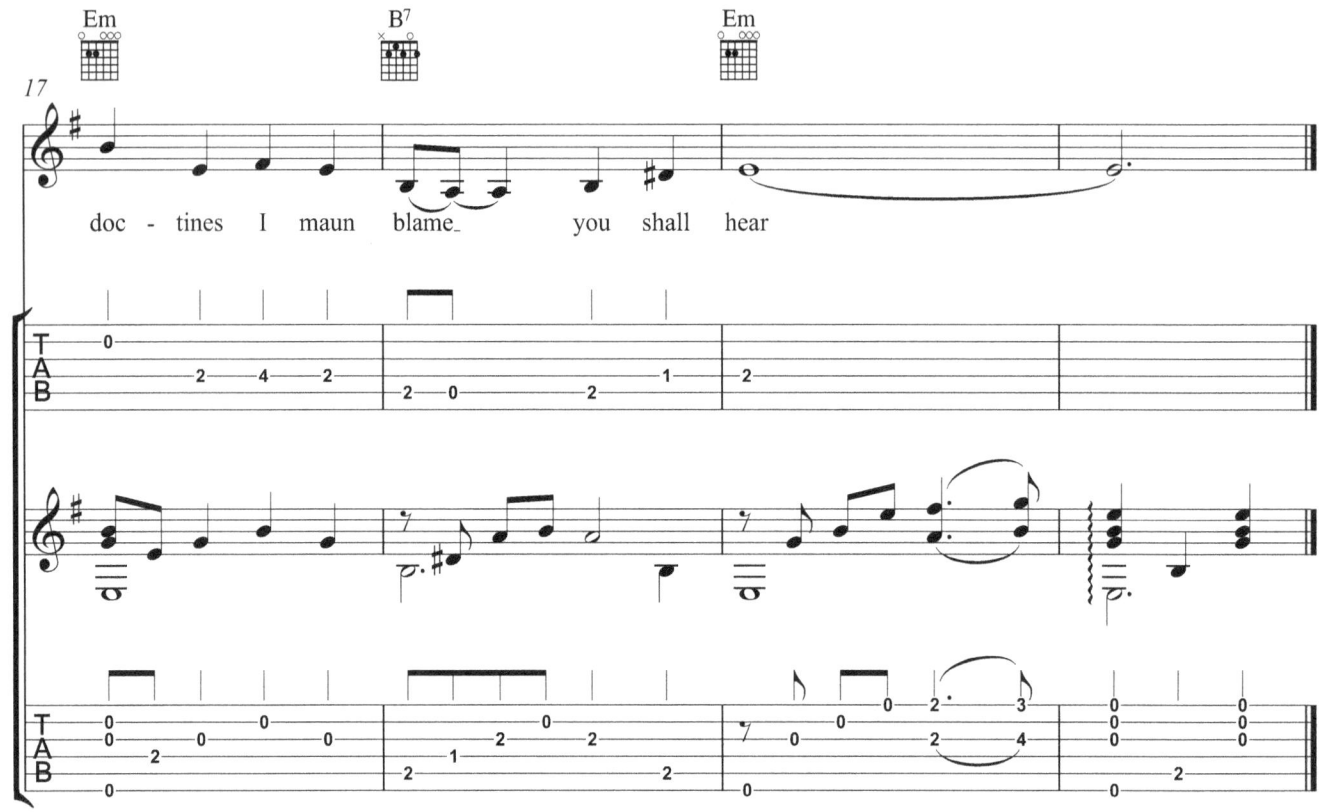

What is Right, and What is Wrang, by the law, by the law?
What is Right and what is Wrang by the law?
What is Right, and what is Wrang?
A weak arm and a strang,
A short sword, and a lang, for to draw, for to draw
A short sword, and a lang, for to draw.

What makes heroic strife, famed afar, famed afar?
What makes heroic strife famed afar?
What makes heroic strife?
To whet th' assassin's knife,
Or haunt a Parent's life, wi' bluidy war?

Then let your schemes alone, in the state, in the state,
Then let your schemes alone in the state.
So let your schemes alone,
Adore the rising sun,
And leave a man undone, to his fate, to his fate.
And leave a man undone, to his fate.

Robert Burns' Scotland

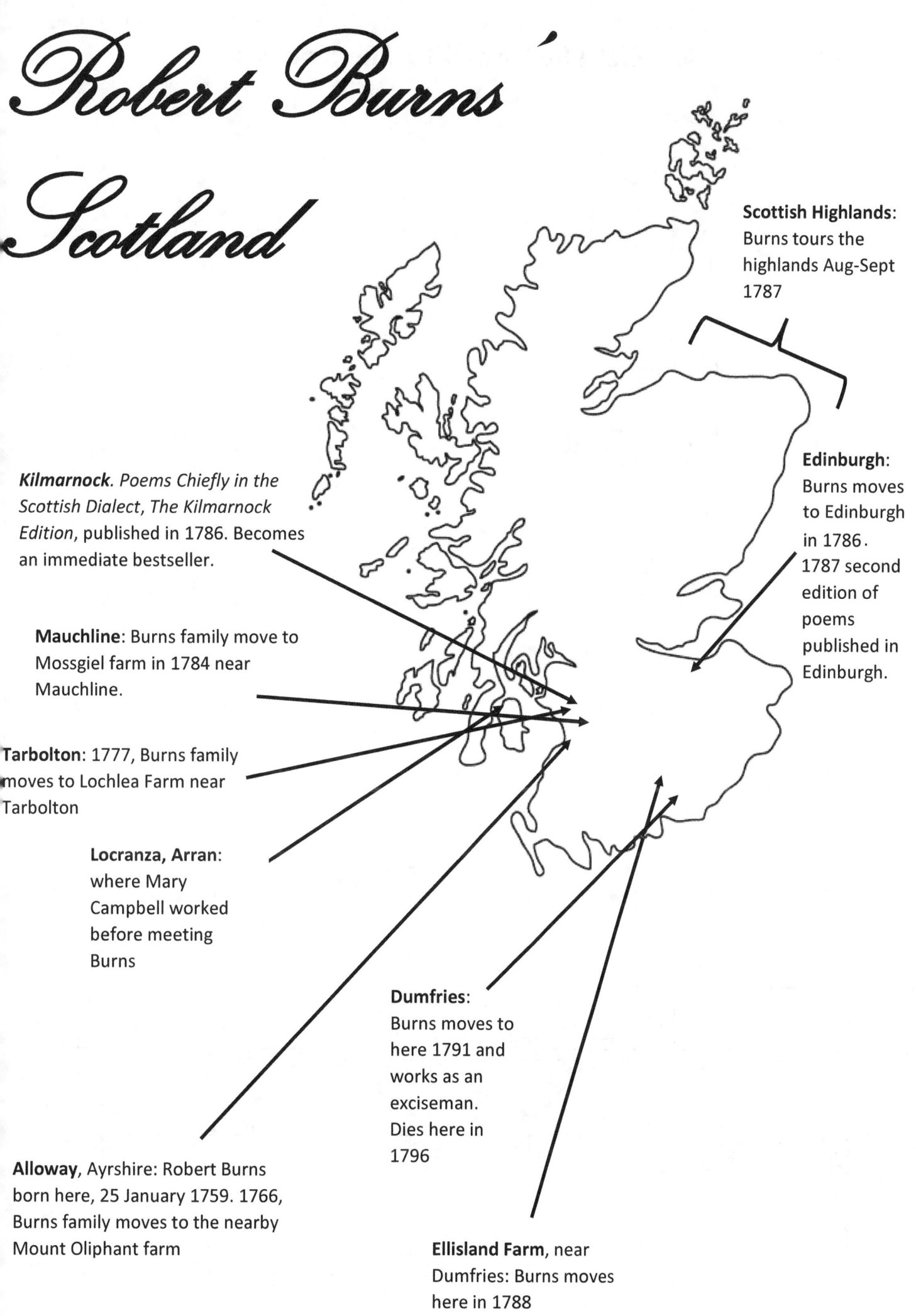

Scottish Highlands: Burns tours the highlands Aug-Sept 1787

Edinburgh: Burns moves to Edinburgh in 1786. 1787 second edition of poems published in Edinburgh.

Kilmarnock. Poems Chiefly in the Scottish Dialect, The Kilmarnock Edition, published in 1786. Becomes an immediate bestseller.

Mauchline: Burns family move to Mossgiel farm in 1784 near Mauchline.

Tarbolton: 1777, Burns family moves to Lochlea Farm near Tarbolton

Locranza, Arran: where Mary Campbell worked before meeting Burns

Dumfries: Burns moves to here 1791 and works as an exciseman. Dies here in 1796

Alloway, Ayrshire: Robert Burns born here, 25 January 1759. 1766, Burns family moves to the nearby Mount Oliphant farm

Ellisland Farm, near Dumfries: Burns moves here in 1788

Ca' The Yowes To The Knowes

Robert Burns

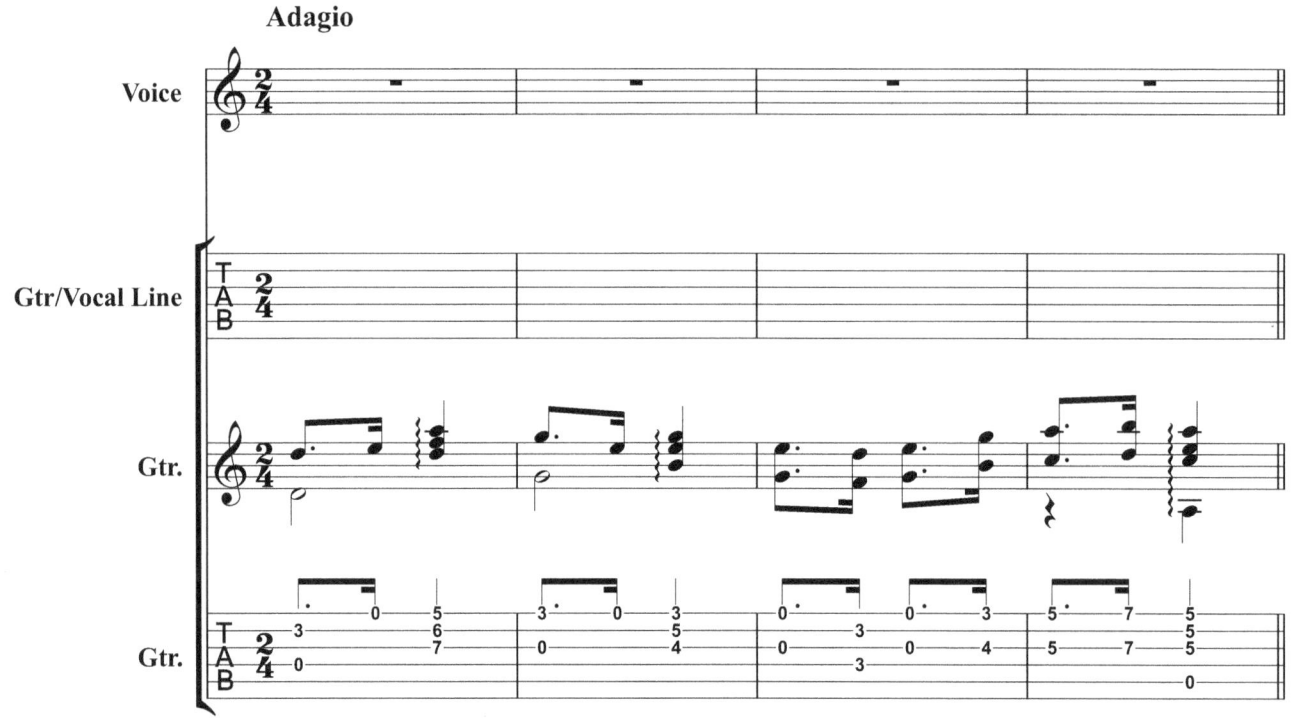

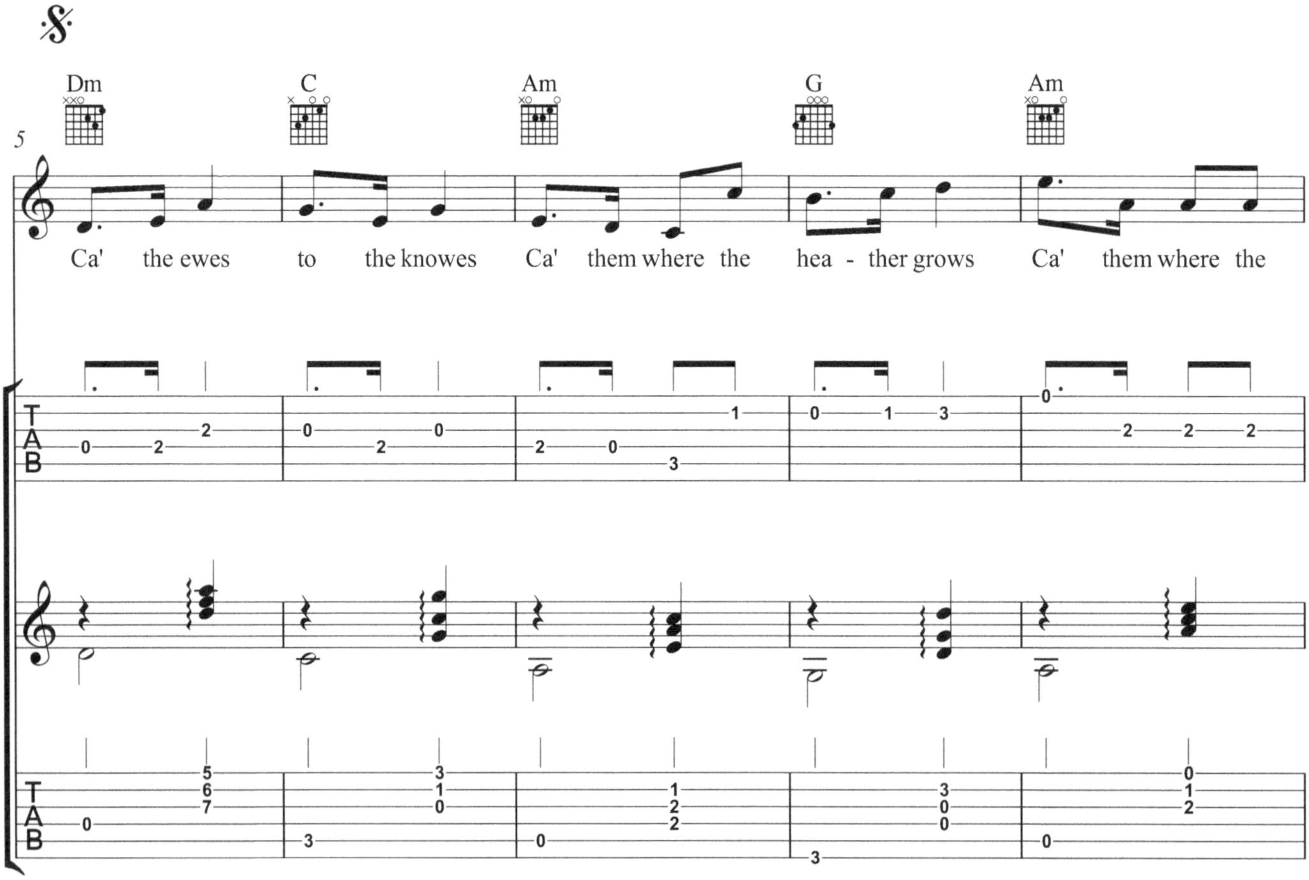

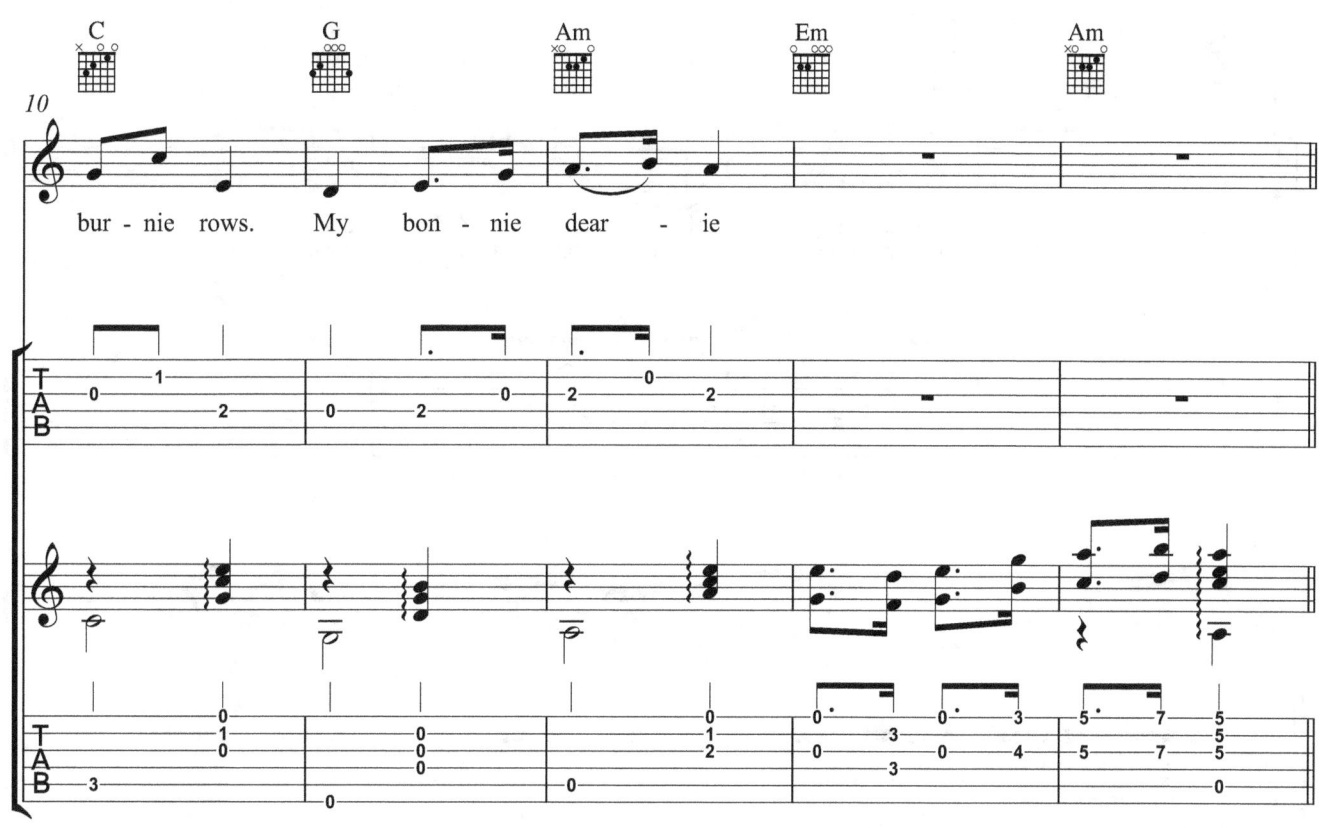

bur - nie rows. My bon - nie dear - ie

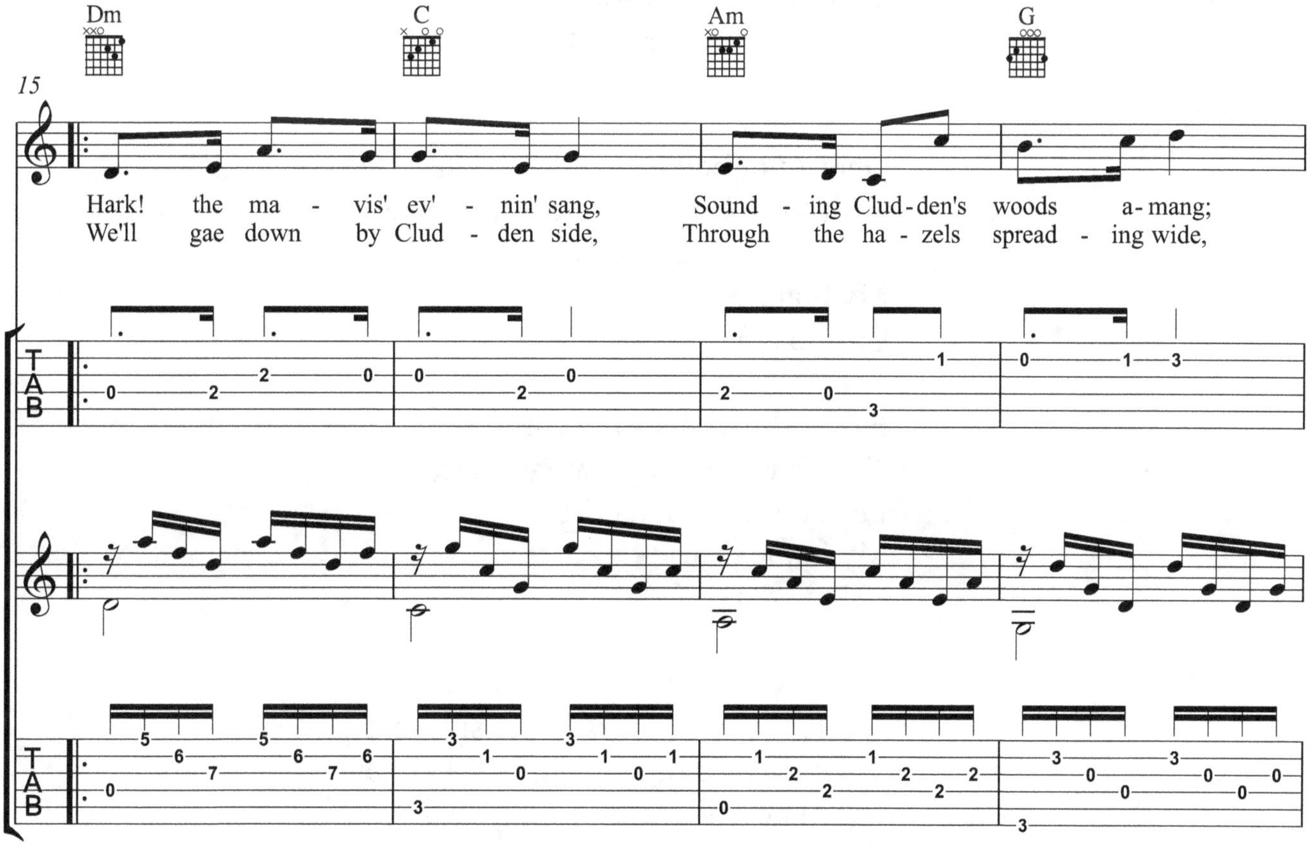

Hark! the ma - vis' ev' - nin' sang,   Sound - ing Clud - den's woods a - mang;

We'll gae down by Clud - den side,   Through the ha - zels spread - ing wide,

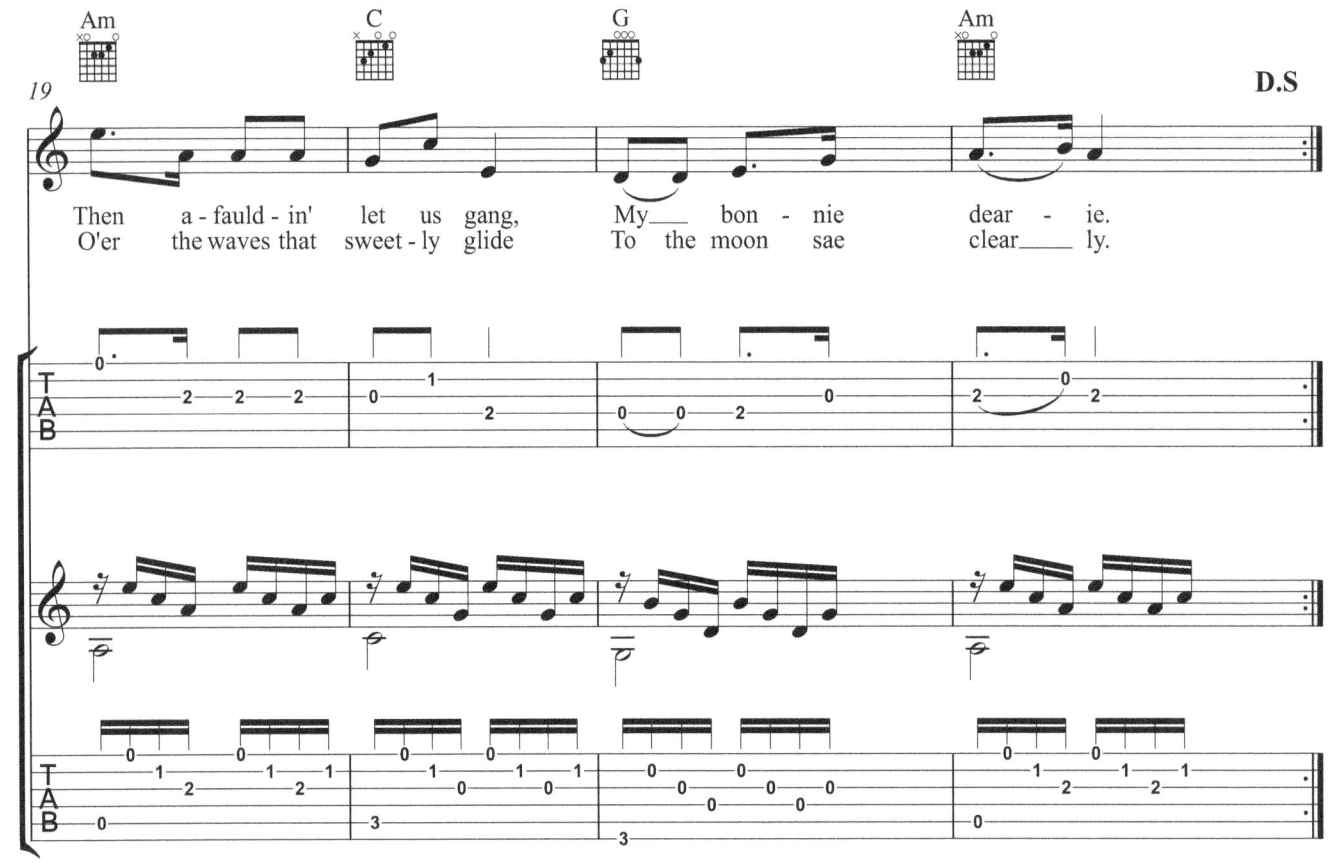

Then a - fauld - in' let us gang, My___ bon - nie dear - ie.
O'er the waves that sweet - ly glide To the moon sae clear___ ly.

Yonder Clouden's silent towers
Where, at moonshine's midnight hours,
O'er the dewy bending flowers
Fairies dance sae cheery.
Ca' the.&c

Ghaist nor bogle shalt thou fear
Thou'rt to Love and Heav'n sae dear
Nocht of ill may come thee near,
My bonnie dearie.
Ca' the.&c

Fair and lovely as thou art,
Thou hast stown my very heart;
I can die-but canna part,
My bonie dearie
Ca' the.&c

As the waters wimple to the sea
While the day breaks in the sky so high
Till clay-cold death shall blind my eye
I shall be thy dearie
Ca' the.&c

Tam Glen

Robert Burns

Moderato

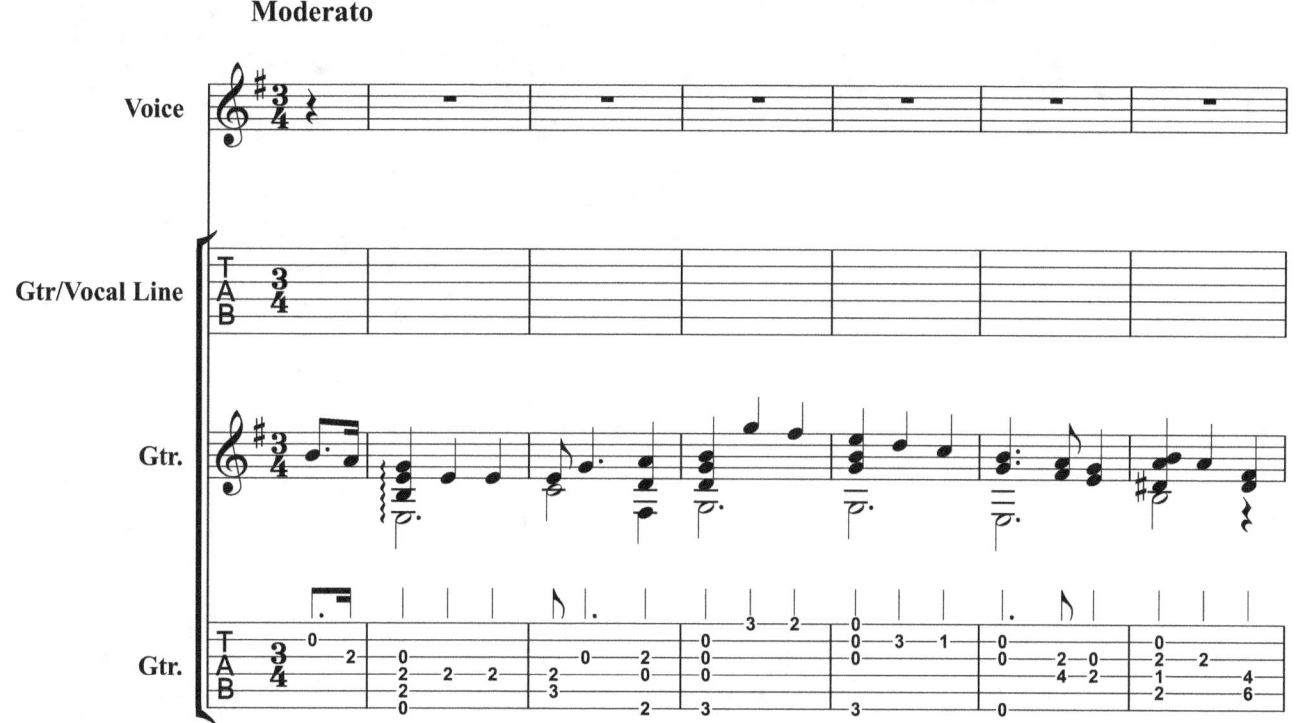

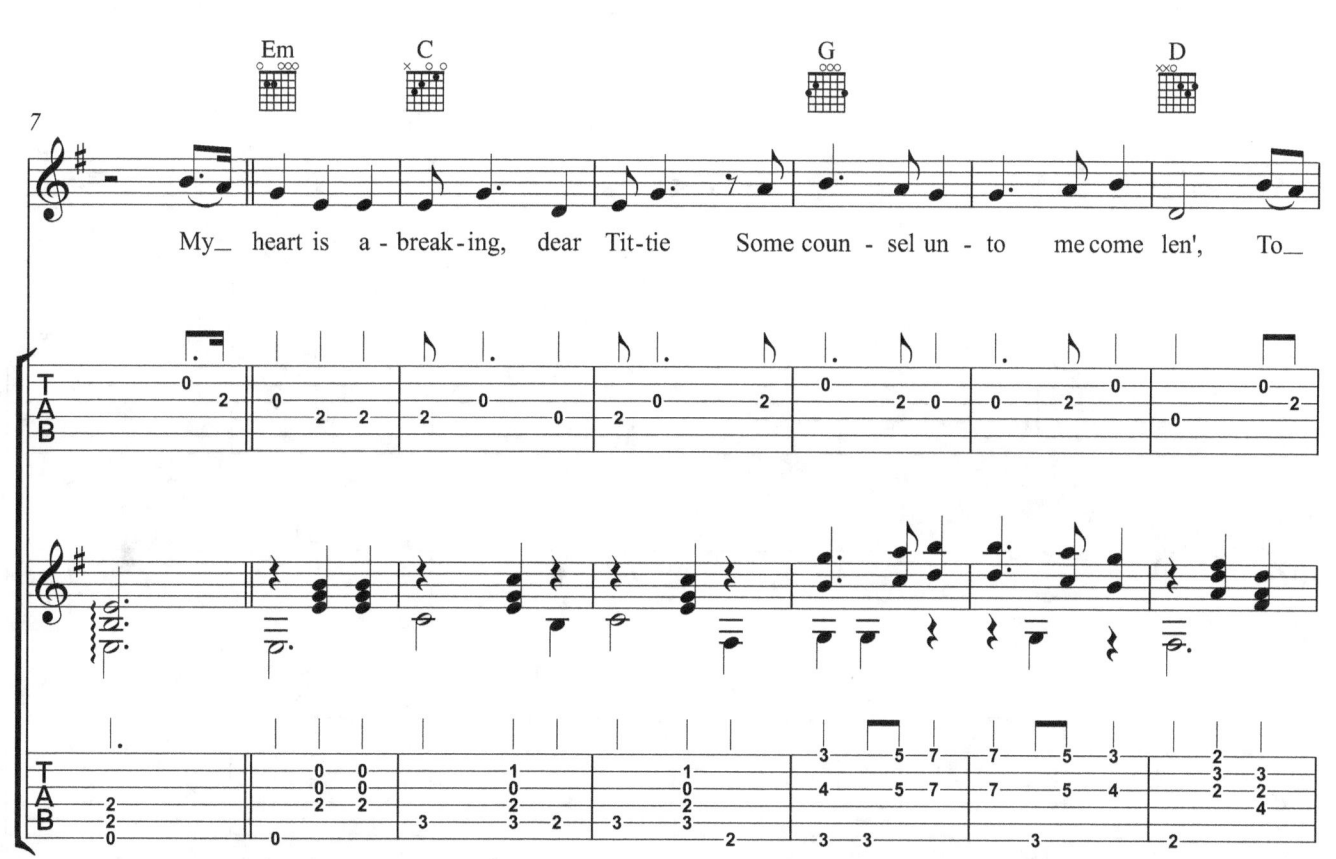

My__ heart is a-break-ing, dear Tit-tie Some coun-sel un-to me come len', To__

14

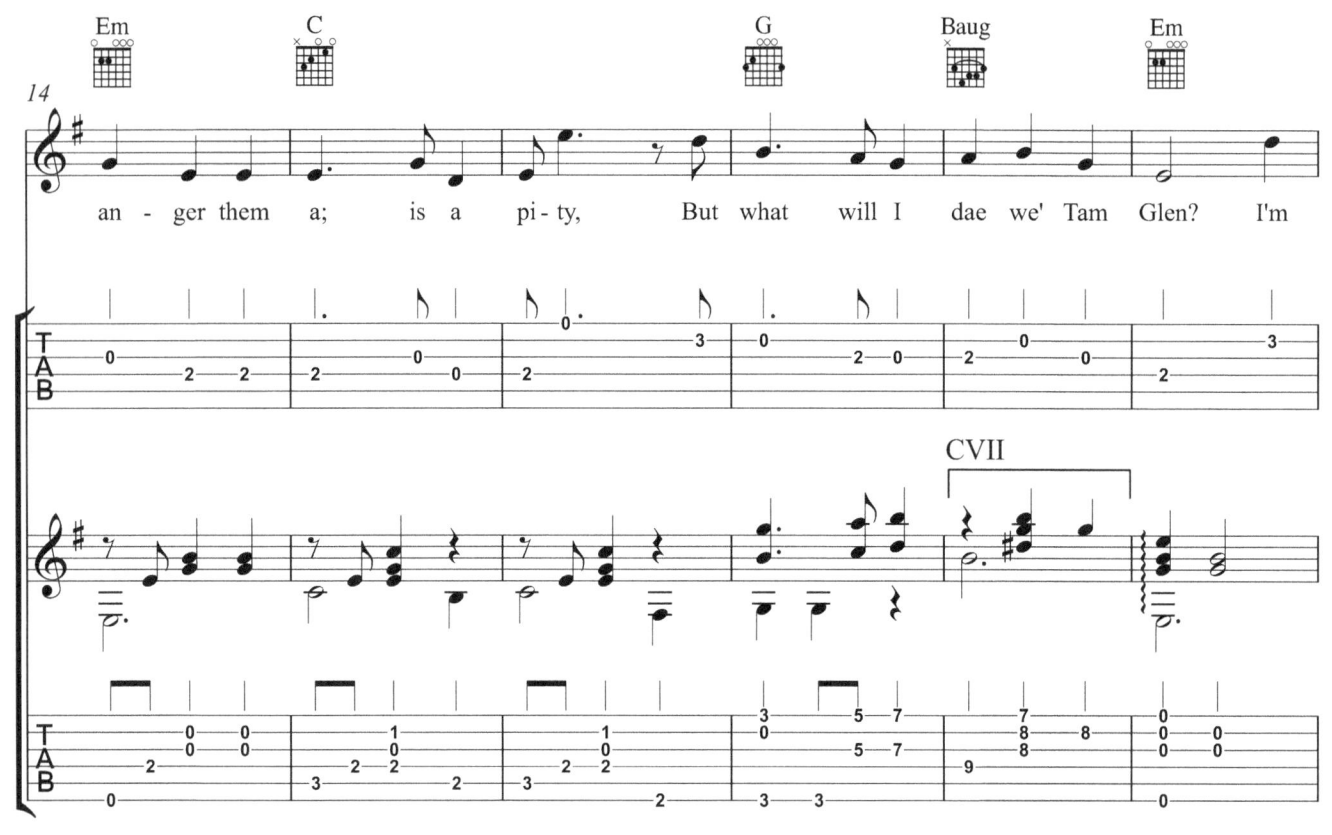

an - ger them a; is a pi - ty, But what will I dae we' Tam Glen? I'm

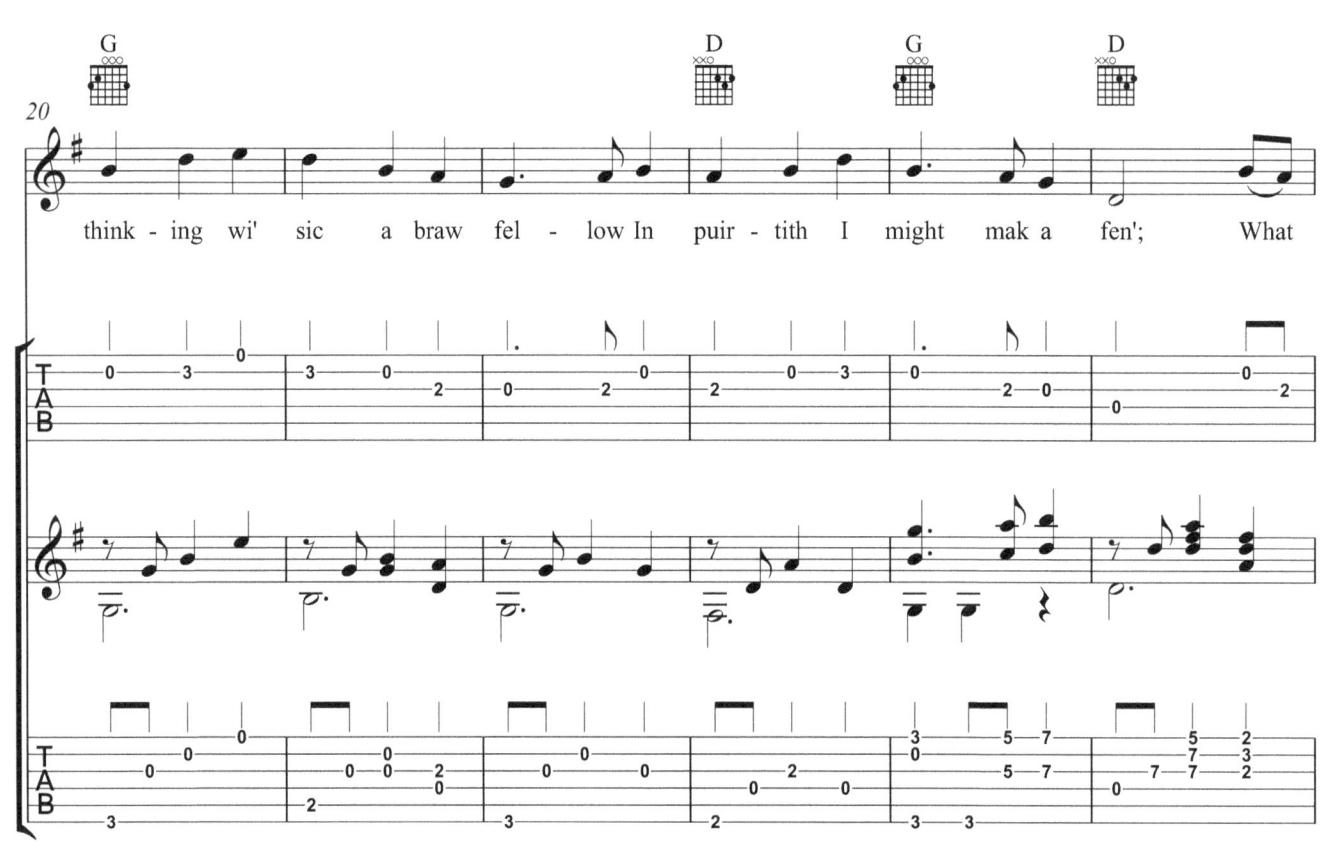

think - ing wi' sic a braw fel - low In puir - tith I might mak a fen'; What

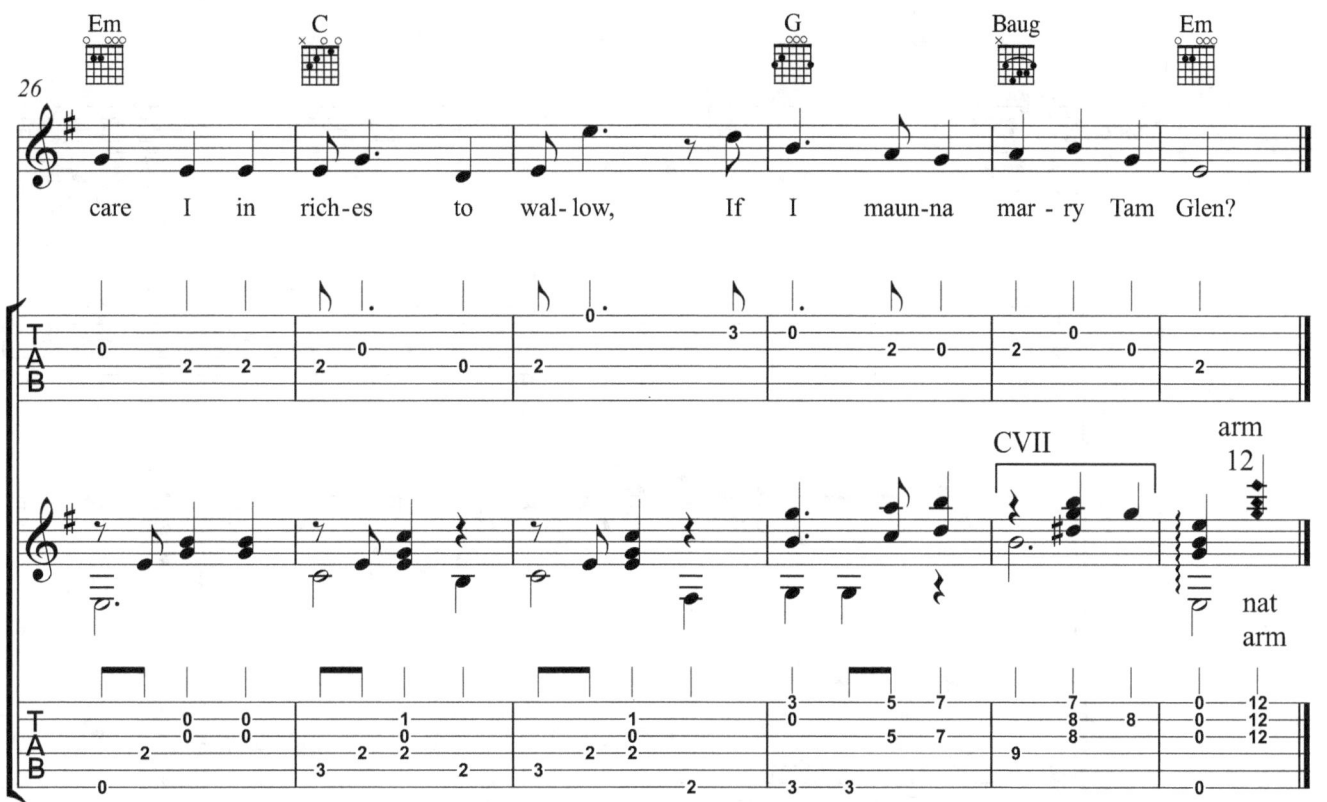

3

There's Lowrie the laird o' Dumeller:
'Guid day to you'- brute! he comes ben,
He brags and he blaws o' his siller,
But when will he dance like Tam Glen?
My minnie does constantly deave me,
And bids me beware o young men.
They flatter, she says, to deceive me-
But wha can think sae o' Tam Glen ?

My daddie says, gin I'll forsake him,
He'd gie me guid hunder marks ten.
But if it's ordain'd I maun take him,
0, wha will I get but Tam Glen?
Yestreen at the Valentines' dealing,
My heart to my mou gied a sten,
For thrice I drew ane without failing,
And thrice it was written, Tam Glen!'

The last Halloween I was waukin
My droukit sark-sleeve, as ye ken-
His likeness came up the house staukin,
And the very grey breeks o' Tam Glen!
Come, counsel, dear Tittie, don't tarry!
I'll gie ye my bonie black hen,
Gif ye will advise me to marry
The lad, I lo'e dearly, Tam Glen.

To Mary In Heaven

Robert Burns

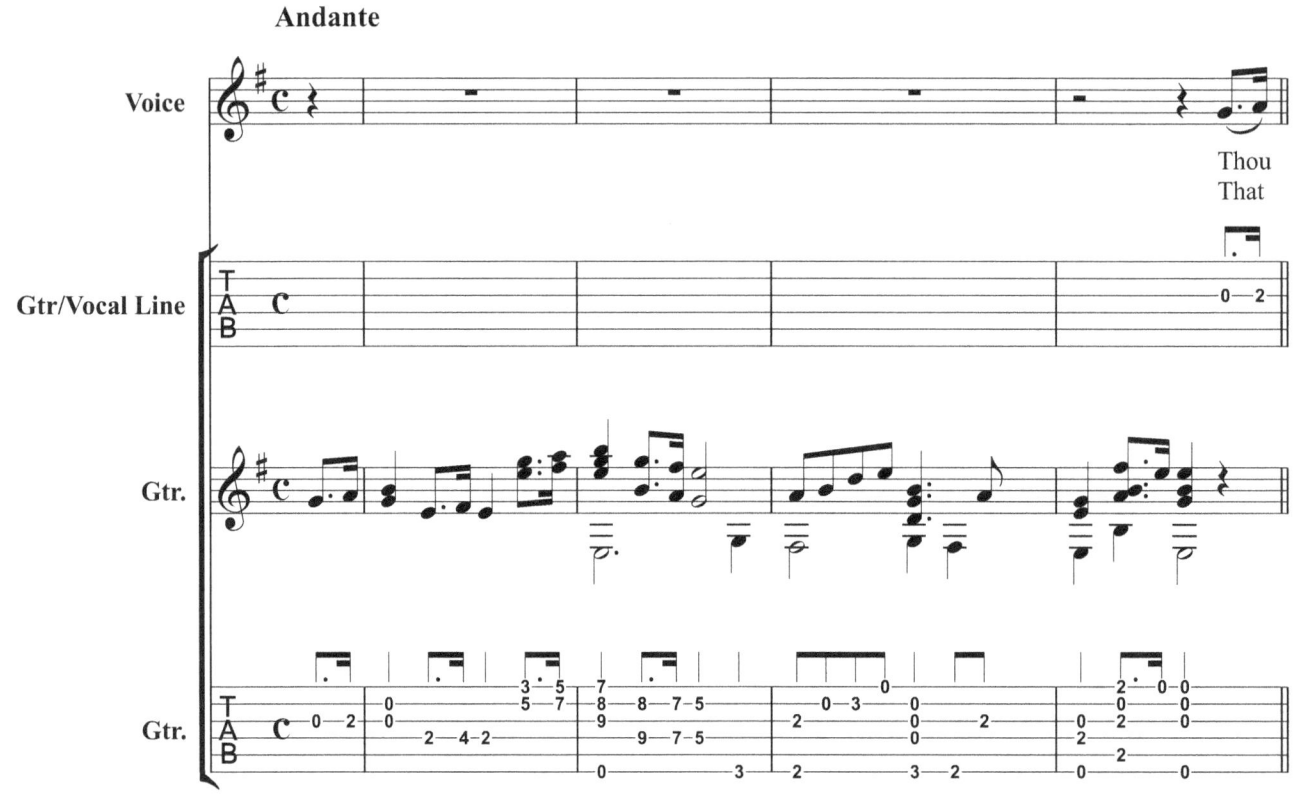

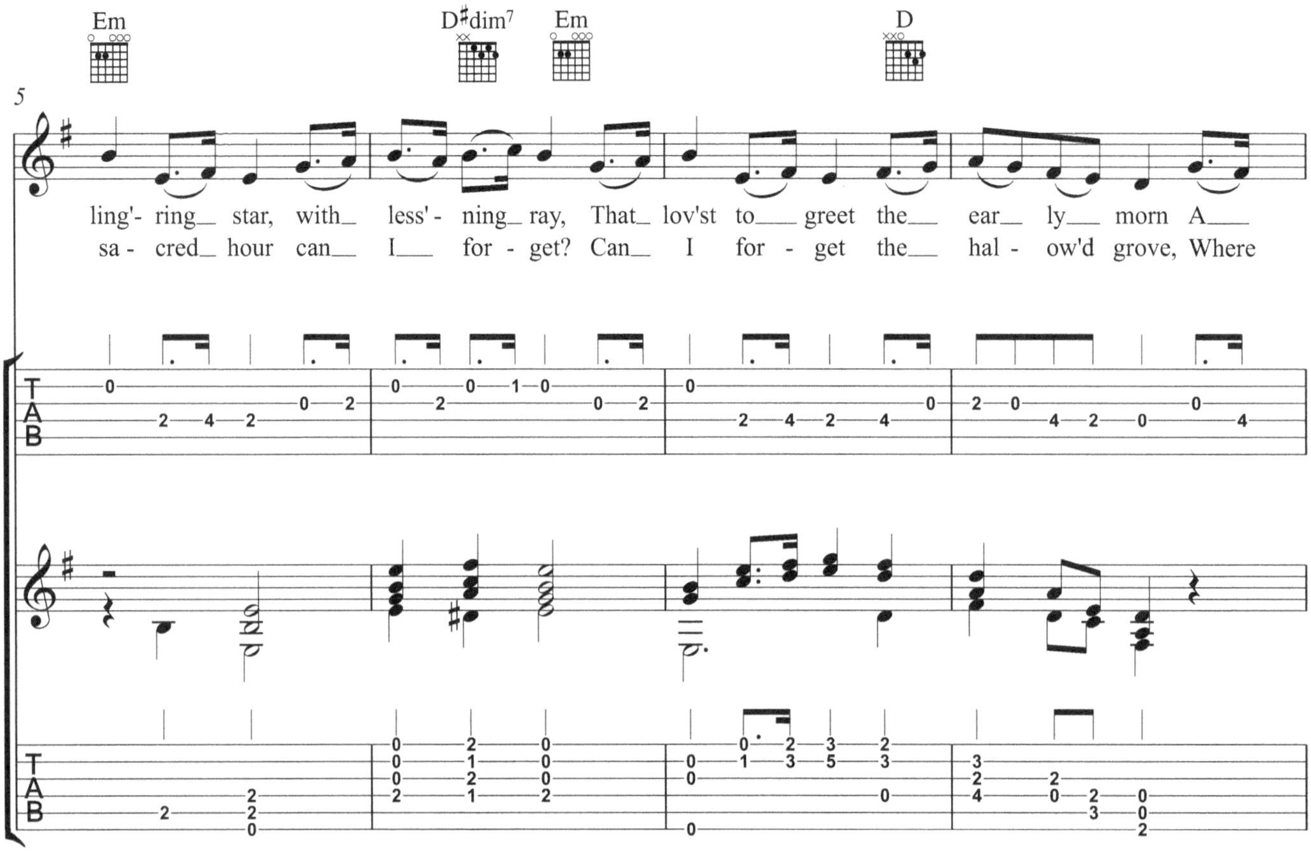

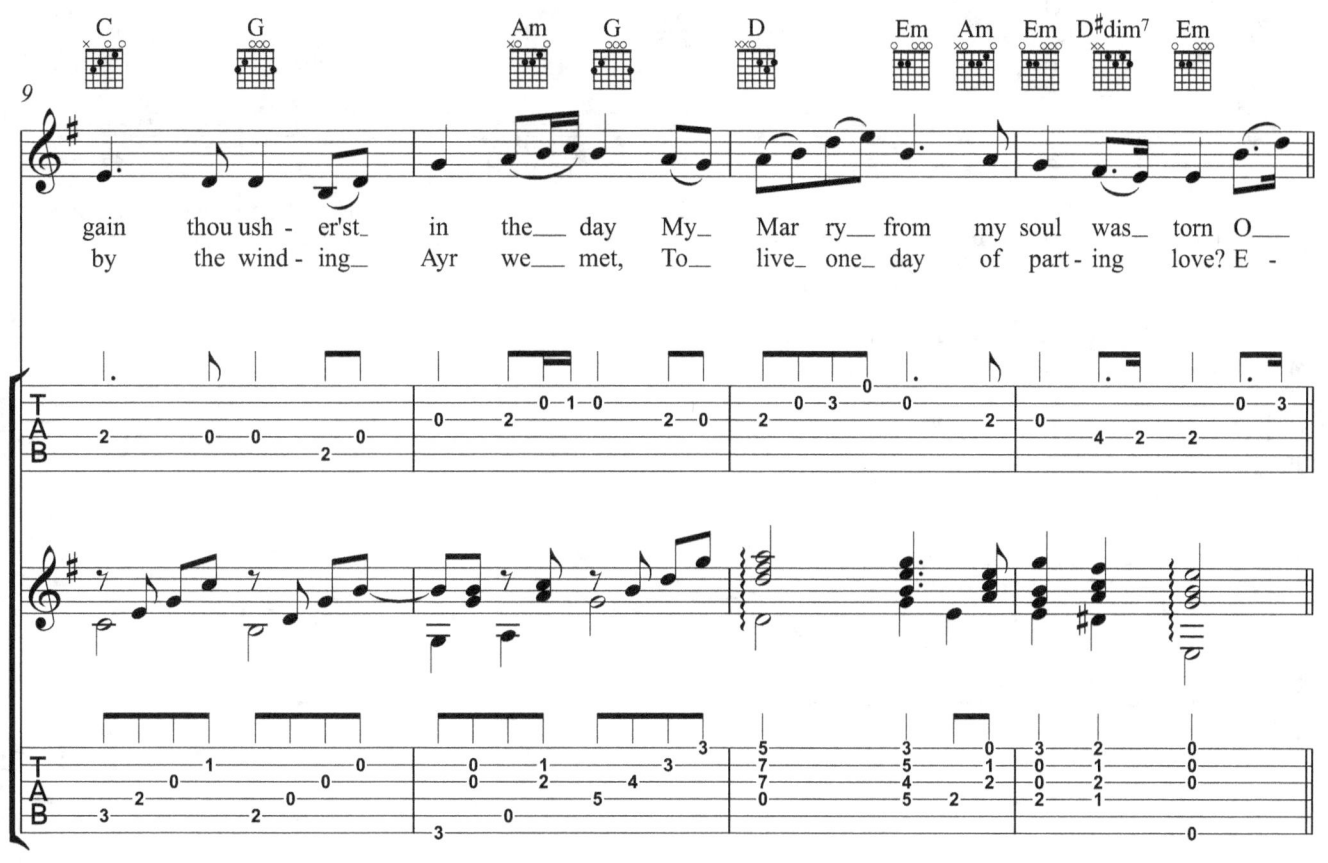

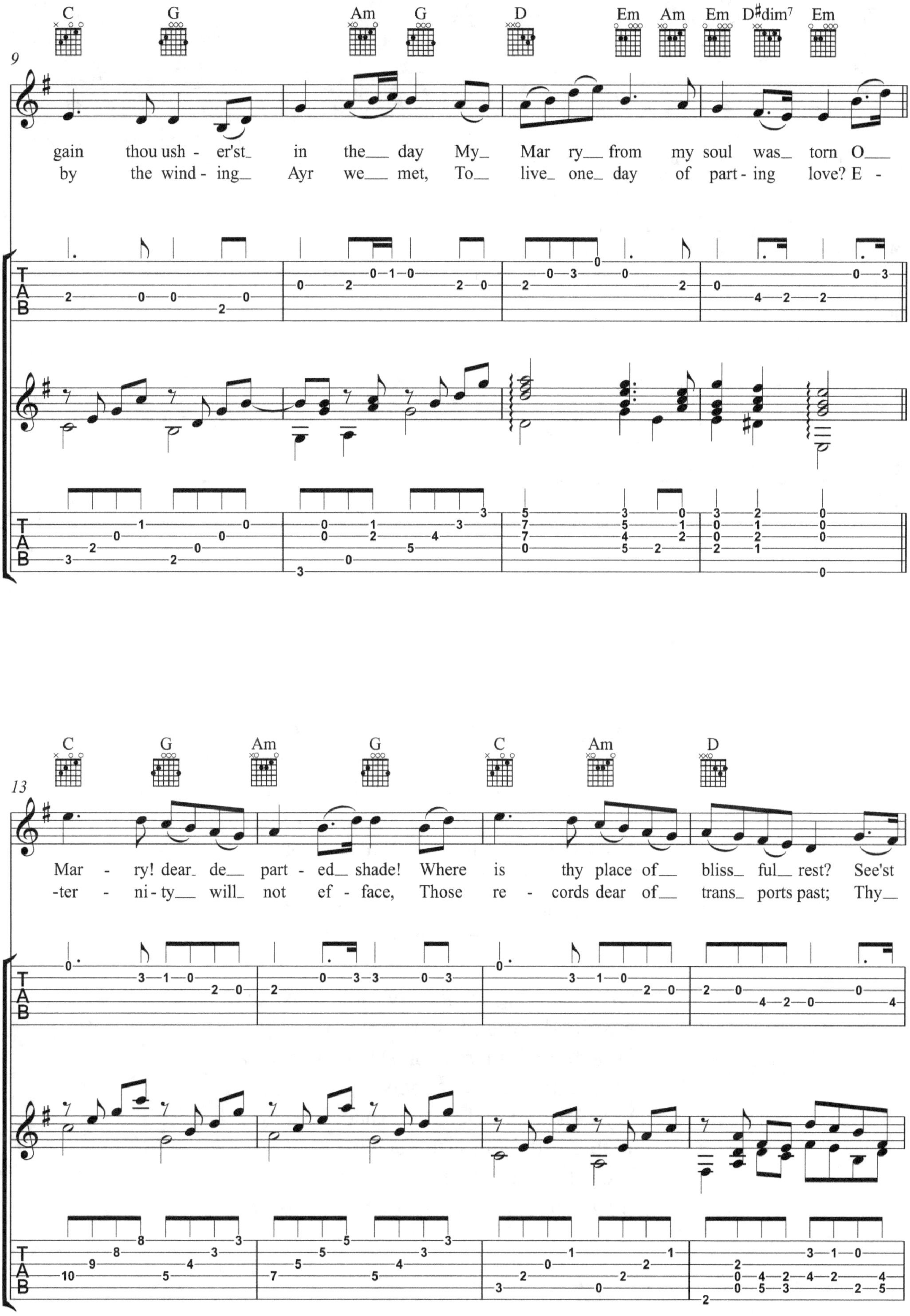

gain thou ush - er'st in the___ day My___ Mar ry___ from my soul was___ torn O___
by the wind - ing___ Ayr we___ met, To___ live___ one___ day of part - ing love? E -

Mar - ry! dear_ de_ part - ed_ shade! Where is thy place of___ bliss_ ful___ rest? See'st
-ter - ni - ty___ will___ not ef - face, Those re - cords dear of___ trans_ ports past; Thy___

18

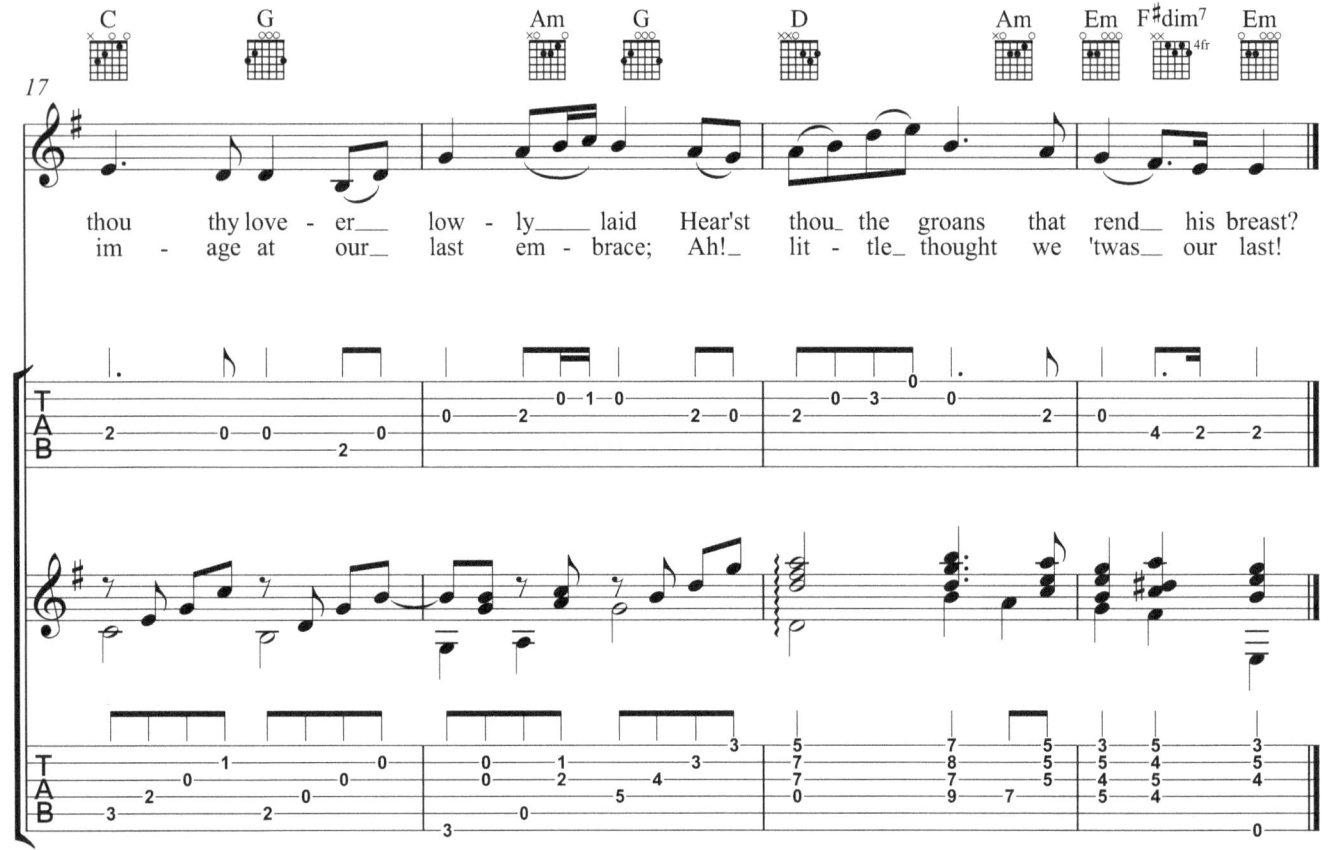

Ayr, gurgling, kiss'd his pebbled shore,
O'erhung with wild-woods, thickening green;
The fragrant birch and hawthorn hoar,
'Twin'd amorous round the raptur'd scene:
The flowers sprang wanton to be prest,
The birds sang love on every spray;
Till too, too soon, the glowing west,
Proclaim'd the speed of winged day.

Still o'er these scenes my mem'ry wakes,
And fondly broods with miser-care;
Time but th' impression stronger makes,
As streams their channels deeper wear,
My Mary! dear departed shade!
Where is thy blissful place of rest?
See'st thou thy lover lowly laid?
Hear'st thou the groans that rend his breast?

Musing On The Roaring Ocean

Robert Burns

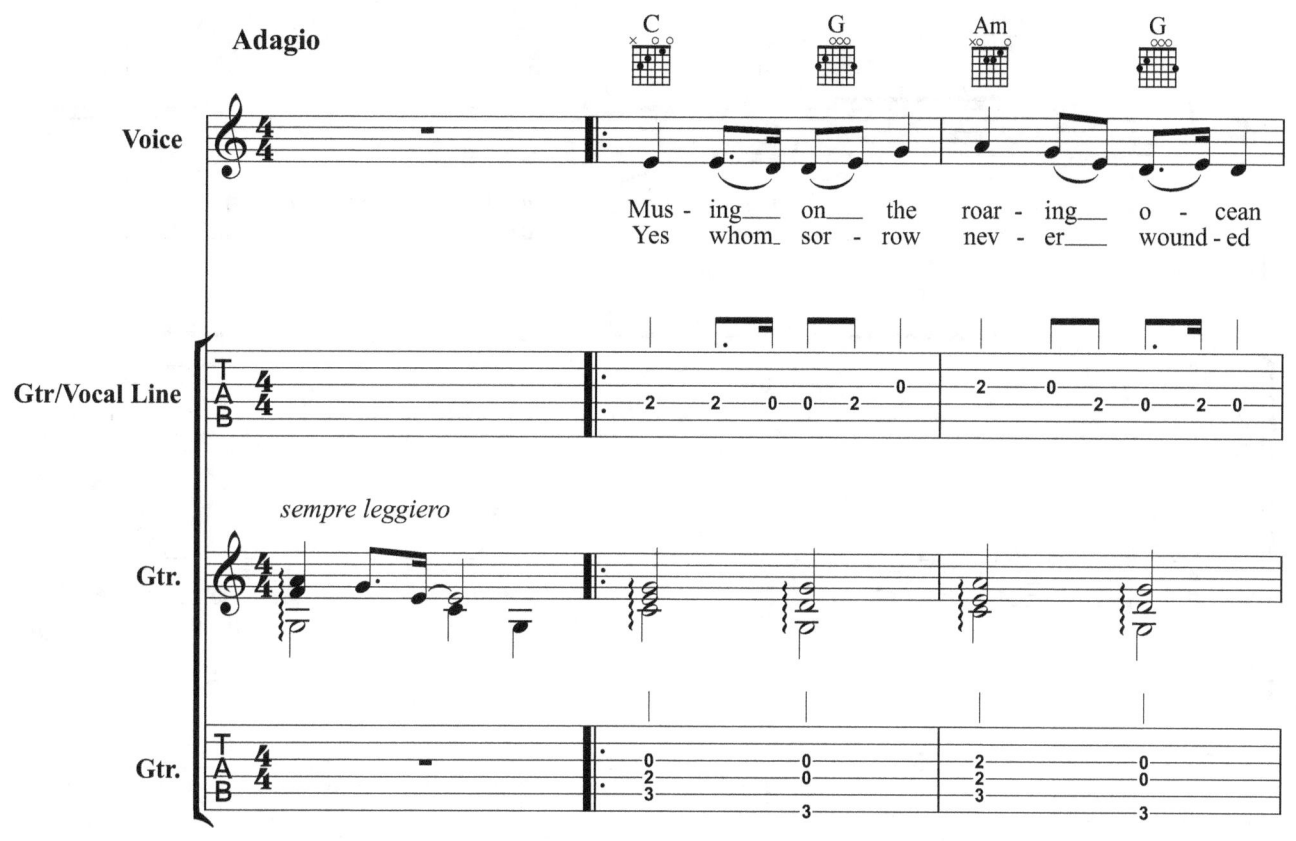

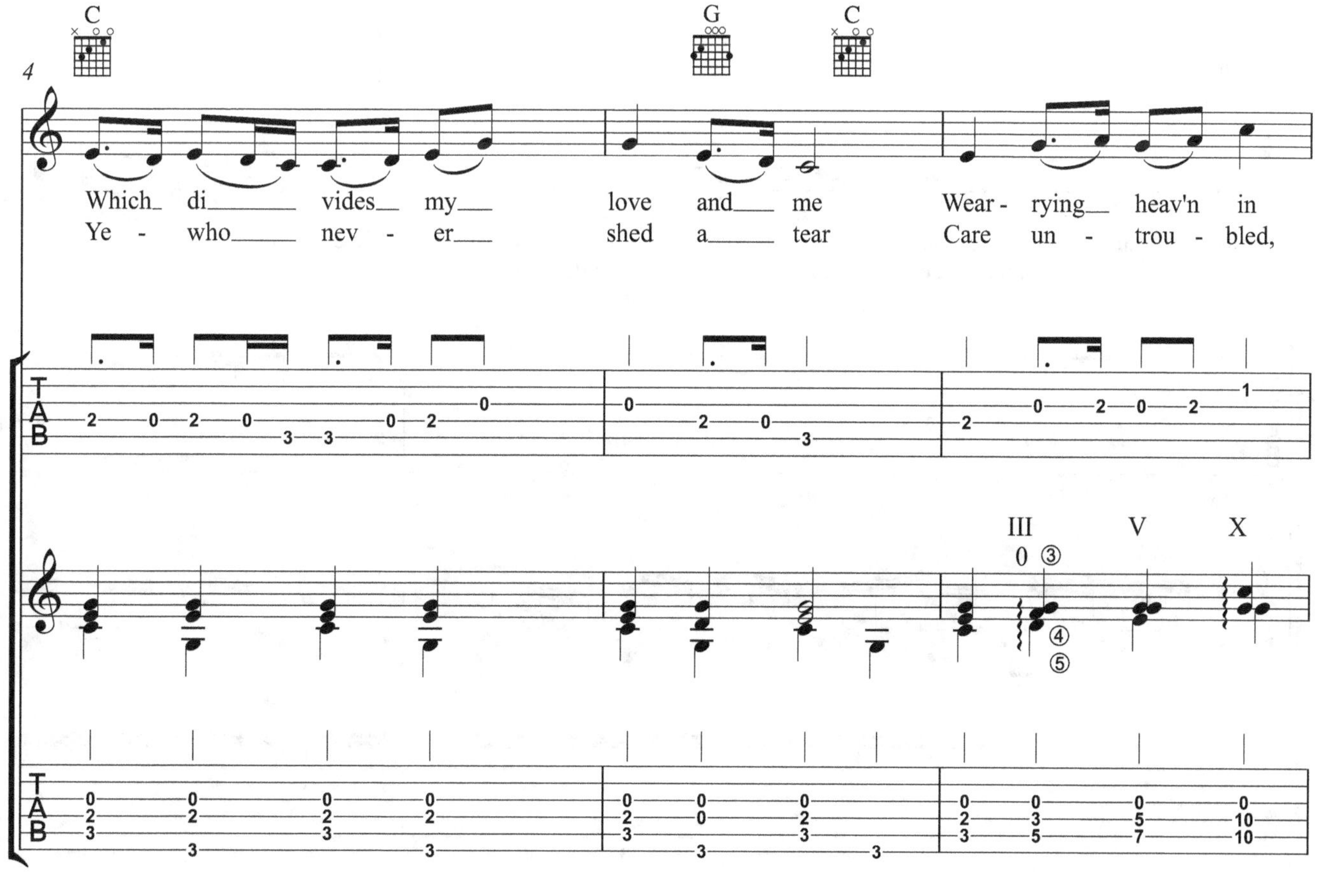

Voice lyrics (measure 1–3):
Mus - ing__ on_ the roar - ing_ o - cean
Yes whom_ sor - row nev - er__ wound - ed

Voice lyrics (measure 4–6):
Which_ di____ vides_ my__ love and_ me Wear - rying_ heav'n in
Ye - who__ nev - er__ shed a_ tear Care un - trou - bled,

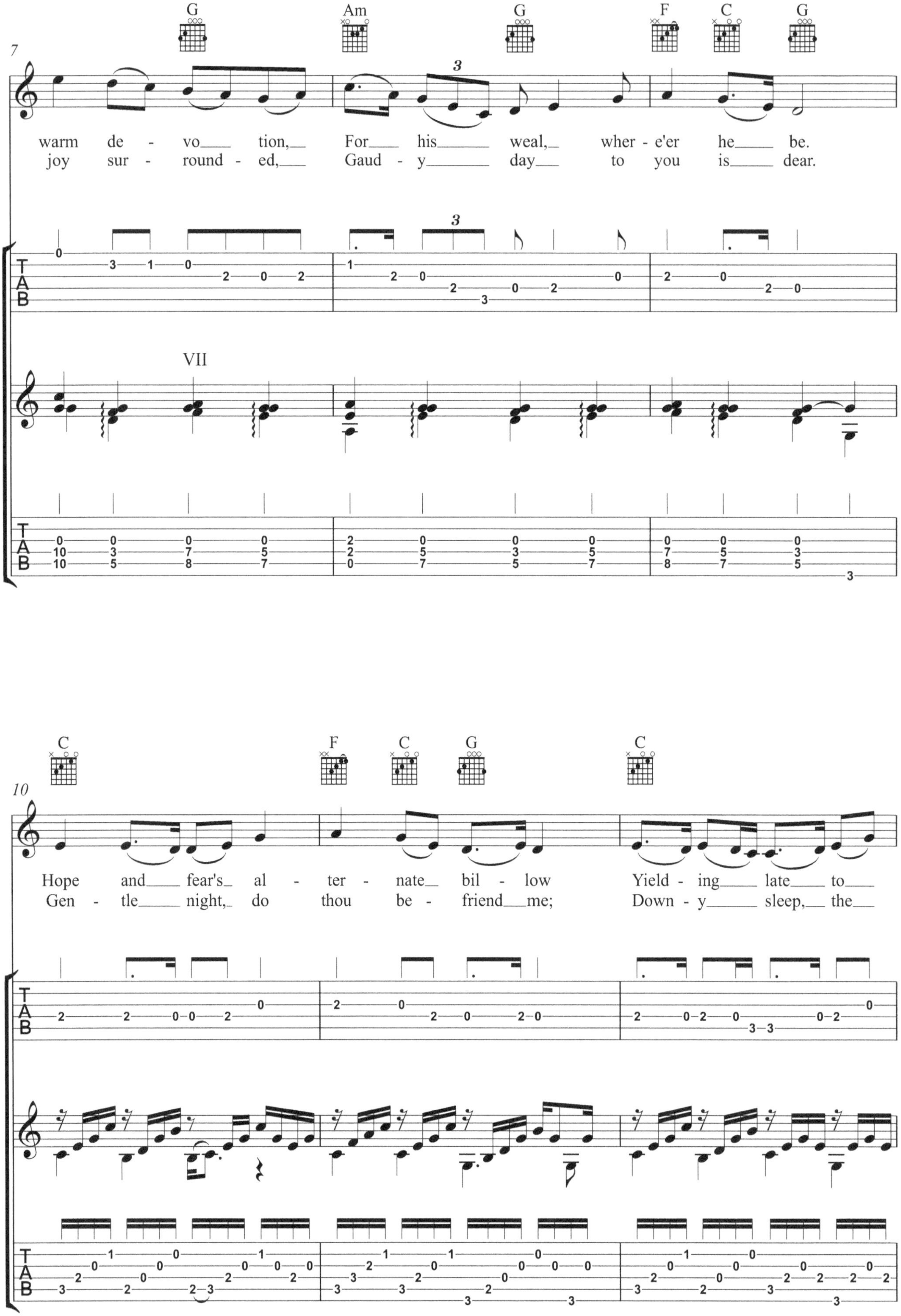

warm de - vo___ tion,___ For___ his___ weal, wher - e'er he___ be.
joy sur - round - ed,___ Gaud - y___ day___ to you is___ dear.

Hope and___ fear's___ al - ter - nate___ bil - low Yield - ing___ late___ to
Gen - tle___ night,___ do thou be - friend___ me; Down - y___ sleep,___ the___

21

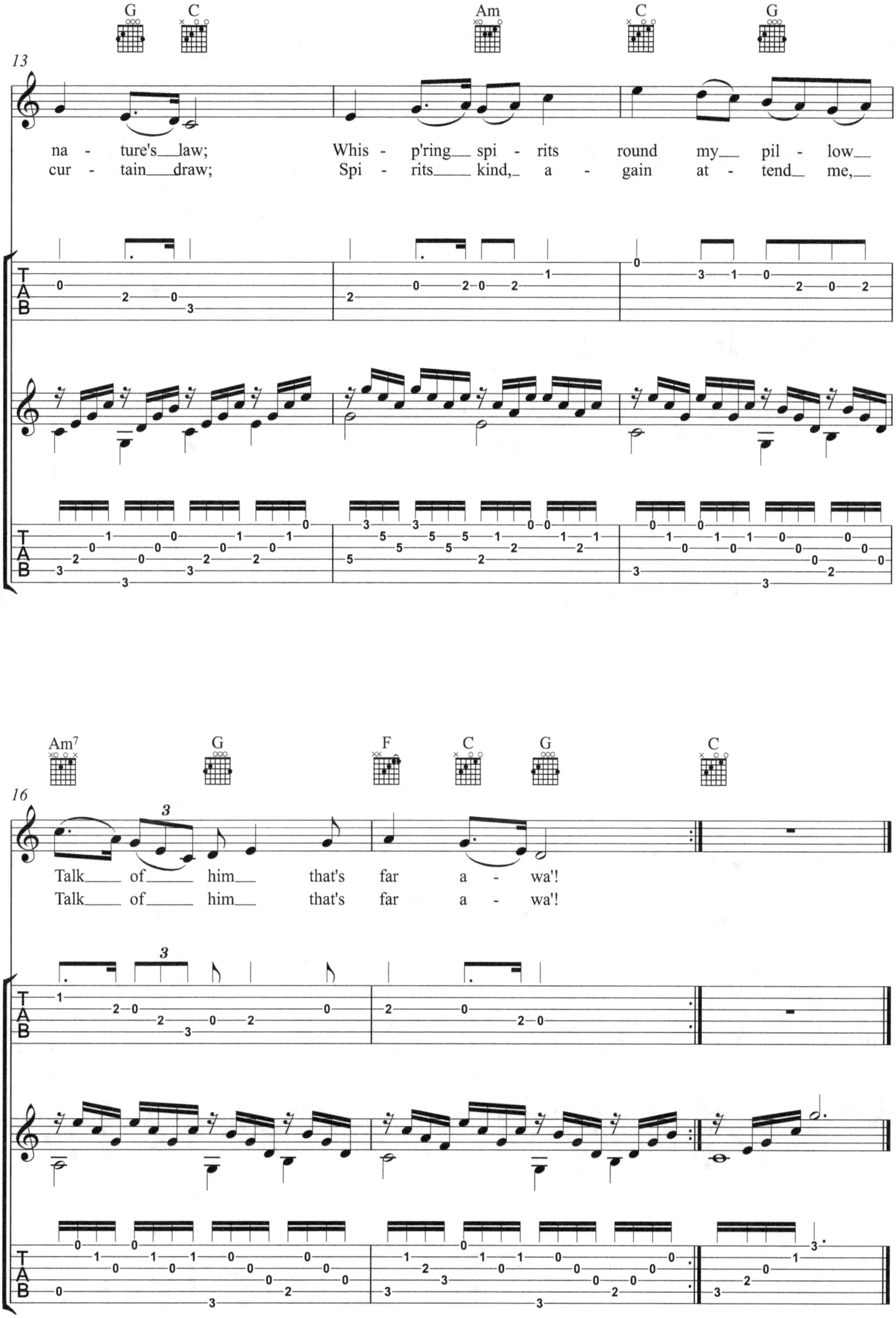

na - ture's___law; Whis - p'ring___spi - rits round my___ pil - low___
cur - tain___draw; Spi - rits___kind, a - gain at - tend___ me,___

Talk___ of___ him___ that's far a - wa'!
Talk___ of___ him___ that's far a - wa'!

Logan Braes

Robert Burns

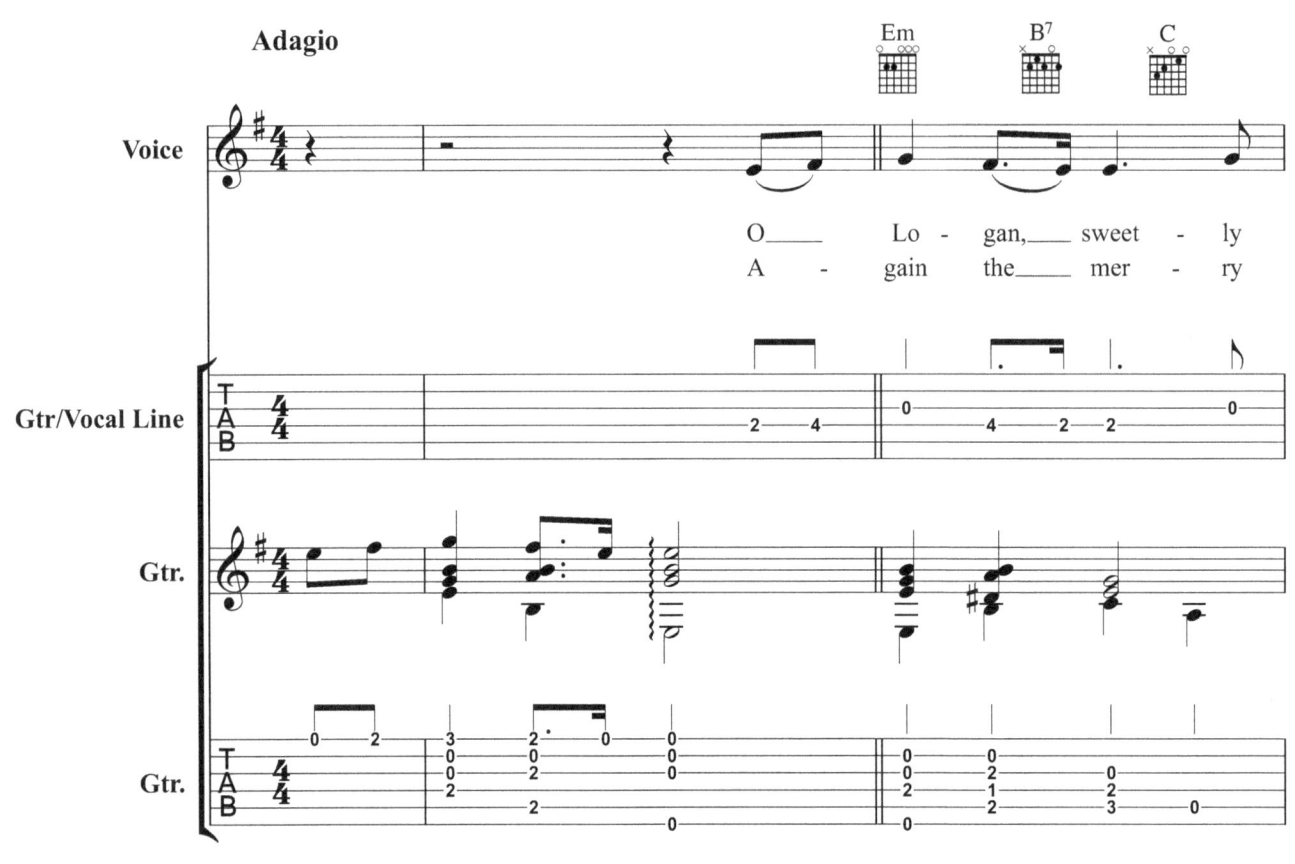

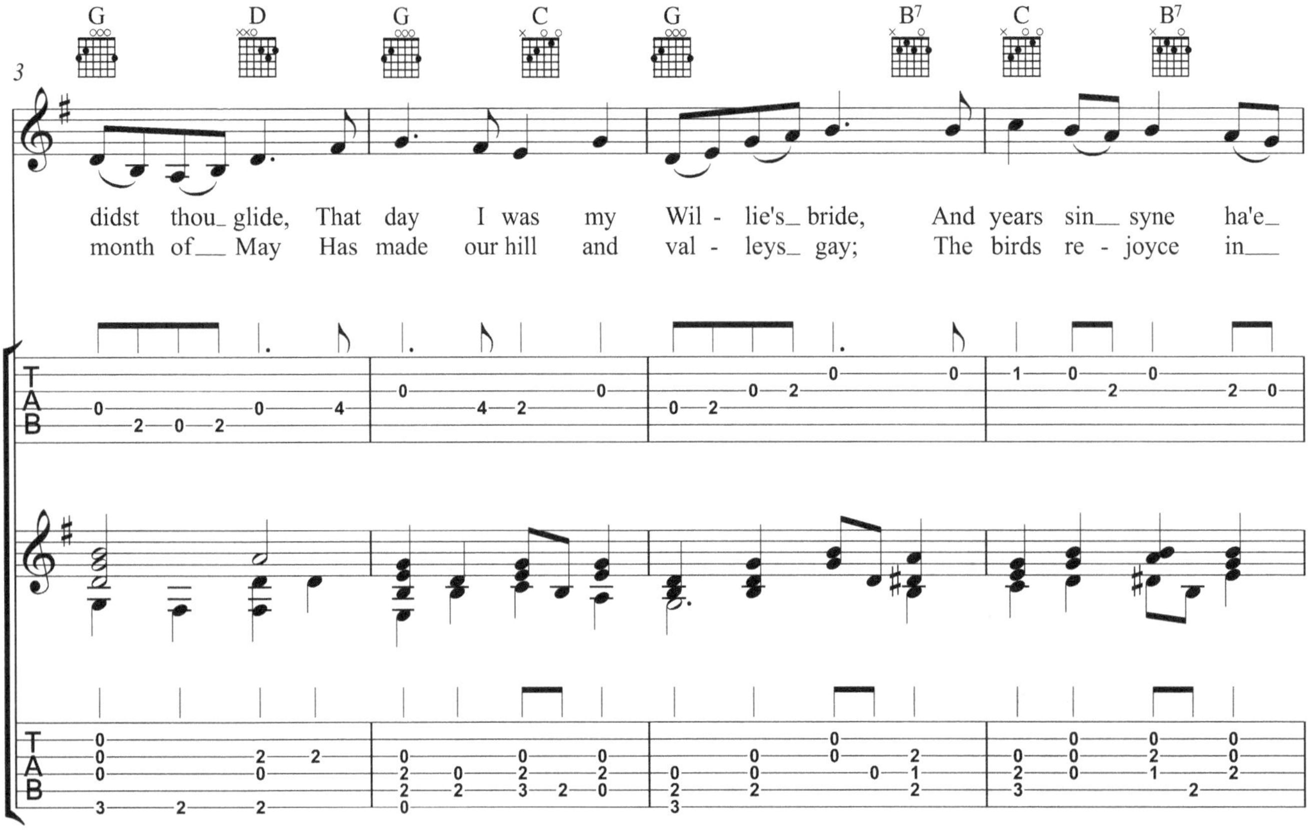

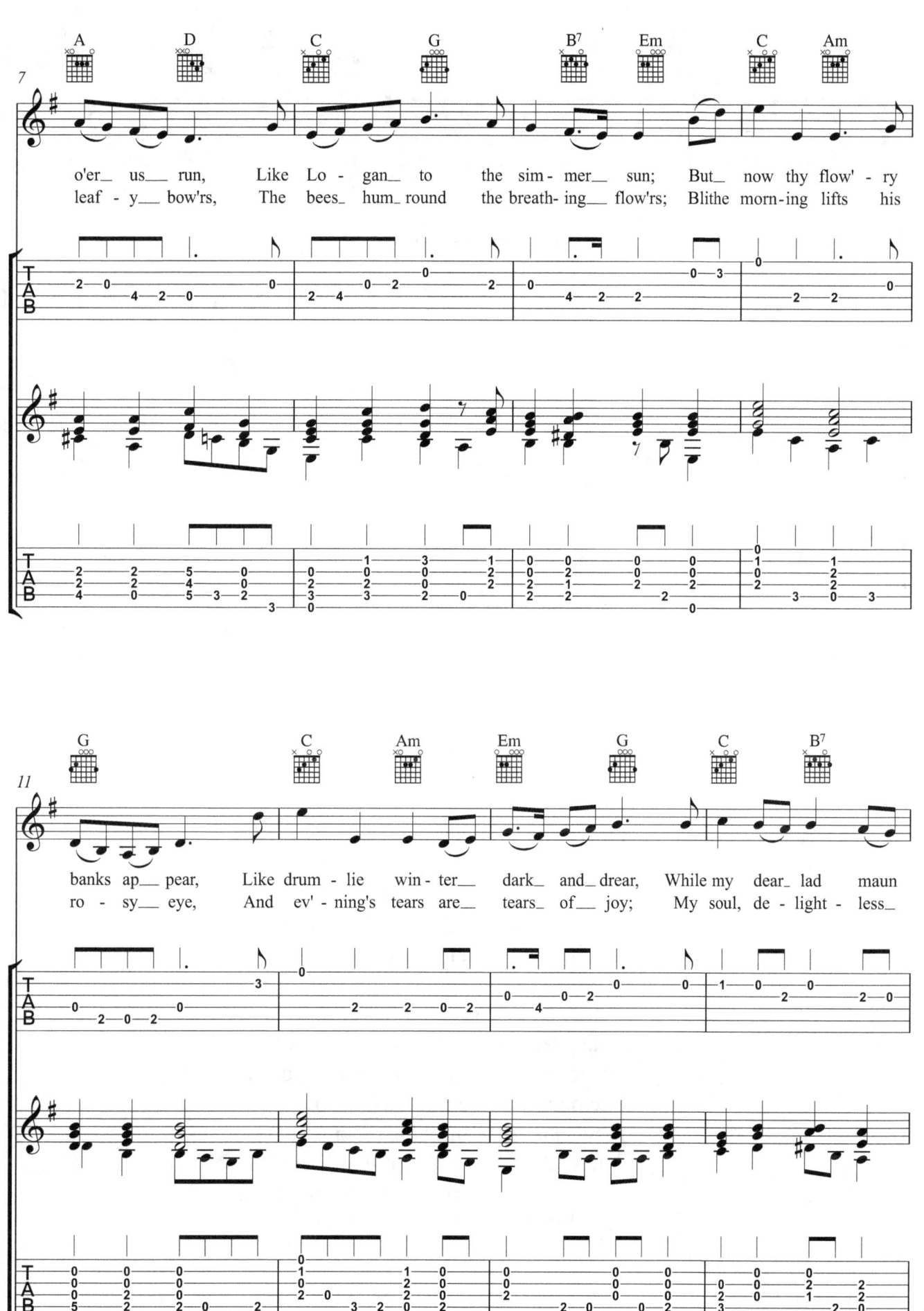

24

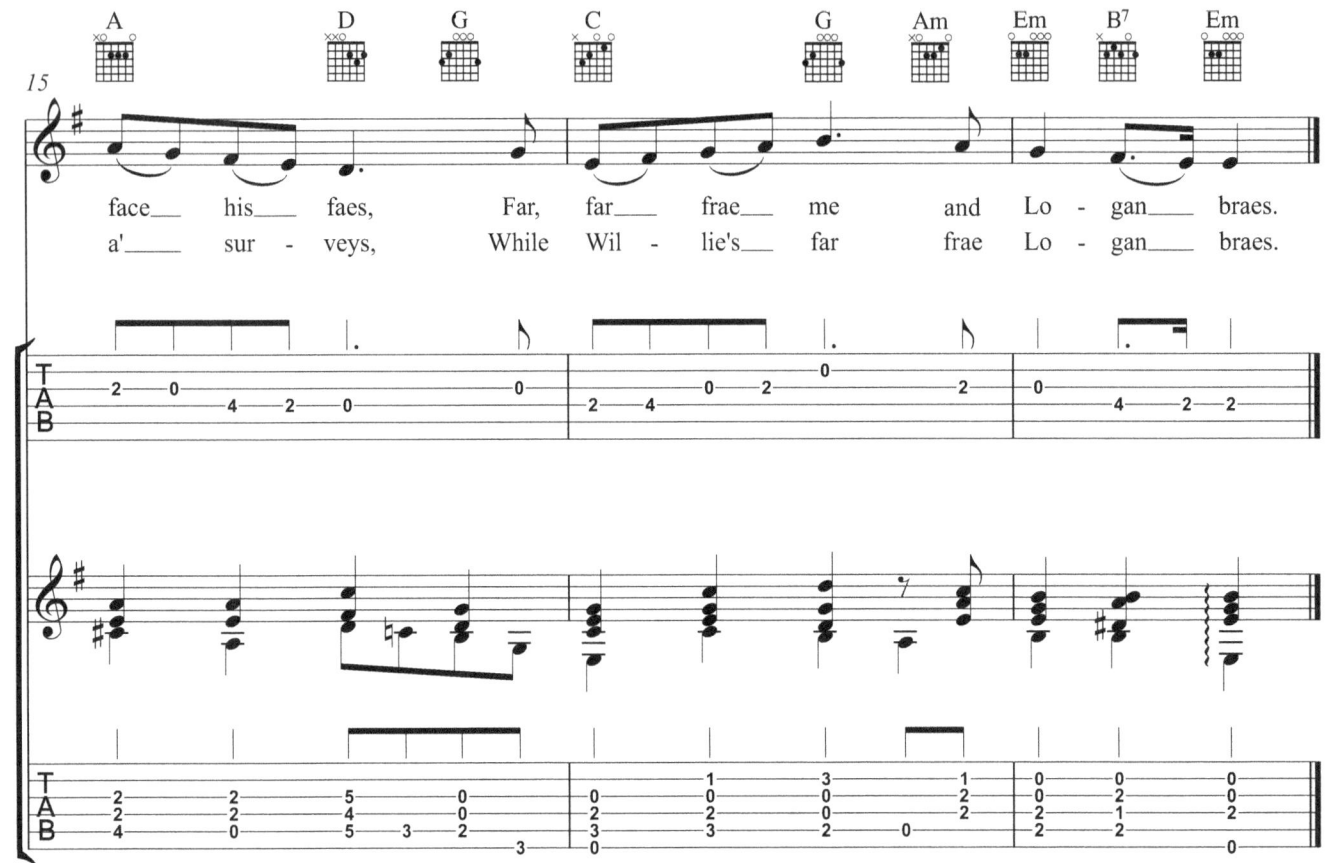

Within yon milk-white hawthorn bush,
Amang her nestlings sits the thrush:
Her faithfu' mate will share her toil,
Or wi' his song her cares beguile;
But I wi' my sweet nurslings here,
Nae mate to help, nae mate to cheer,
Pass widow'd nights and joyless days,
While Willie's far frae Logan braes.

O wae be to you, Men o' State,
That brethren rouse to deadly hate!
As ye make mony a fond heart mourn,
Sae may it on your heads return!
How can your flinty hearts enjoy
The widow's tear, the orphan's cry?
But soon may peace bring happy days,
And Willie hame to Logan braes

O, Willie Brew'd A Peck O' Maut

Robert Burns

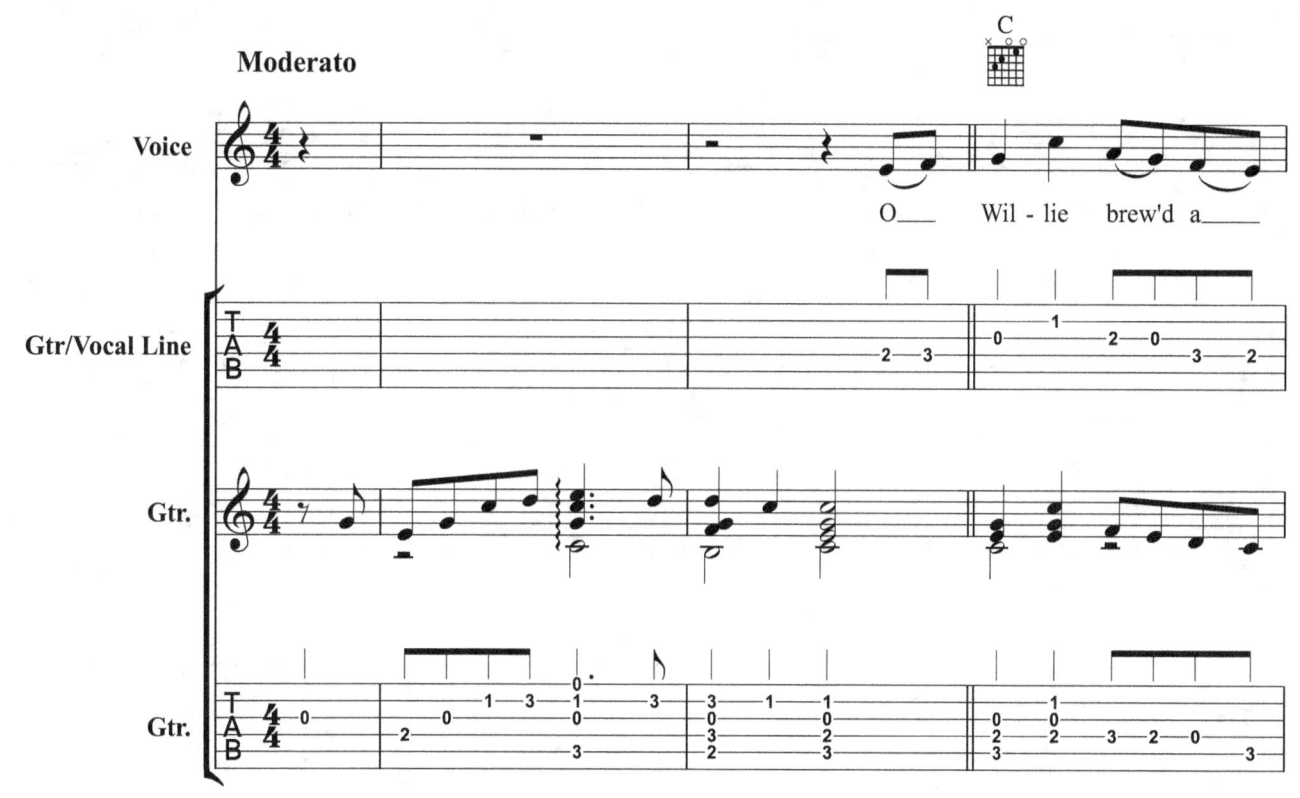

O___ Wil - lie brew'd a___

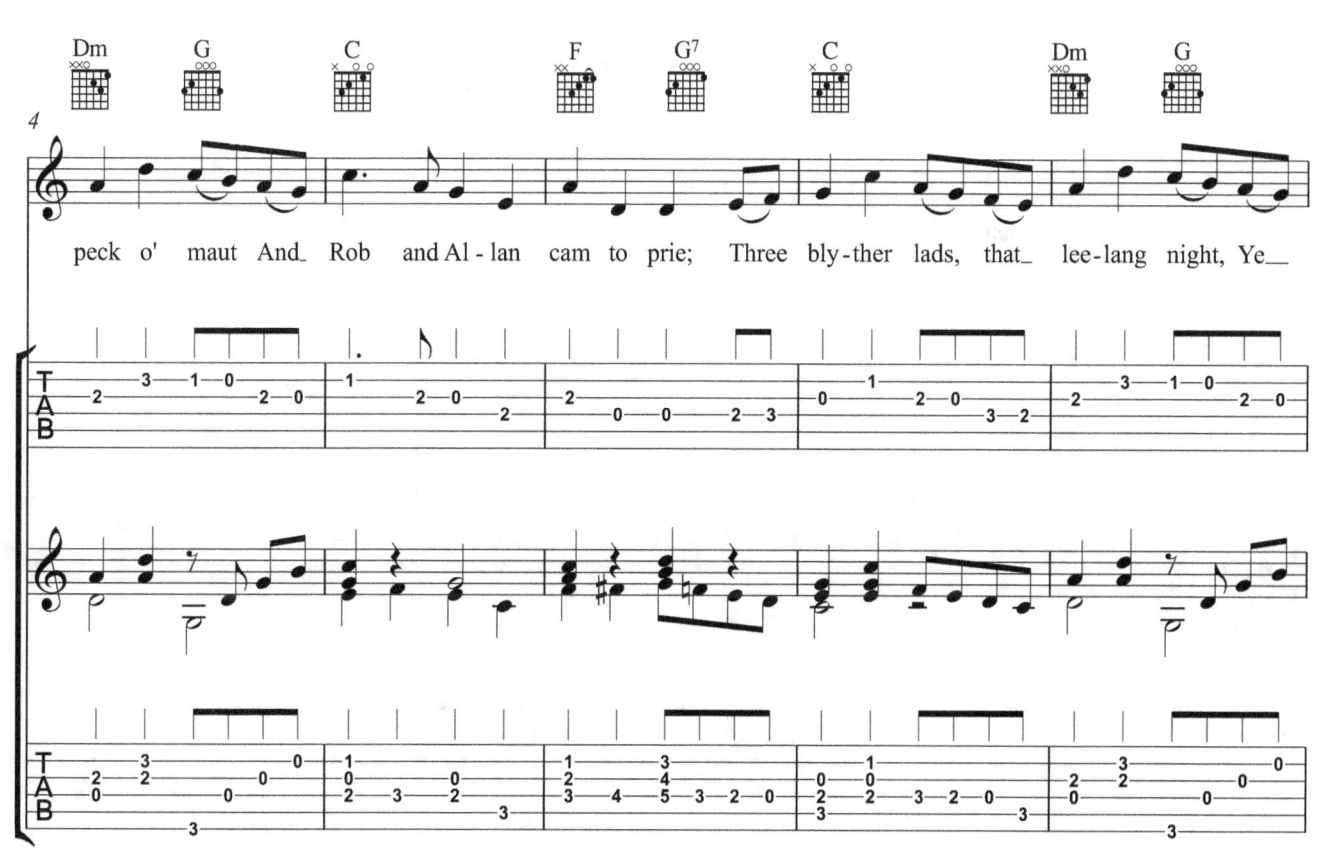

peck o' maut And_ Rob and Al - lan cam to prie; Three bly-ther lads, that_ lee-lang night, Ye___

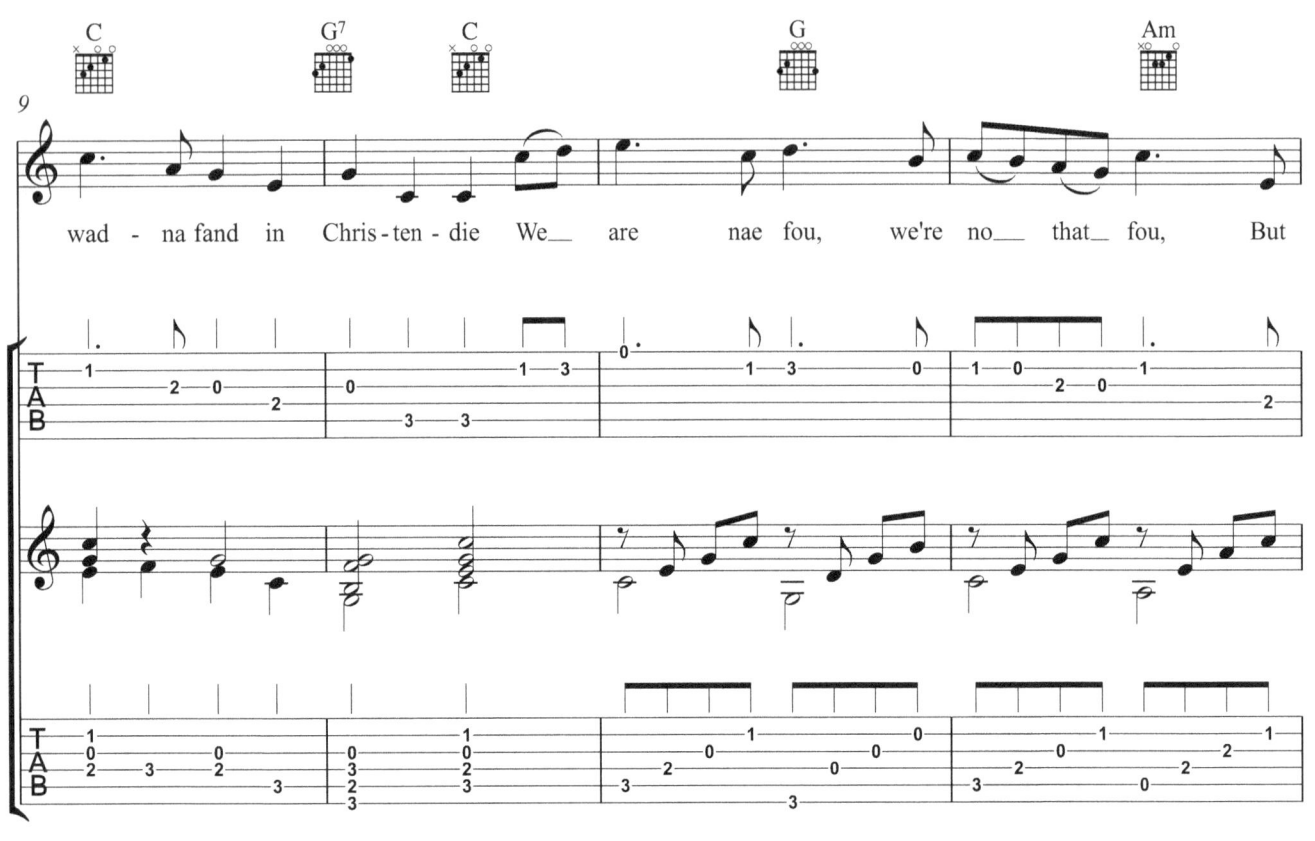

wad - na fand in Chris - ten - die We__ are nae fou, we're no__ that__ fou, But

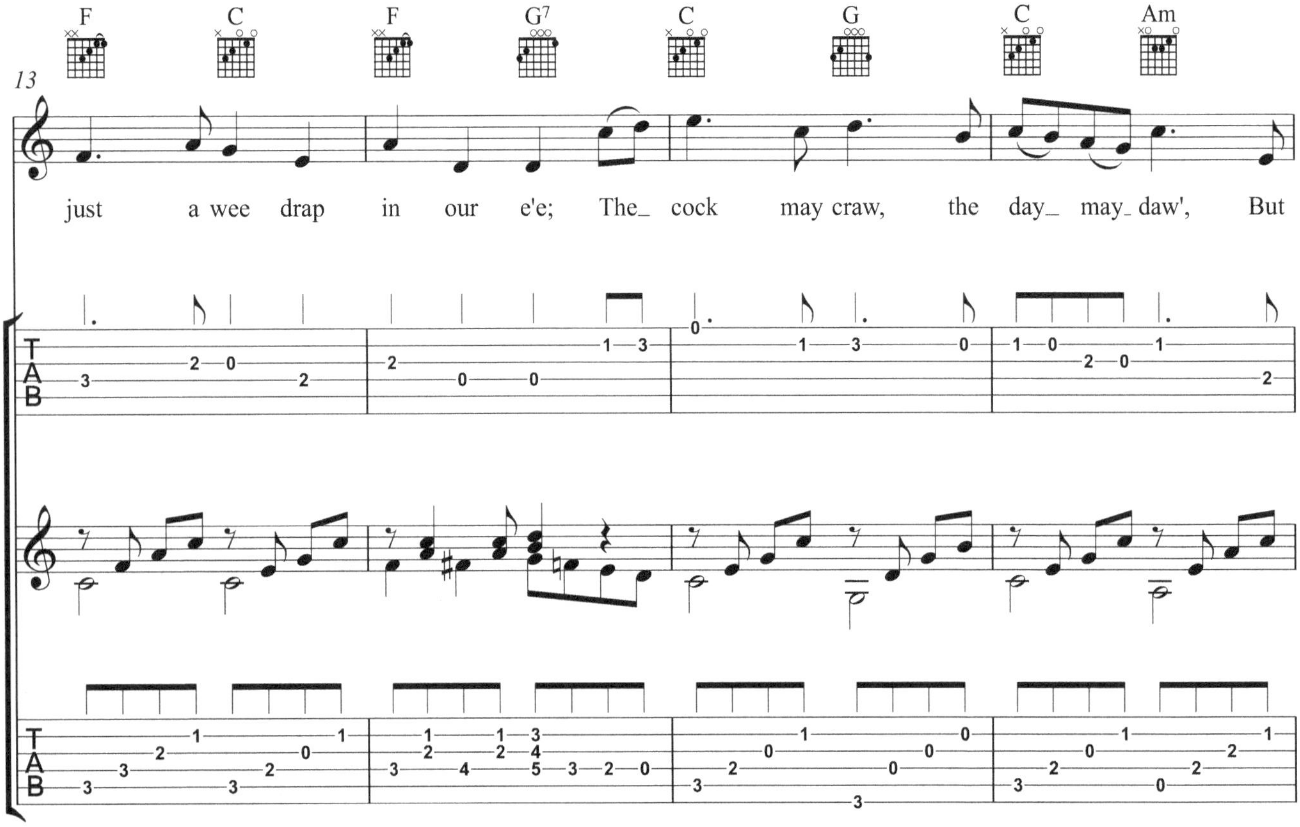

just a wee drap in our e'e; The__ cock may craw, the day__ may__ daw', But

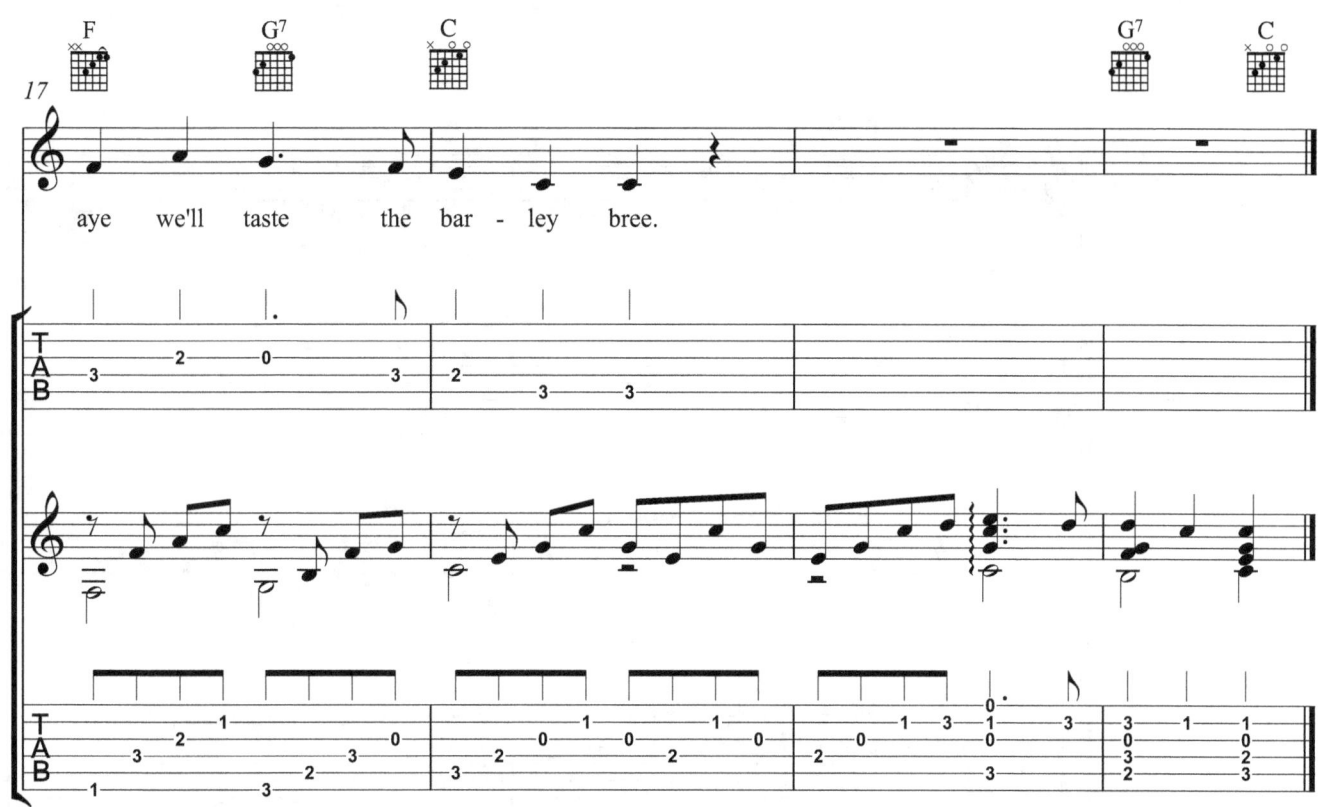

aye we'll taste the bar - ley bree.

Here are we met, three merry boys,
Three merry boys I trow are we;
And mony a night we 've merry been,
And mony mae we hope to be!
Chos. We are na fou, &c.

It is the moon, I ken her horn,
That 's blinkin in the lift sae hie;
She shines sae bright to wyle us hame,
But by my sooth she'll wait a wee!
Chos. We are na fou, &c.

Wha first shall rise to gang awa,
A cuckold, coward loun is he!
Wha first beside his chair shall fa',
He is the king amang us three!
Chos. We are na fou, &c.

O A' The Airts The Wind Can Blaw

Robert Burns

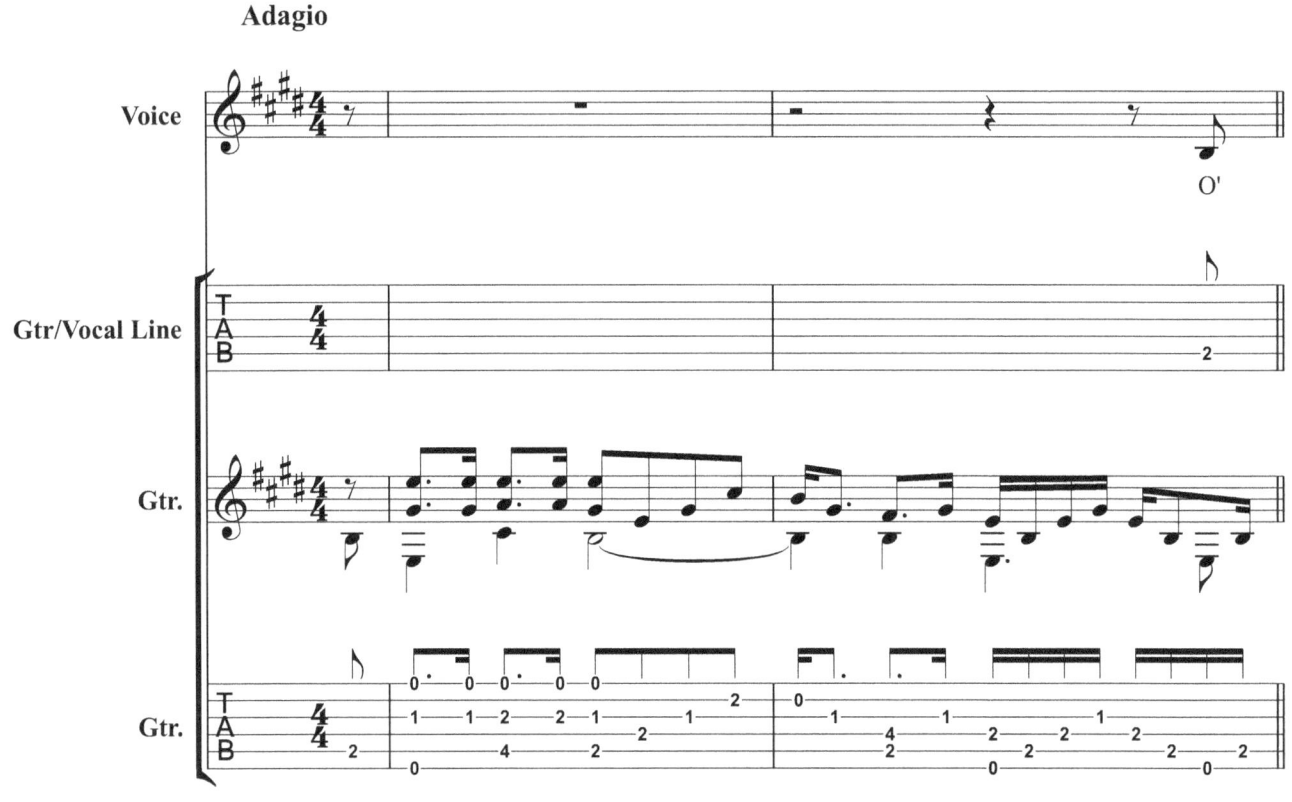

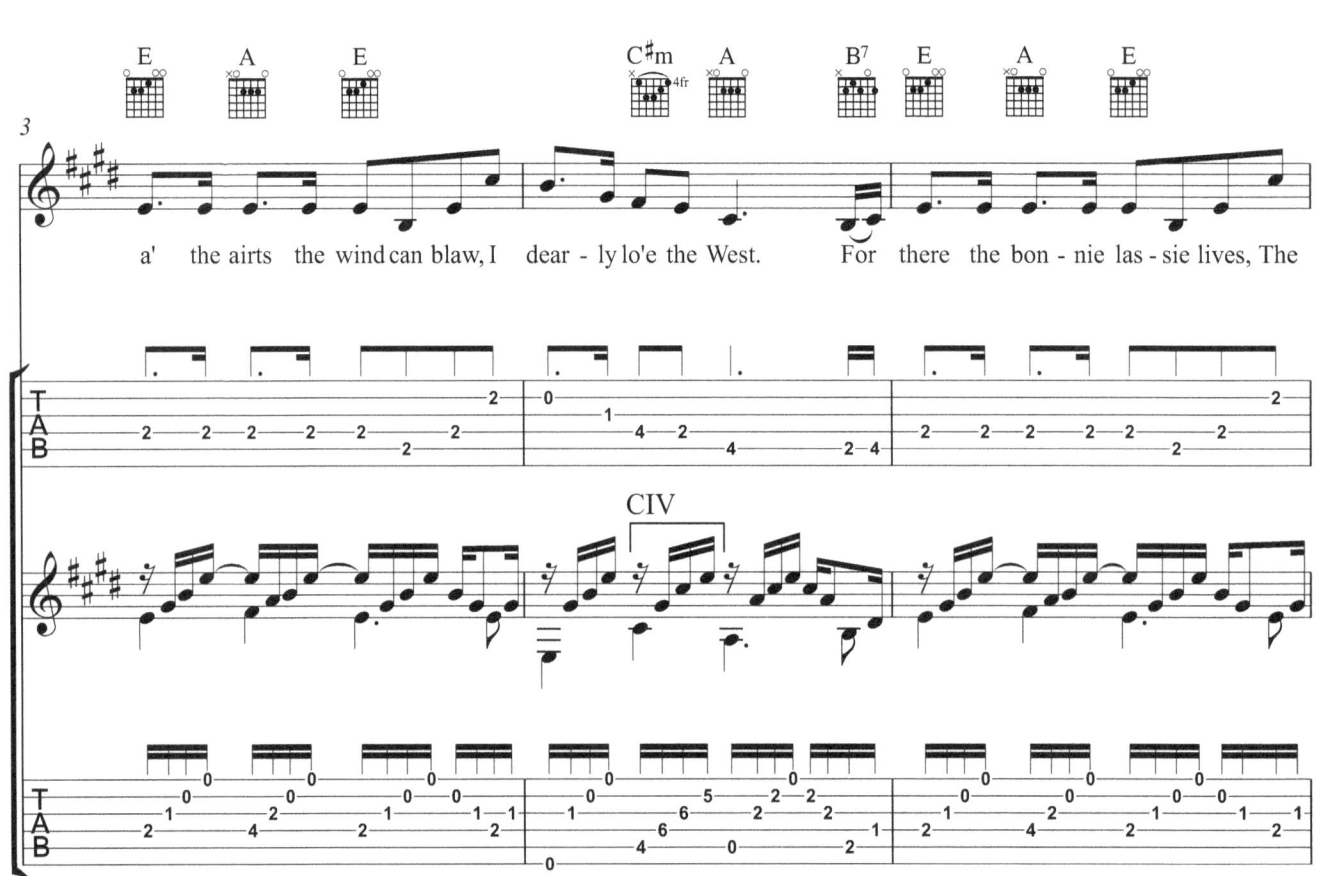

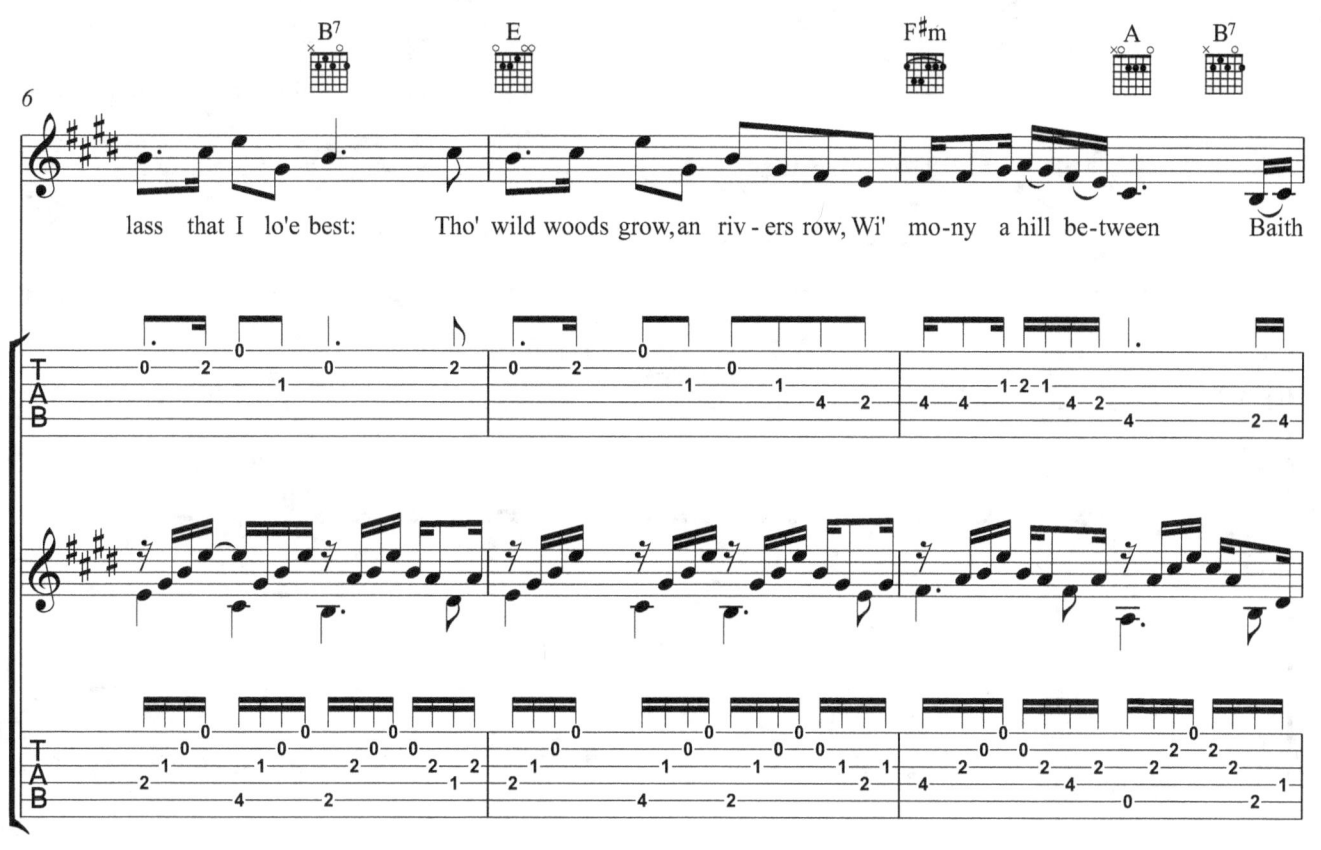

lass that I lo'e best: Tho' wild woods grow, an riv-ers row, Wi' mo-ny a hill be-tween Baith

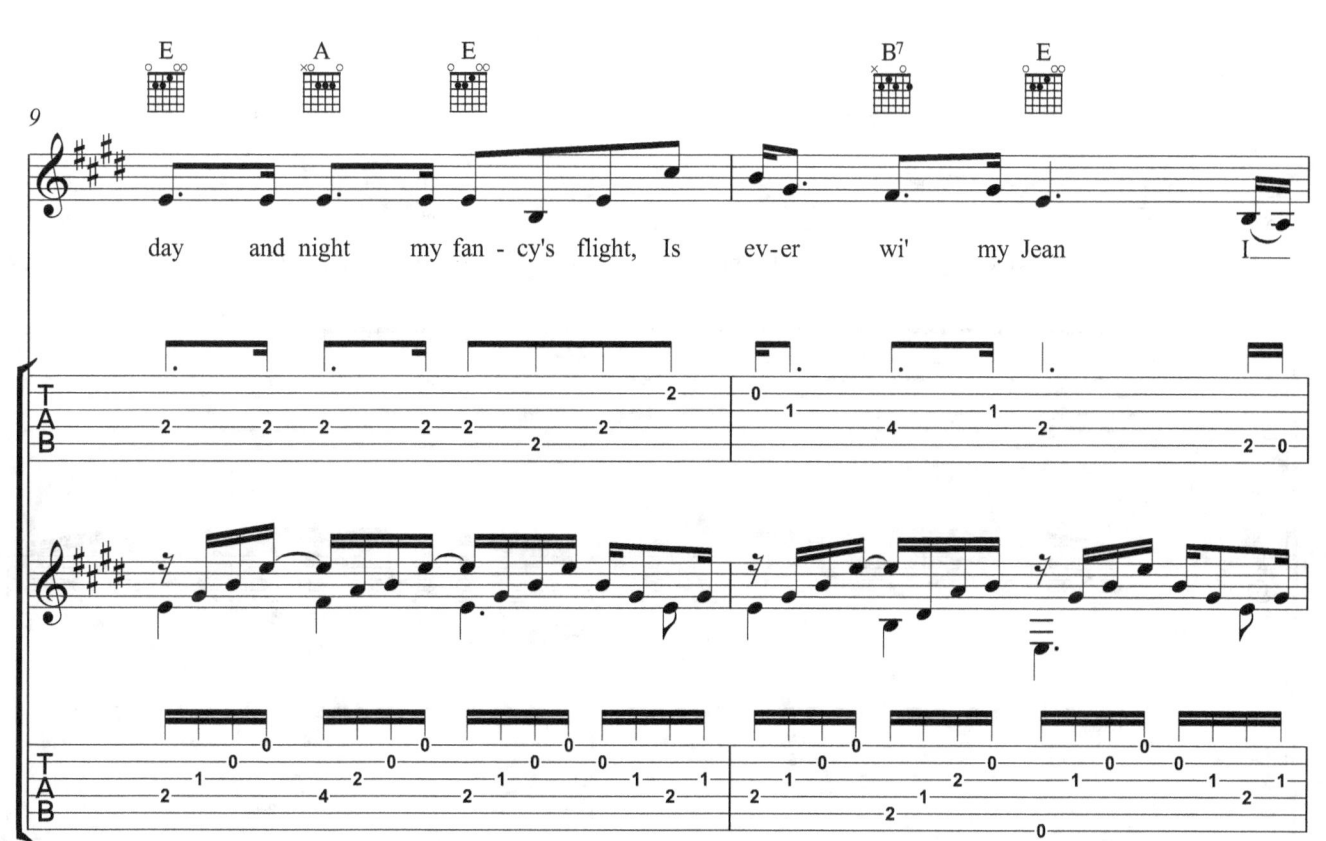

day and night my fan-cy's flight, Is ev-er wi' my Jean I

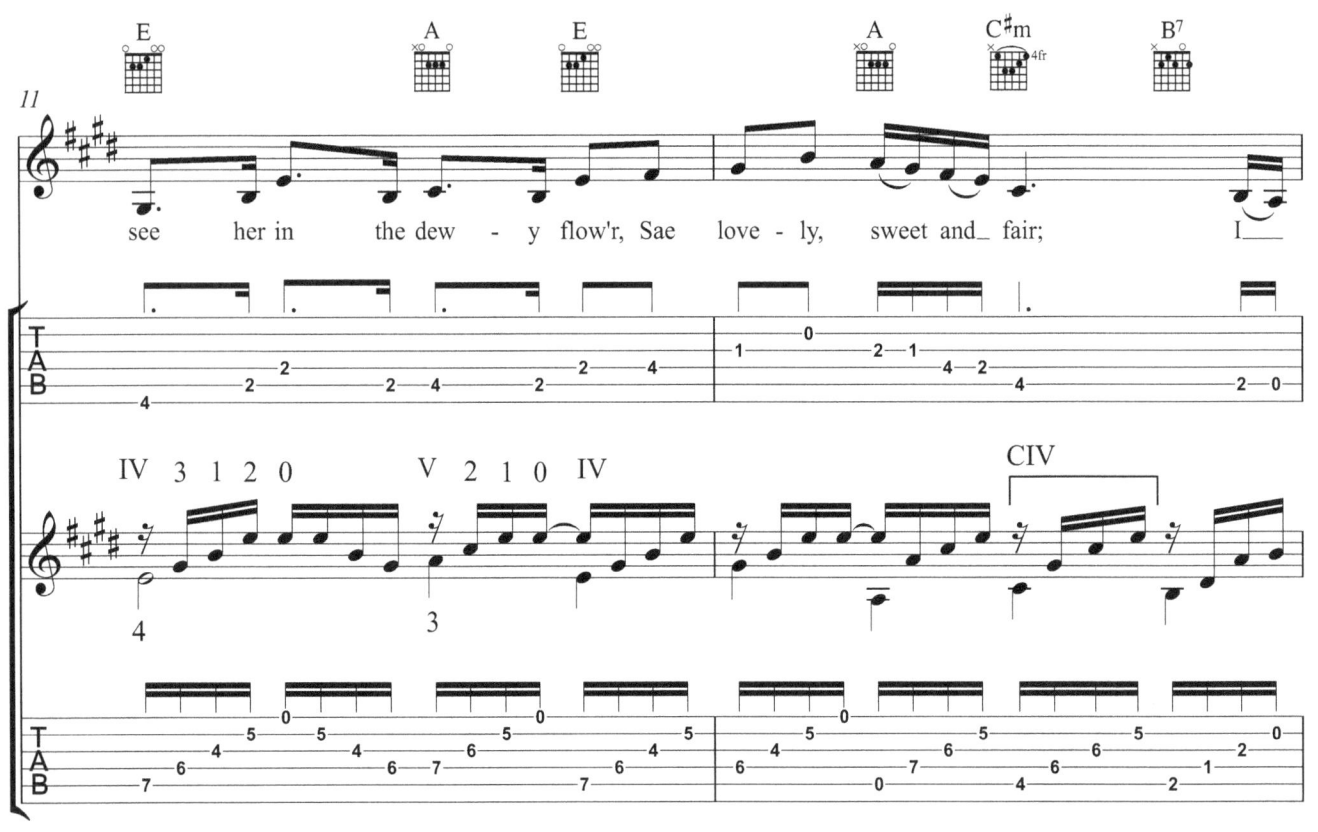

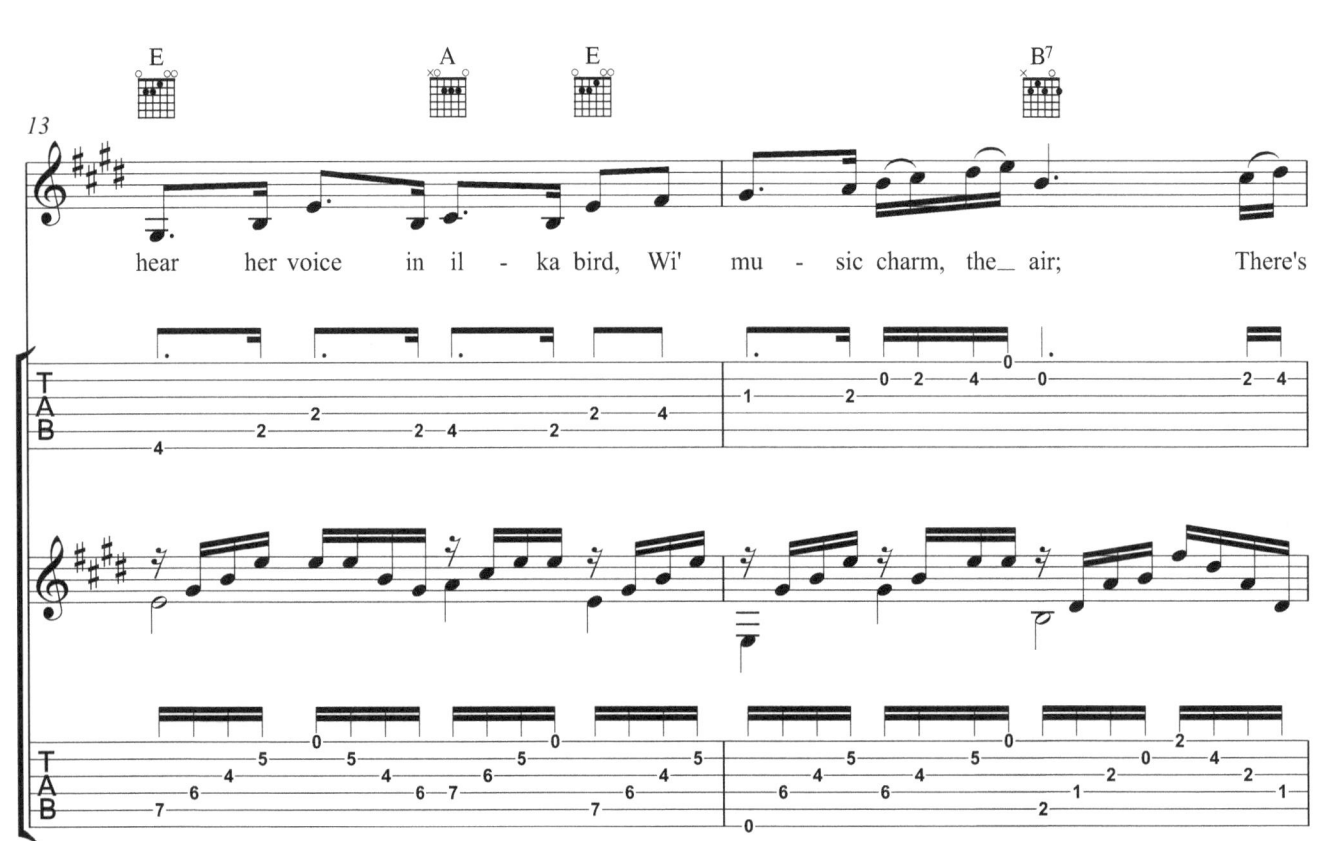

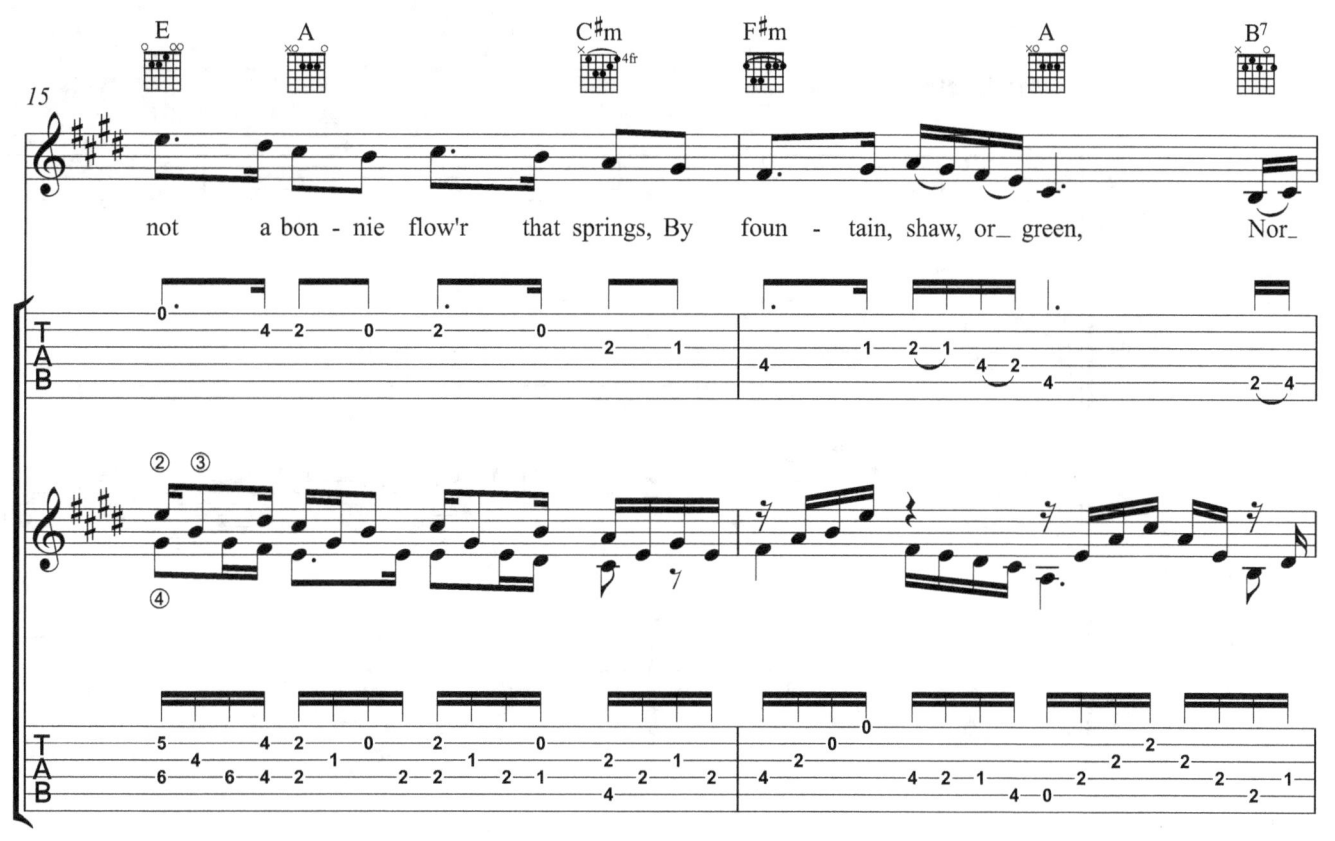

not   a bon - nie flow'r   that springs, By   foun - tain, shaw, or_ green,   Nor_

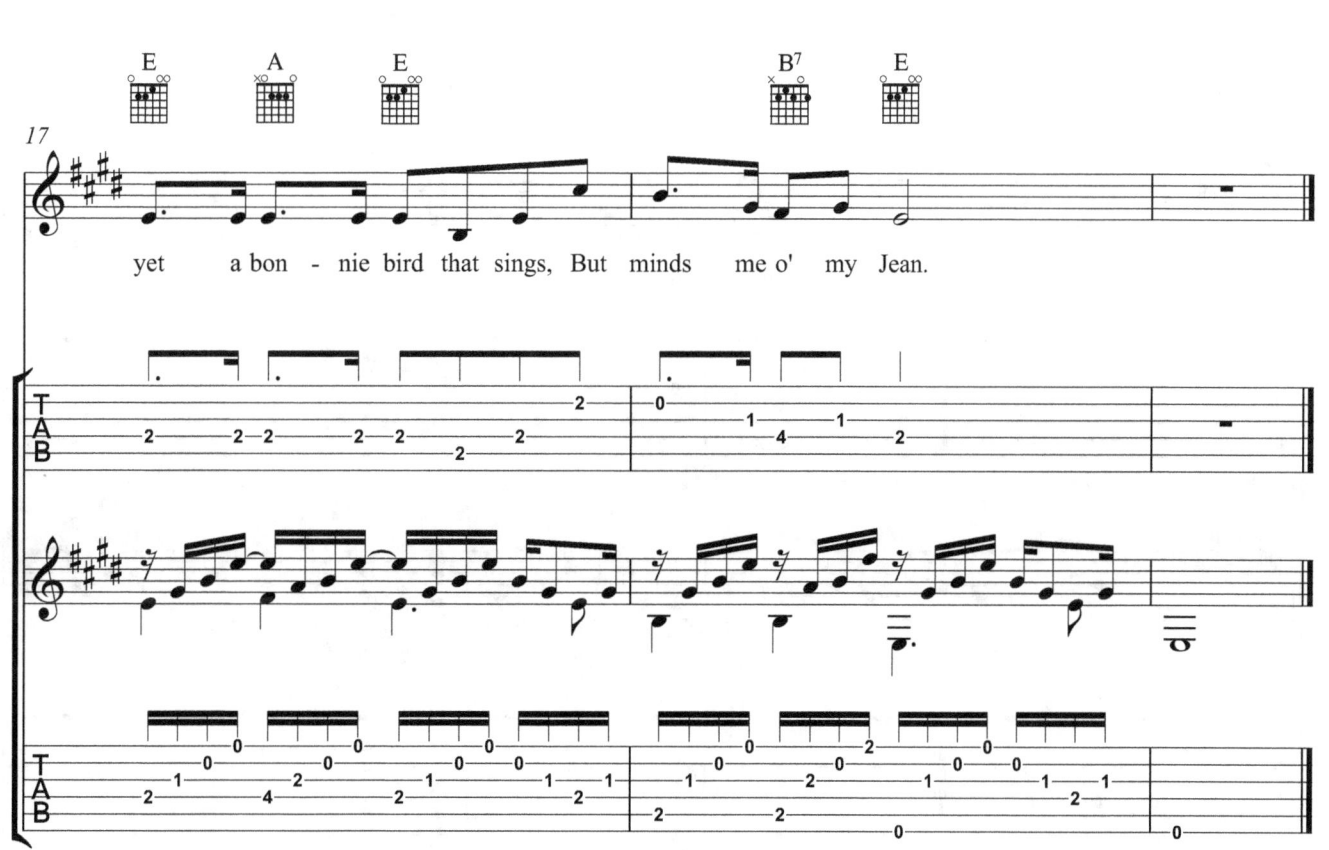

yet   a bon - nie bird that sings, But   minds   me o'   my Jean.

32

Leezie Lindsay

Robert Burns

Moderato

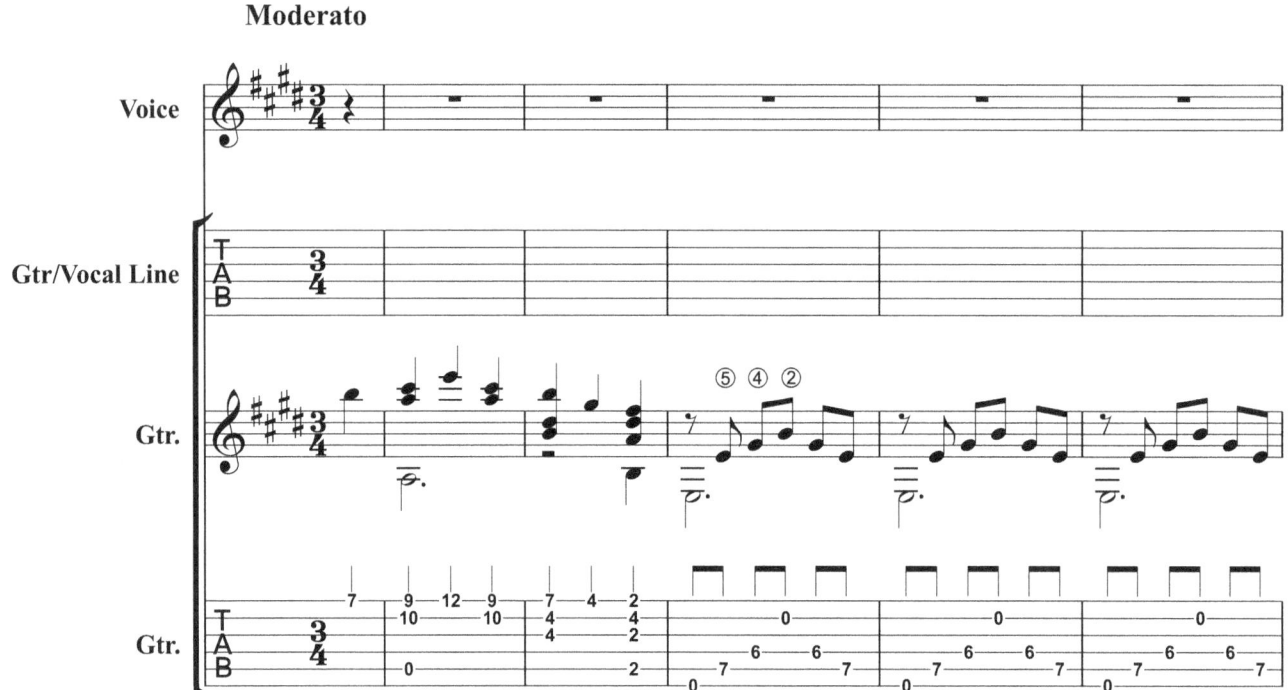

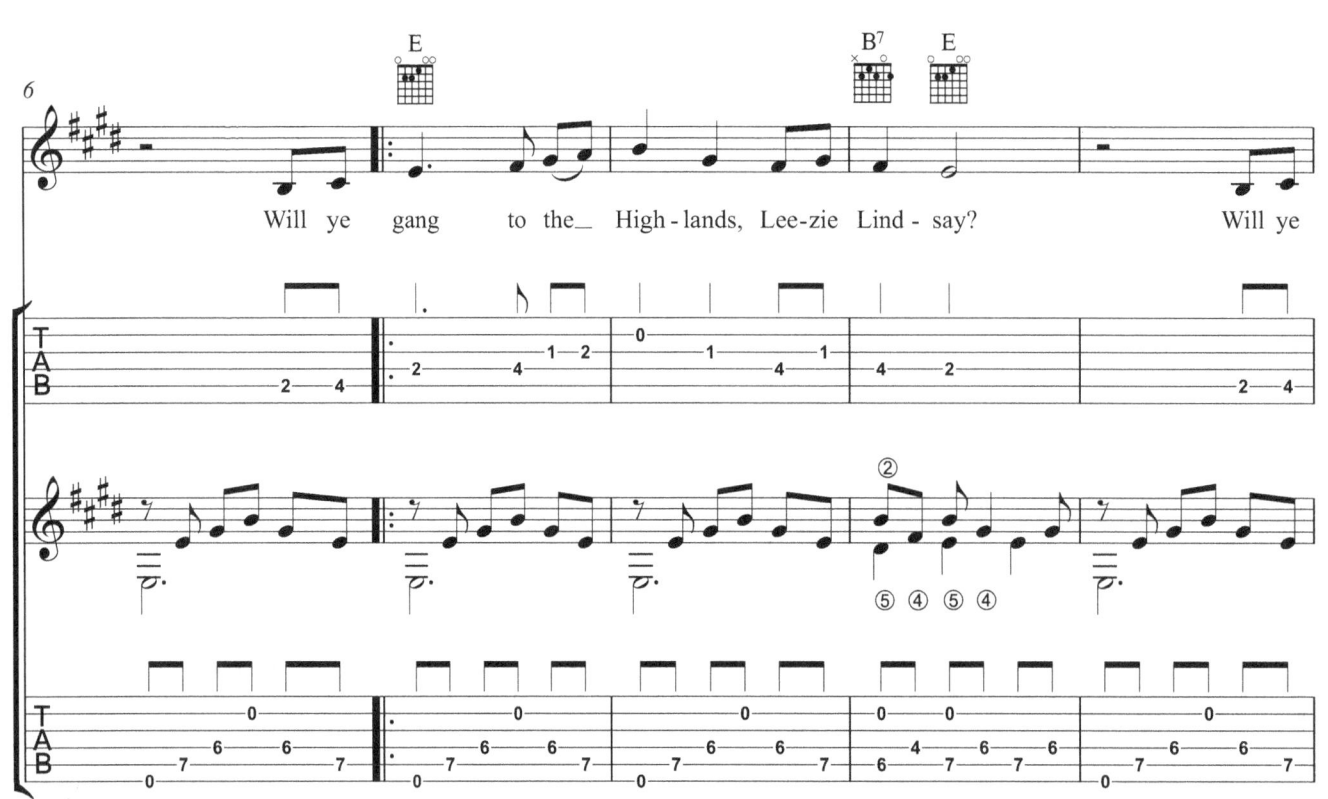

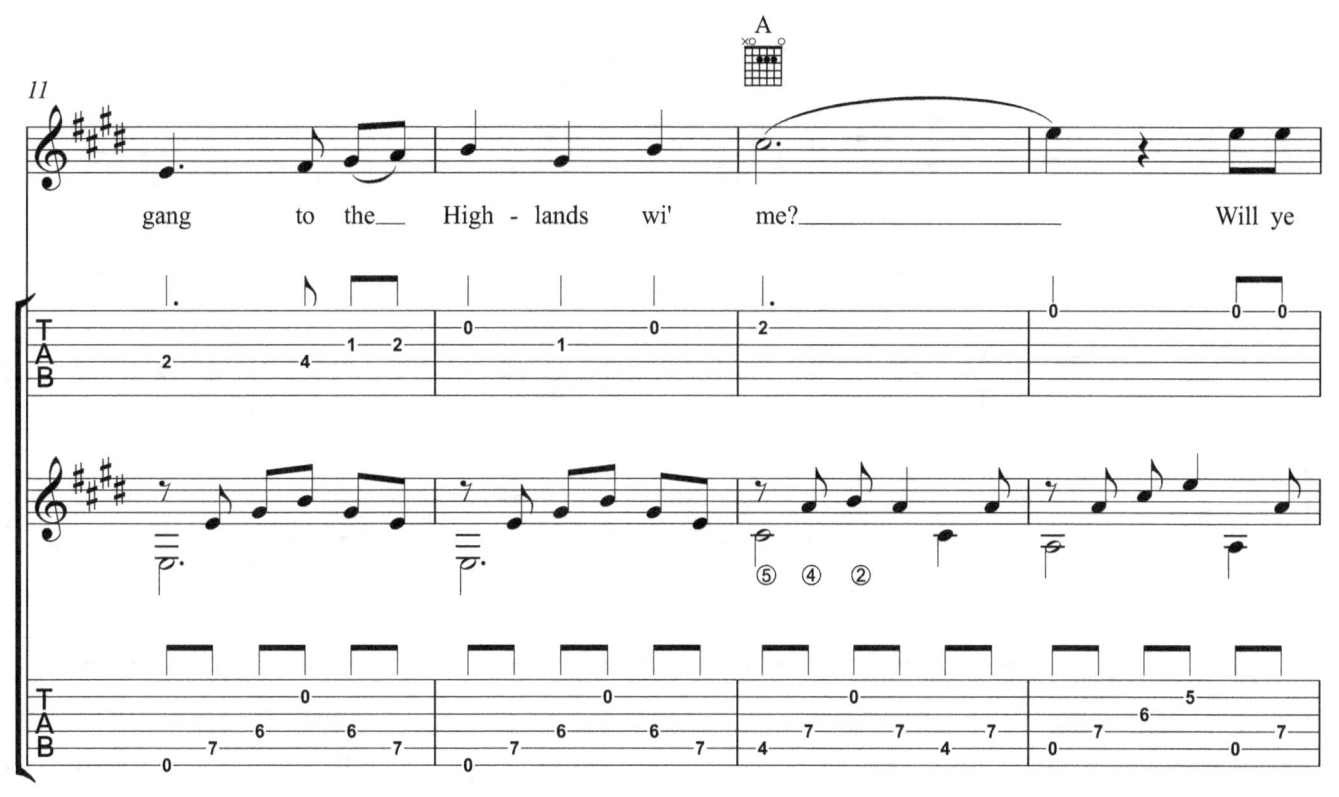

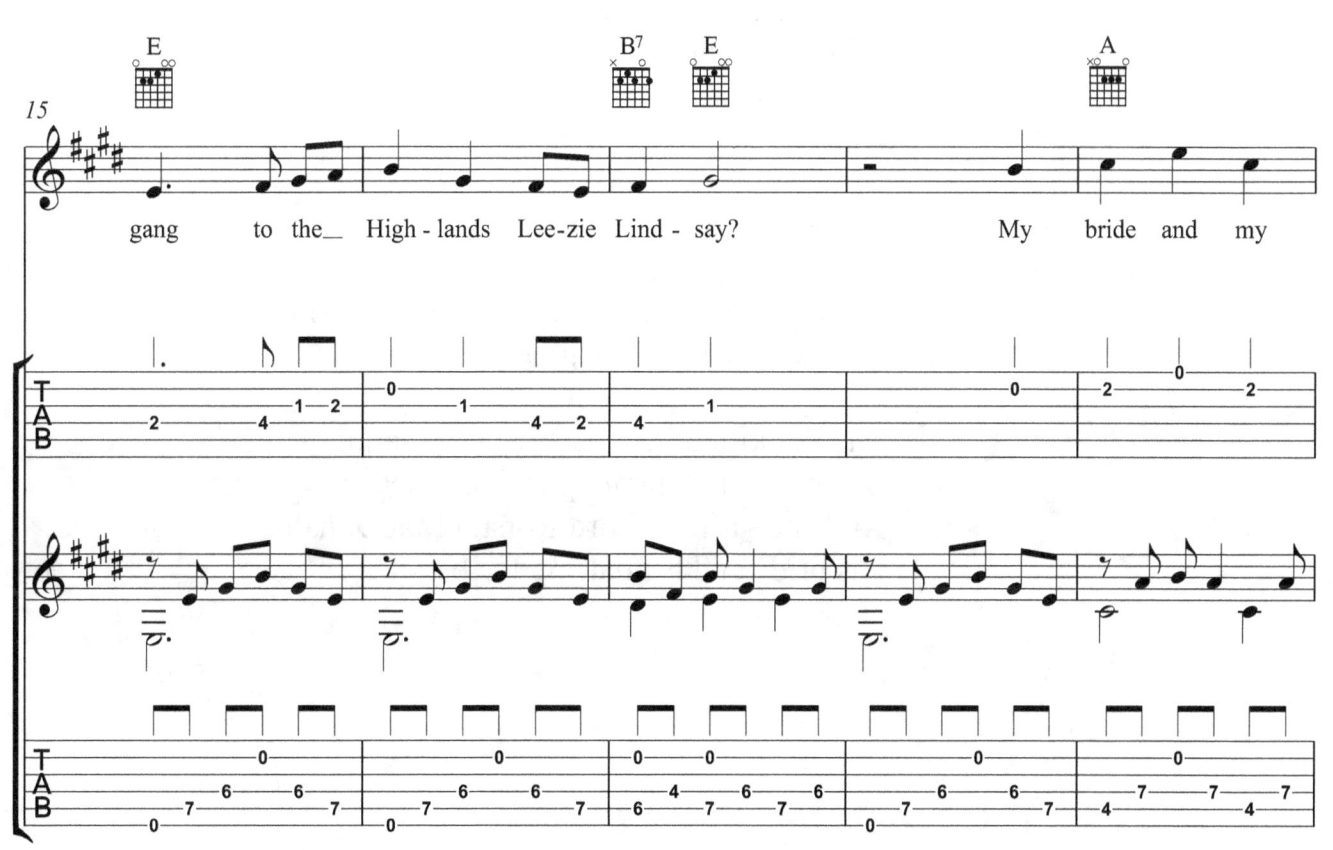

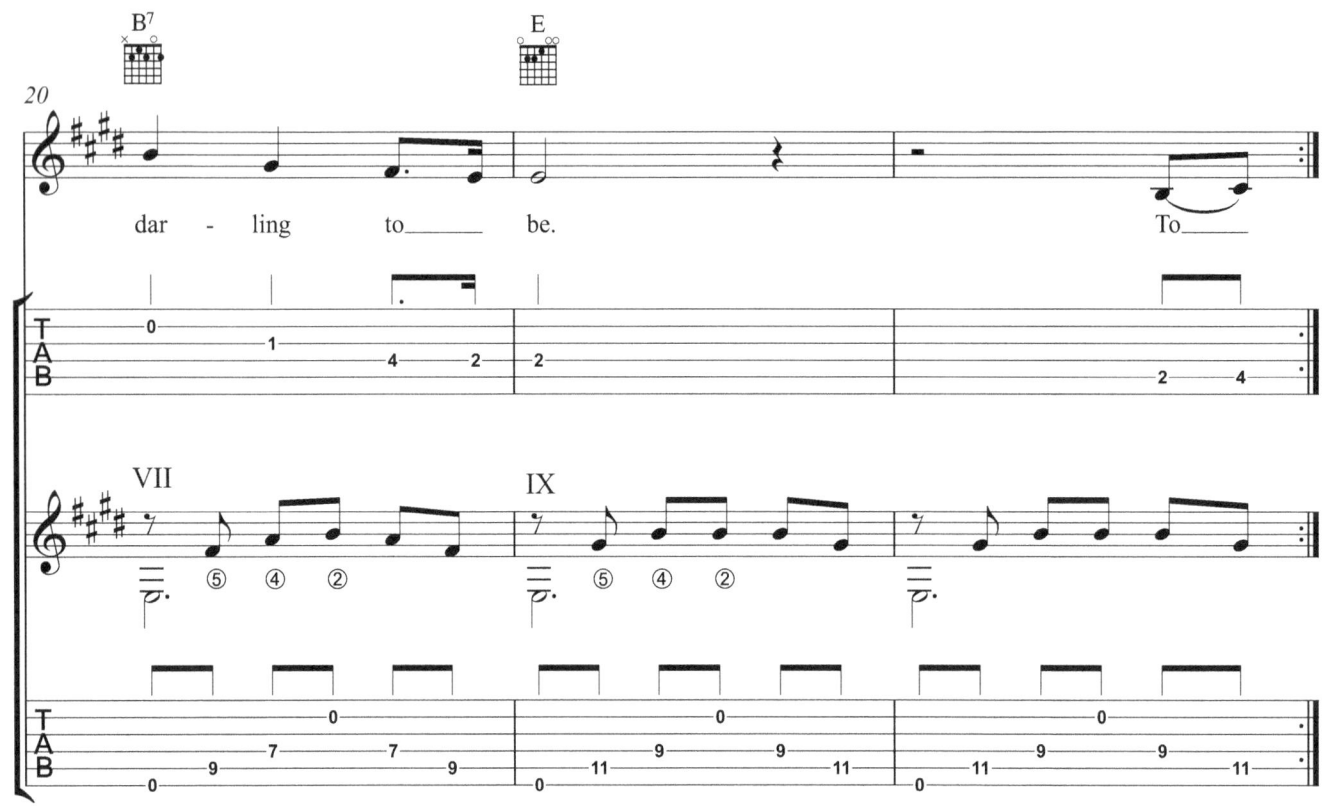

To gang to the Hielands wi' you, sir.
I dinna ken how that may be;
For I ken nae the land that ye live in,
Nor ken I the lad I'm gaun wi'.

O, Leezie, lass, ye maun ken little,
If sae be ye dinna ken me;
For my name is Lord Ronald MacDonald,
A chieftain o' high degree.

She has kilted her coats o' green satin.
She has kilted them up tae her knee,
And she's aff wi' Lord Ronald MacDonald,
His bride and his darling tae be.

Highland Mary

Robert Burns

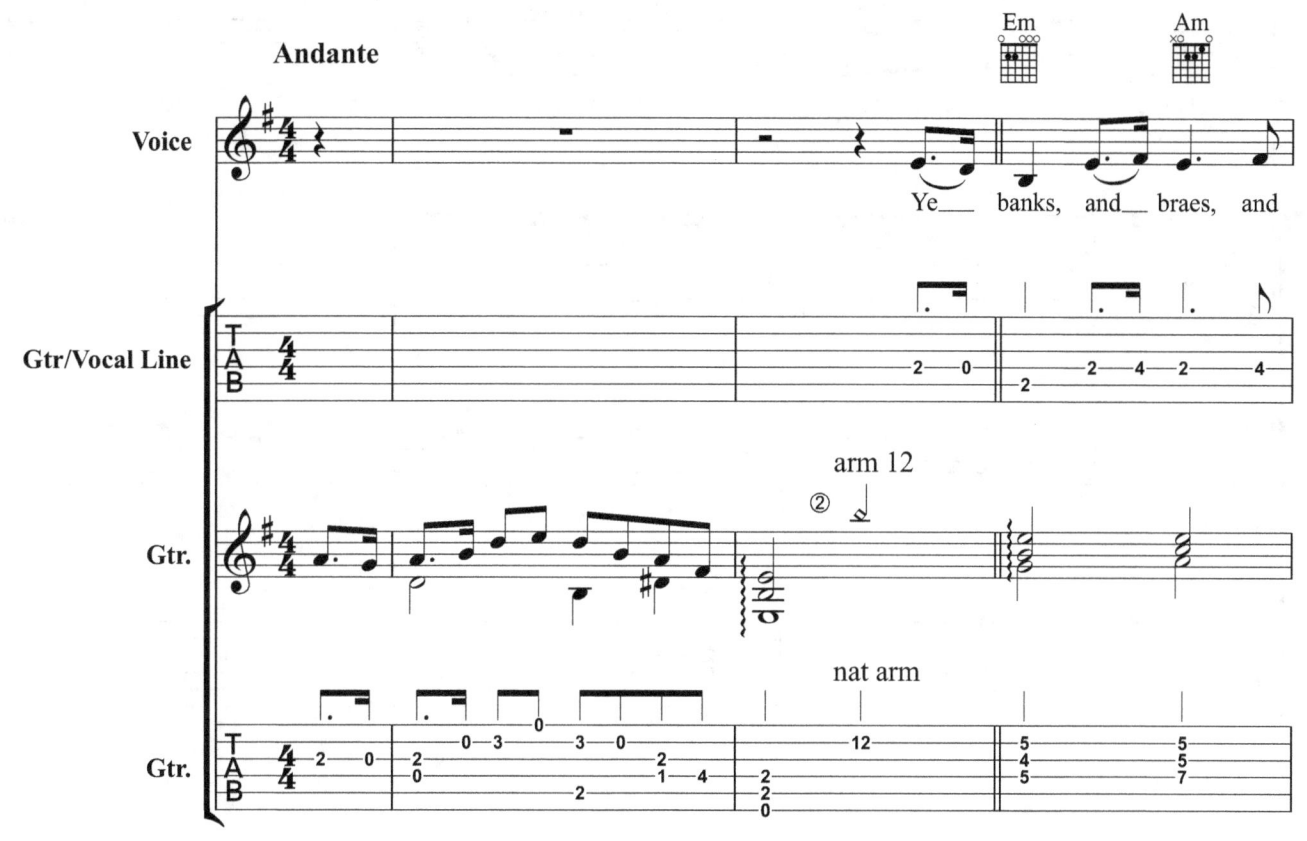

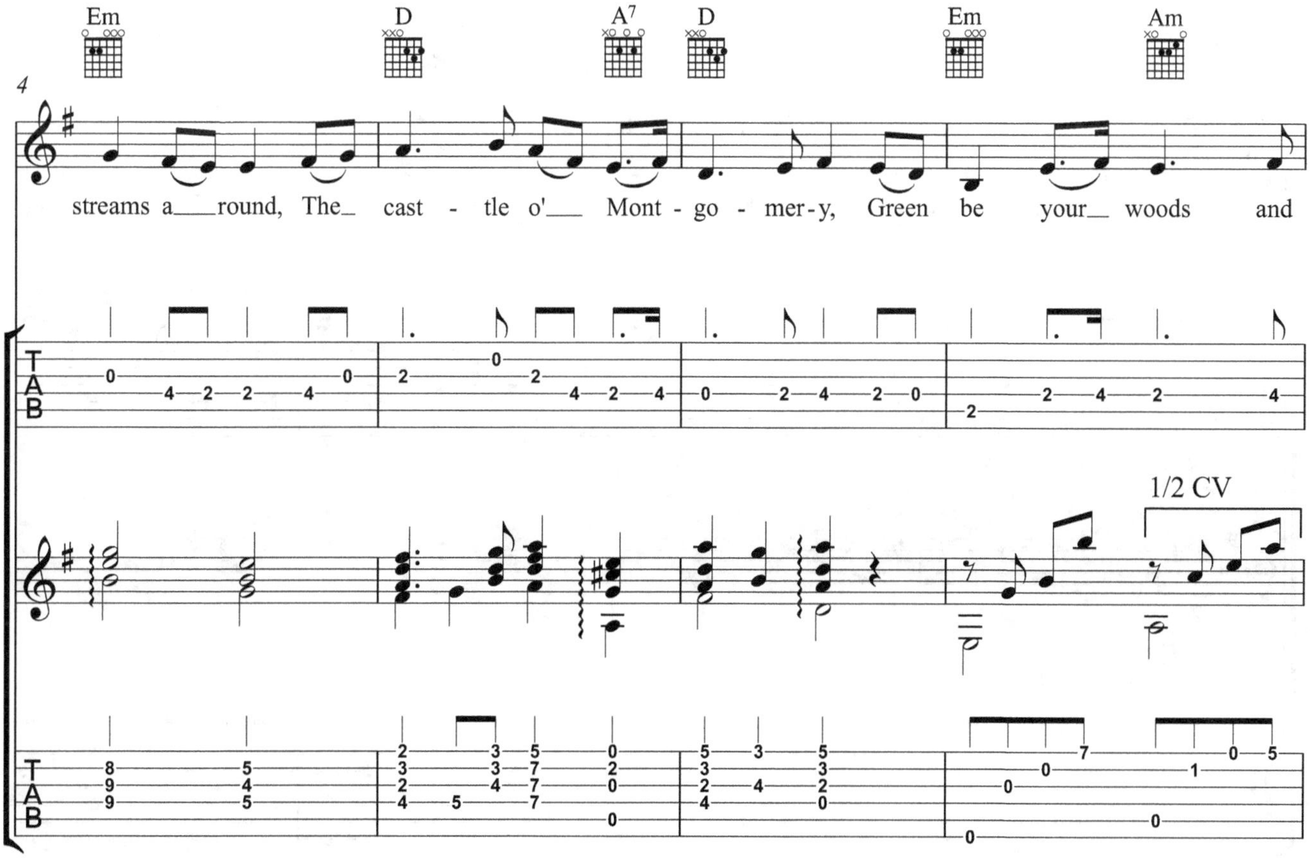

streams a___round, The_ cast - tle o'___ Mont - go - mer-y, Green be your___ woods and

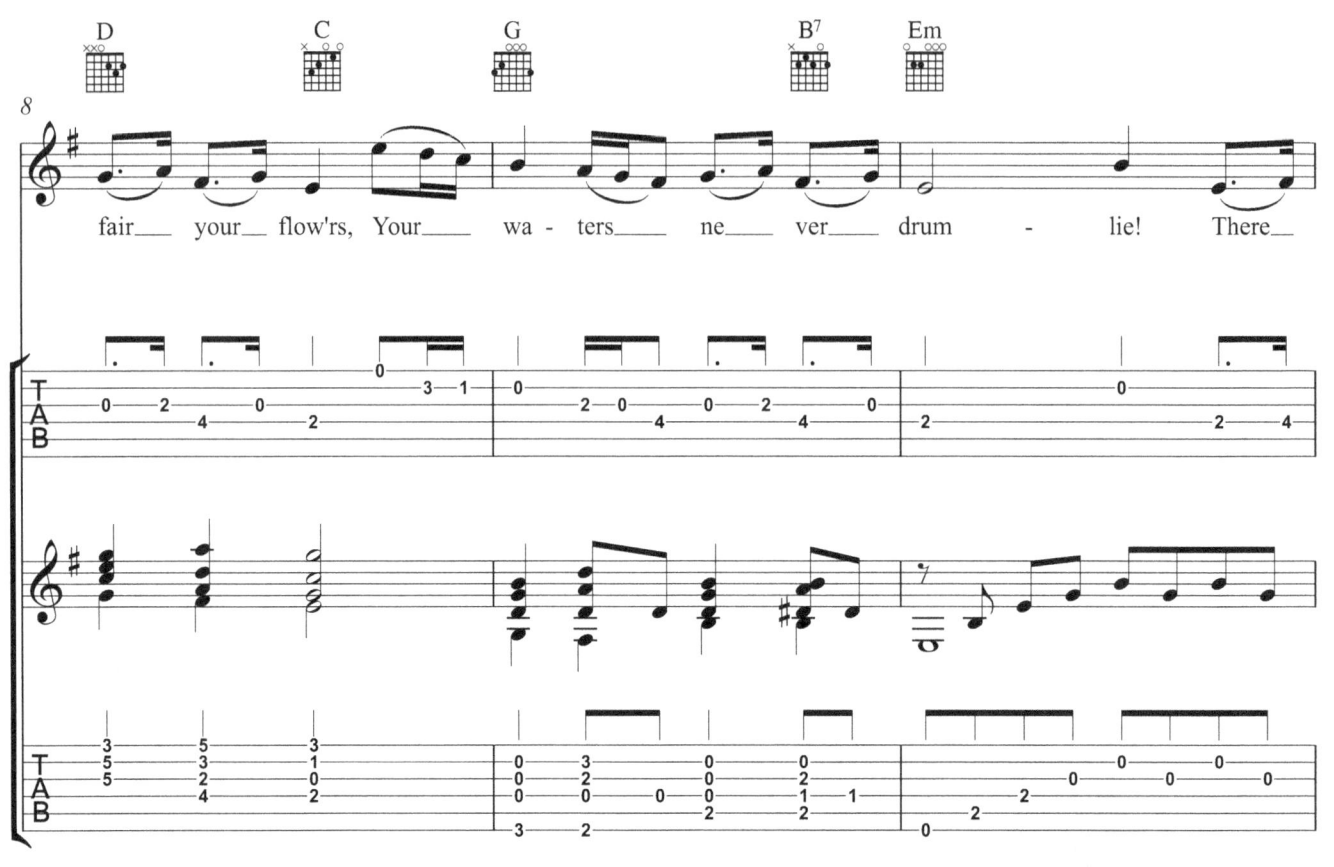

fair__ your__ flow'rs, Your__ wa__ters__ ne__ ver__ drum - lie! There__

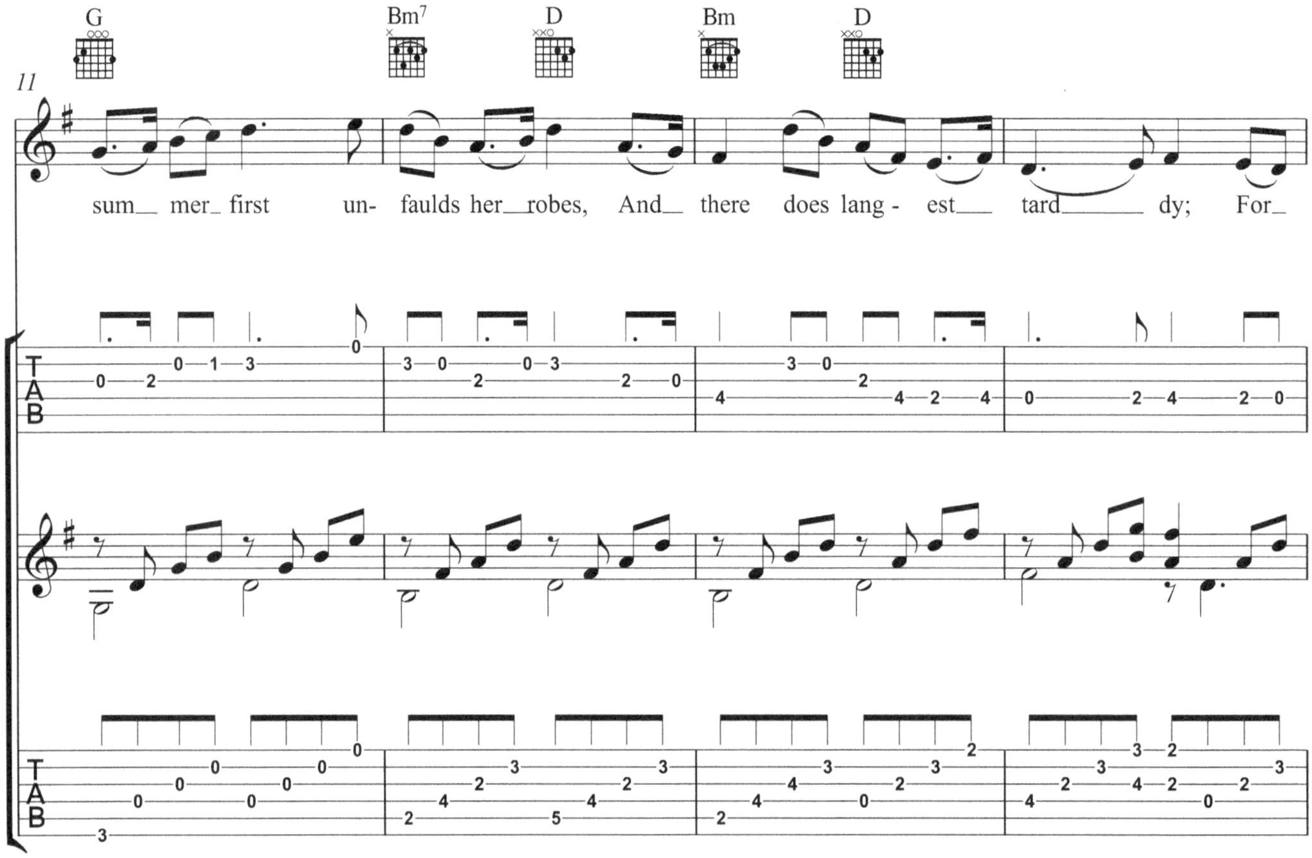

sum__ mer__ first un- faulds her__robes, And__ there does lang- est__ tard__ dy; For__

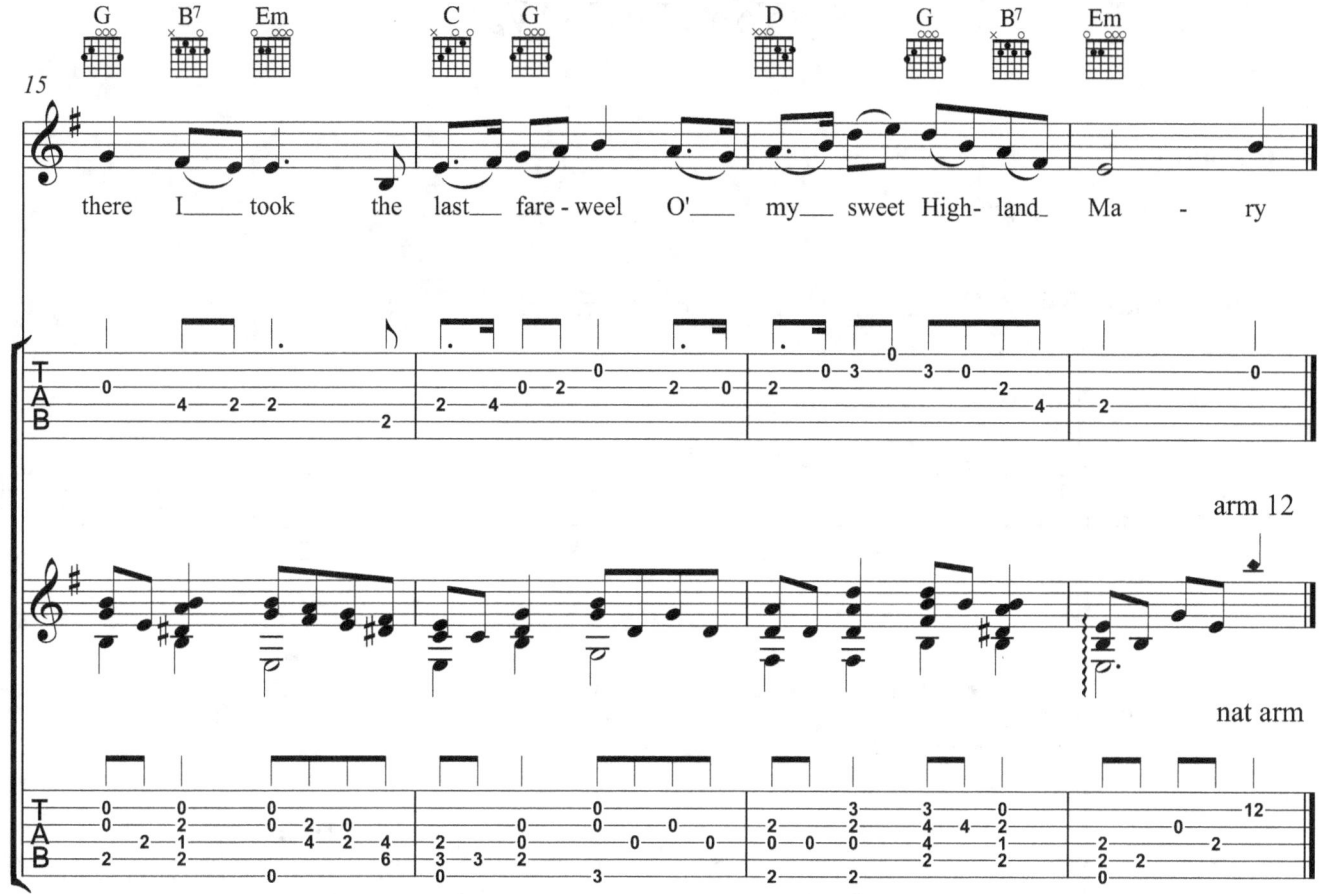

How sweetly bloom'd the gay, green birk,
How rich the hawthorn's blossom;
As underneath their fragrant shade,
I clasp'd her to my bosom!
The golden Hours, on angel wings,
Flew o'er me and my Dearie;
For dear to me as light and life
Was my sweet Highland Mary.

Wi' mony a vow, and lock'd embrace,
Our parting was fu'tender;
And pledging aft to meet again,
We tore oursels asunder:
But Oh, fell Death's untimely frost,
That nipt my Flower sae early!
Now green's the sod, and cauld's the clay,
That wraps my Highland Mary!

0 pale, pale now, those rosy lips
I aft hae kiss'd sae fondly!
And clos'd for ay, the sparkling glance,
That dwalt on me sae kindly!
And mouldering now in silent dust,
That heart that lo'ed me dearly!
But still within my bosom's core
Shall live my Highland Mary.

By Yon Castle Wa'

Robert Burns

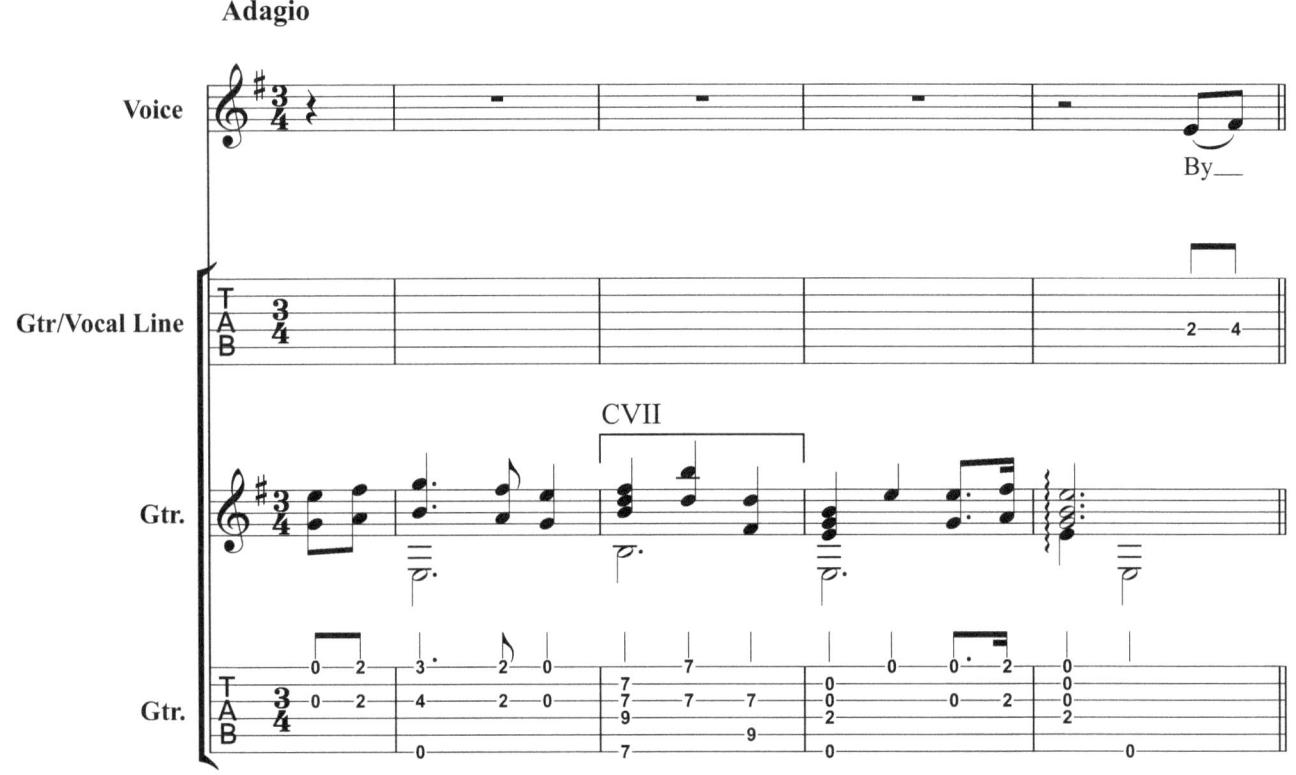

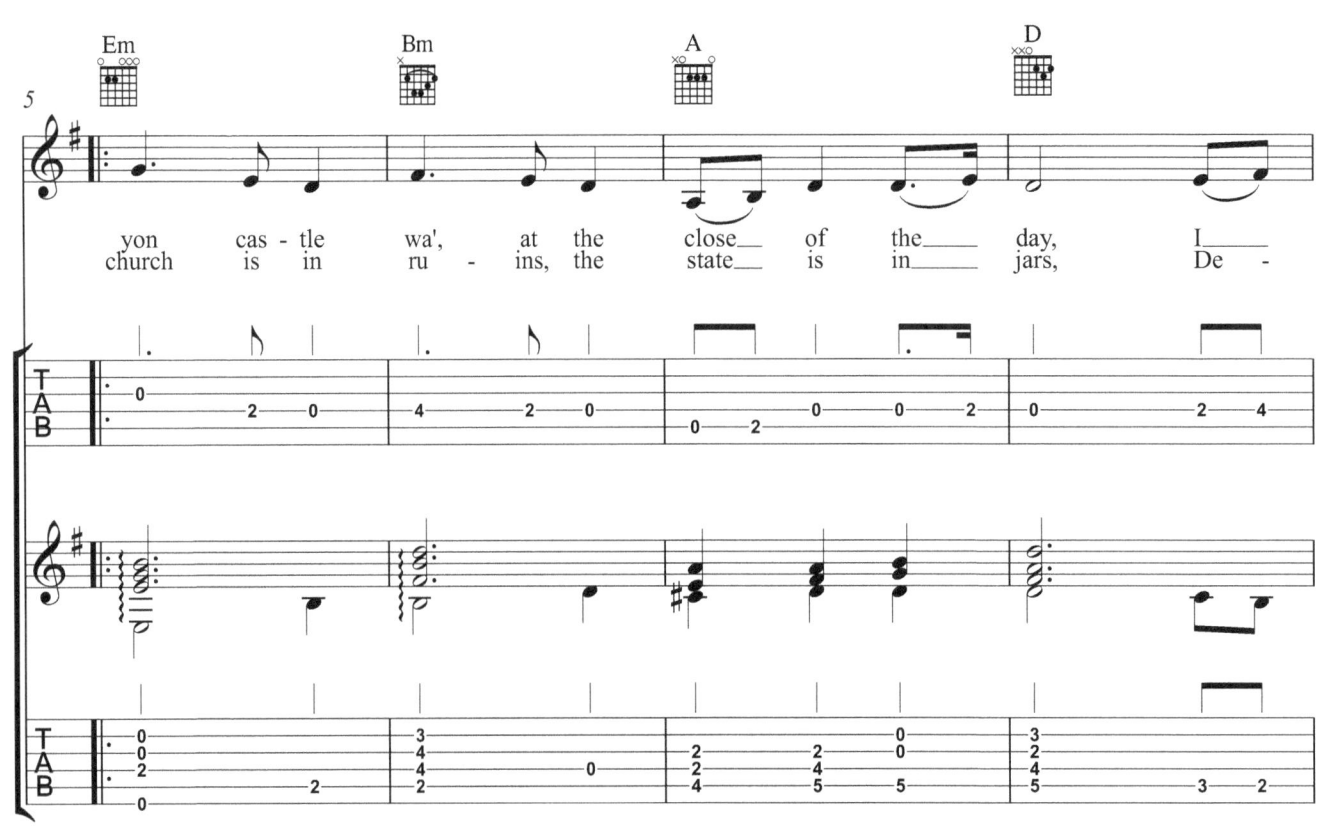

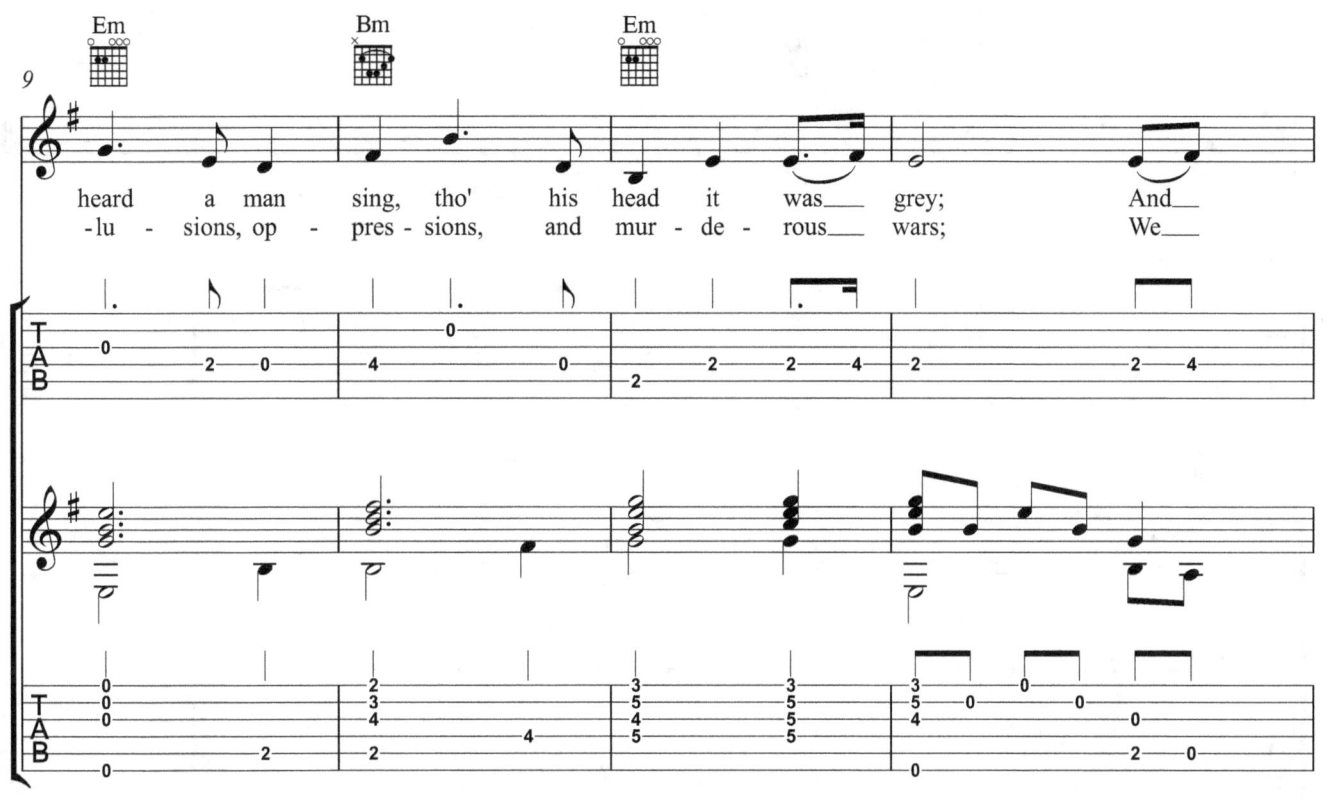

heard   a man   sing, tho' his head it   was___ grey;   And__

-lu - sions, op - pres - sions,   and mur - de - rous___ wars;   We___

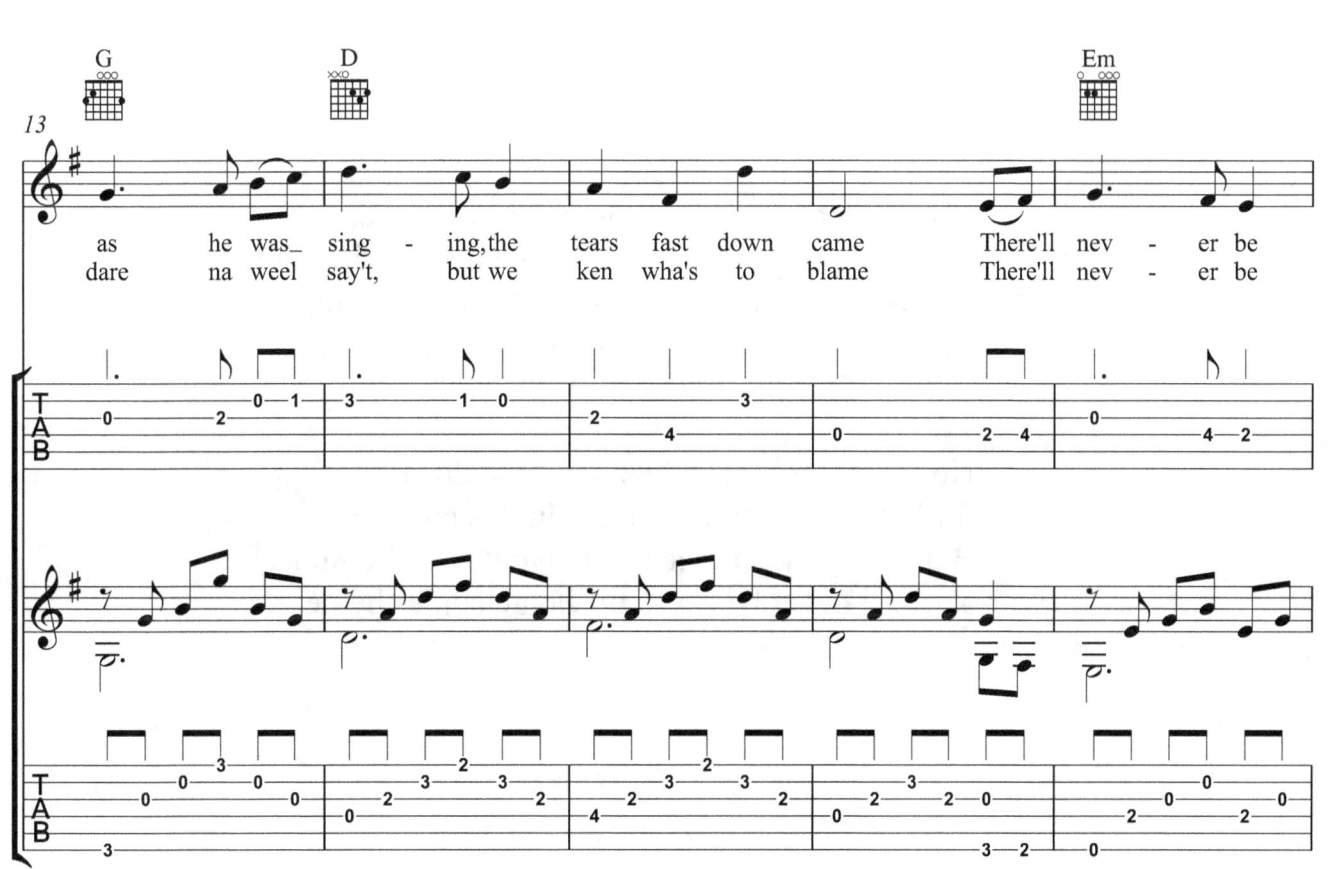

as   he was_ sing - ing,the tears fast down came   There'll nev - er be

dare   na weel say't,   but we   ken wha's to   blame   There'll nev - er be

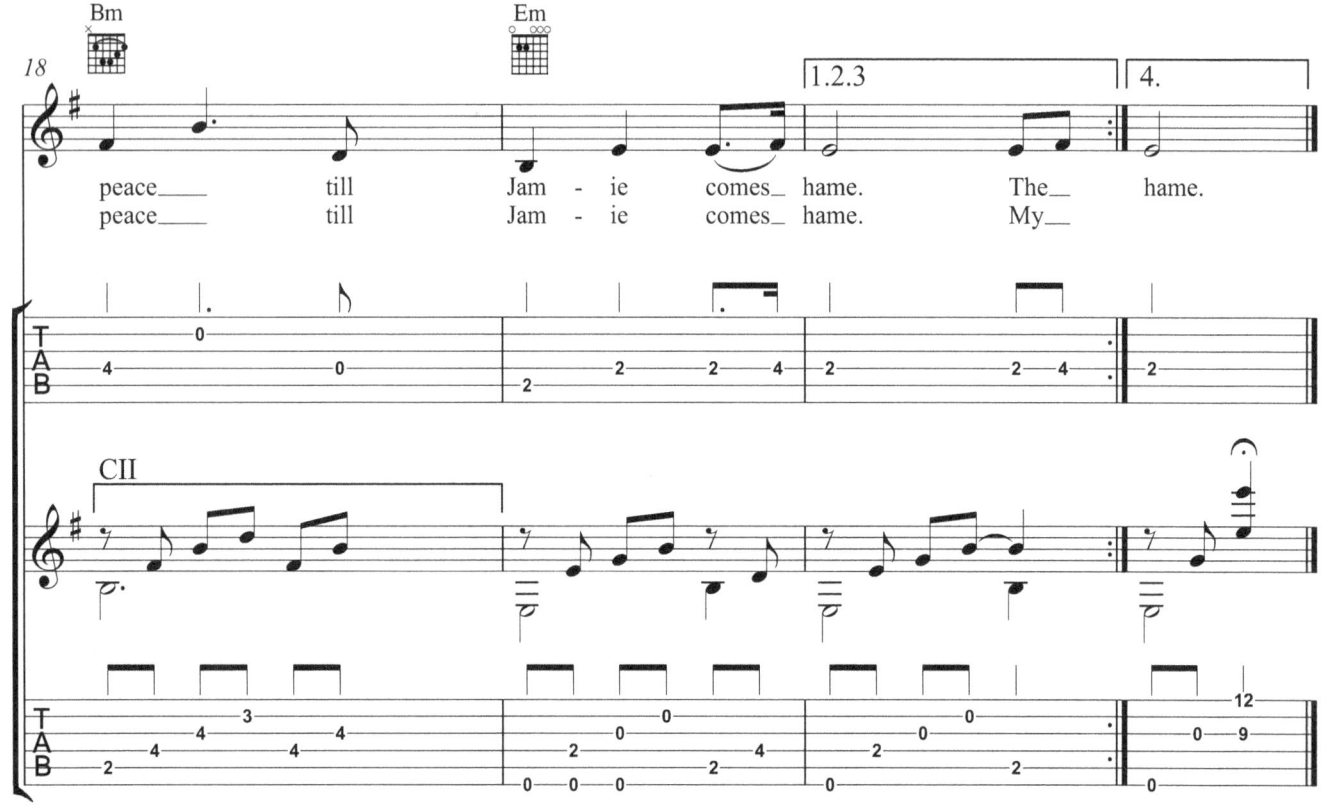

My seven braw sons for Jamie drew sword,
But now I greet round their green beds in the yerd;
It brak the sweet heart o' my faithful and dame,
There'll never be peace till Jamie comes hame.

Now life is a burden that bows me down,
Sin' I tint my bairns, and he tint his crown;
But till my last moments my words are the same,
There'll never be peace till Jamie comes hame.

A Rose-Bud By My Early Walk

Robert Burns

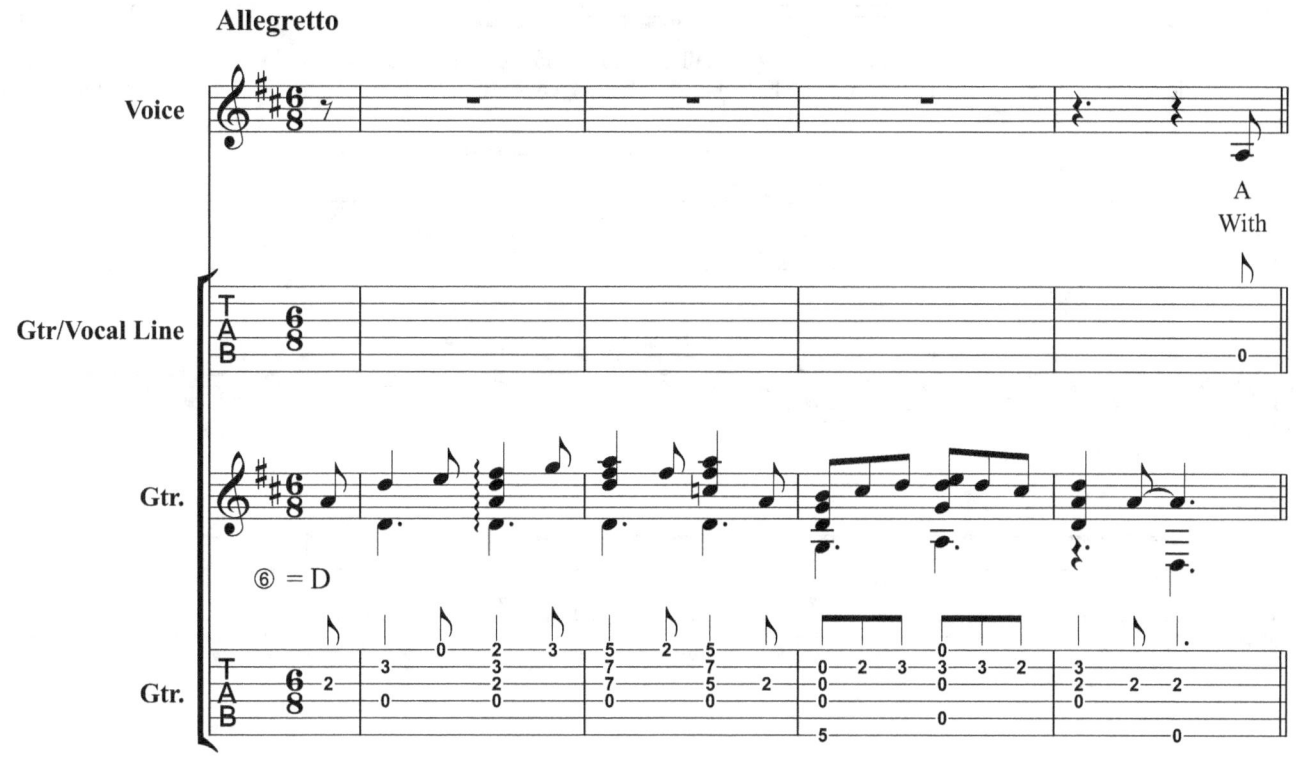

rose - bud by my ear - ly walk,_ A - down_ a corn - en - clos - ed bawk, Sae
in the bush, her cov - ert nest_ A lit - tle lin - et fond - ly prest, The

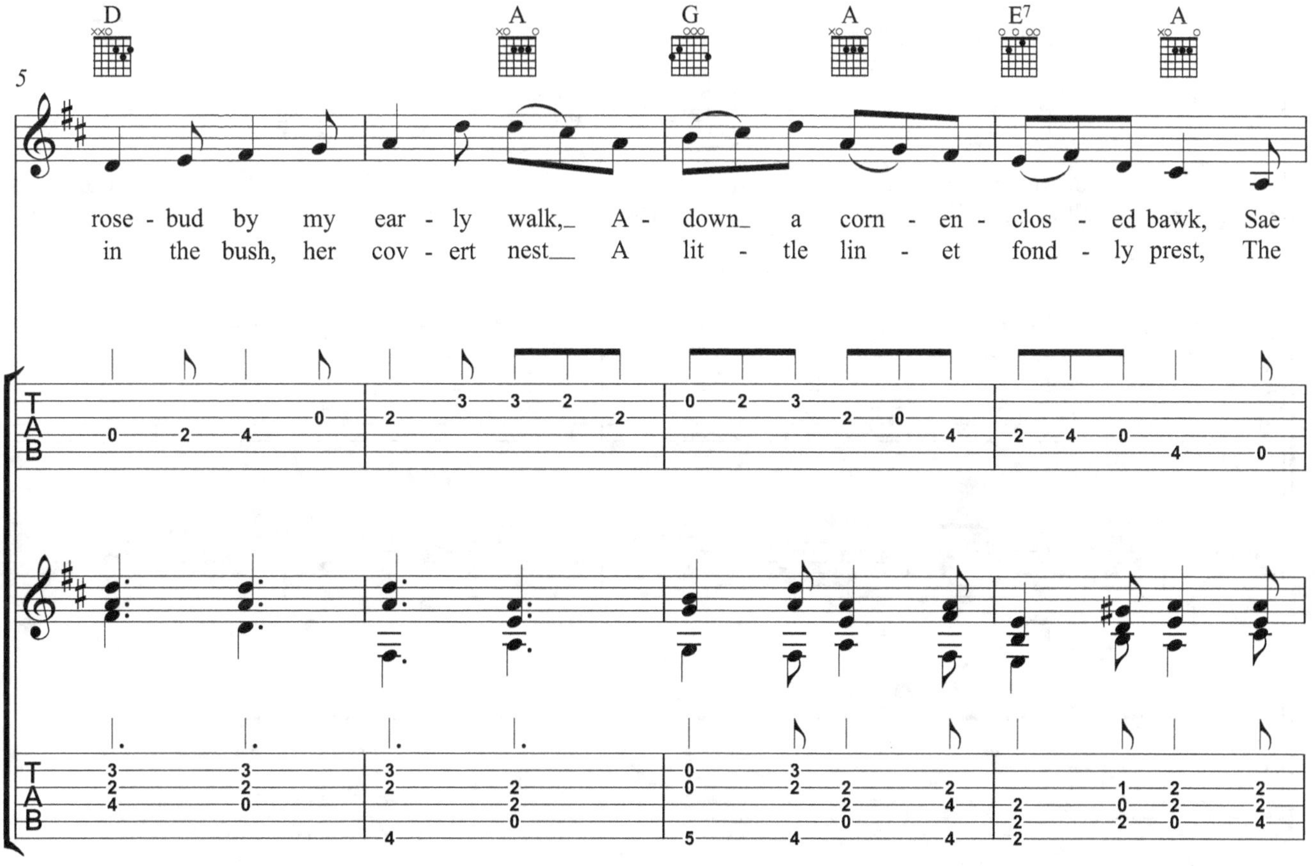

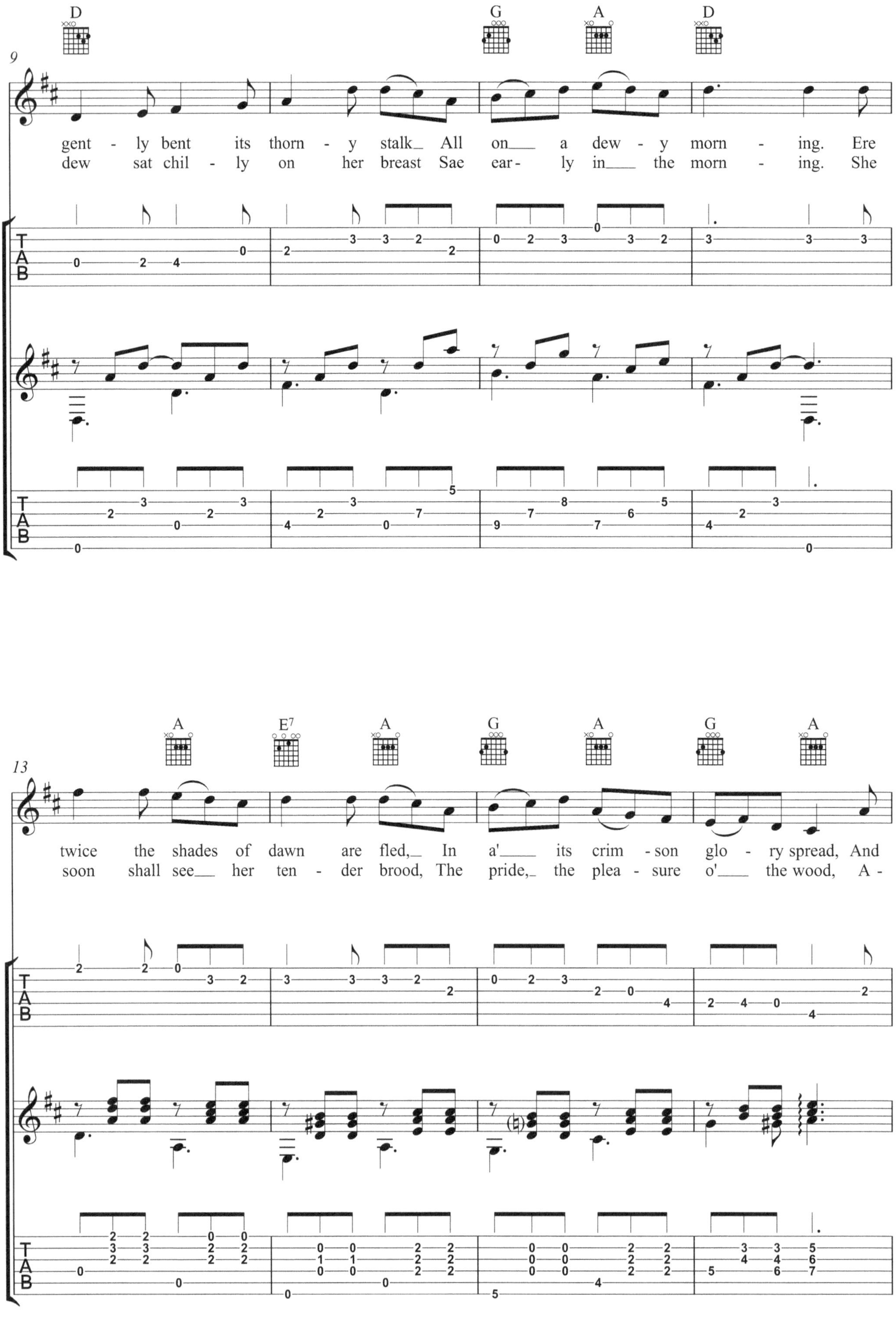

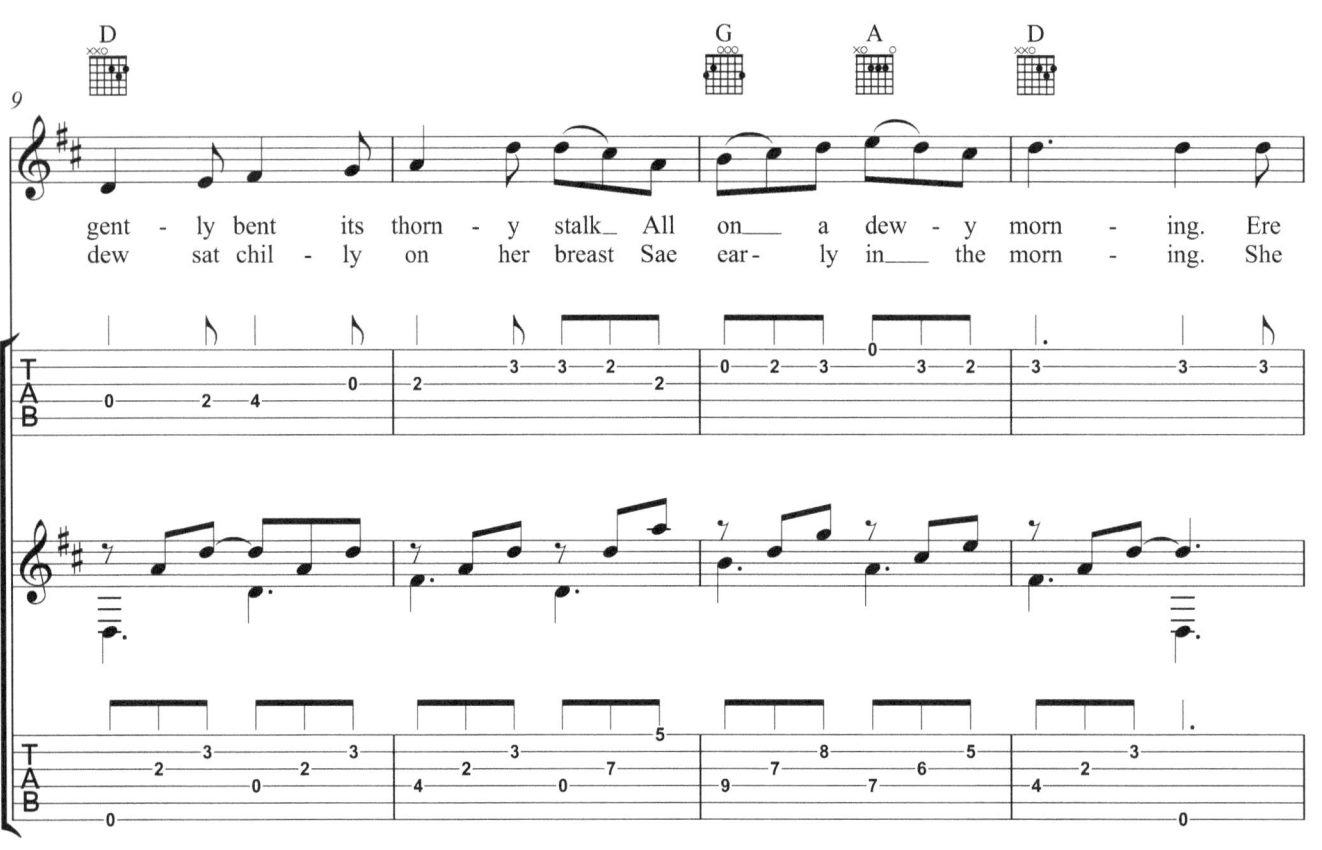

gently bent its thorny stalk All on a dewy morning. Ere
dew sat chilly on her breast Sae early in the morning. She

twice the shades of dawn are fled, In a' its crimson glory spread, And
soon shall see her tender brood, The pride, the pleasure o' the wood, A-

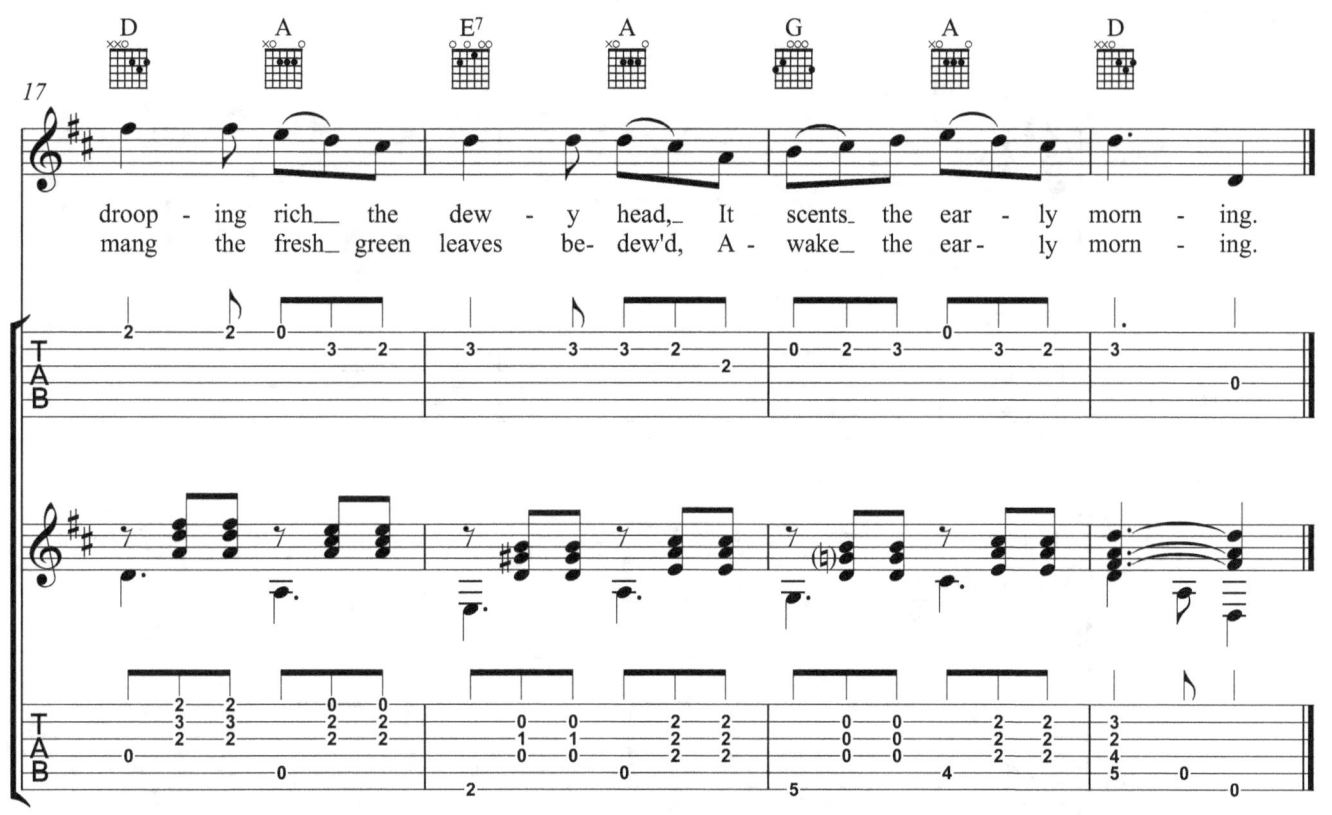

droop - ing rich__ the dew - y head,_ It scents_ the ear - ly morn - ing.
mang the fresh_ green leaves be - dew'd, A - wake_ the ear - ly morn - ing.

So thou, dear bird, young Jeany fair,
On trembling string or vocal air,
Shall sweetly pay the tender care
That tents thy early morning!
So thou, sweet rose-bud, young and gay,
Shalt beauteous blaze upon the day,
And bless the parent's evening ray
That watch'd thy early morning!

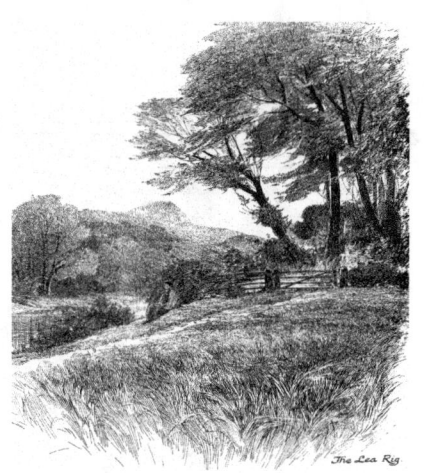

The Lea Rig.

My Heart Is Sair

Robert Burns

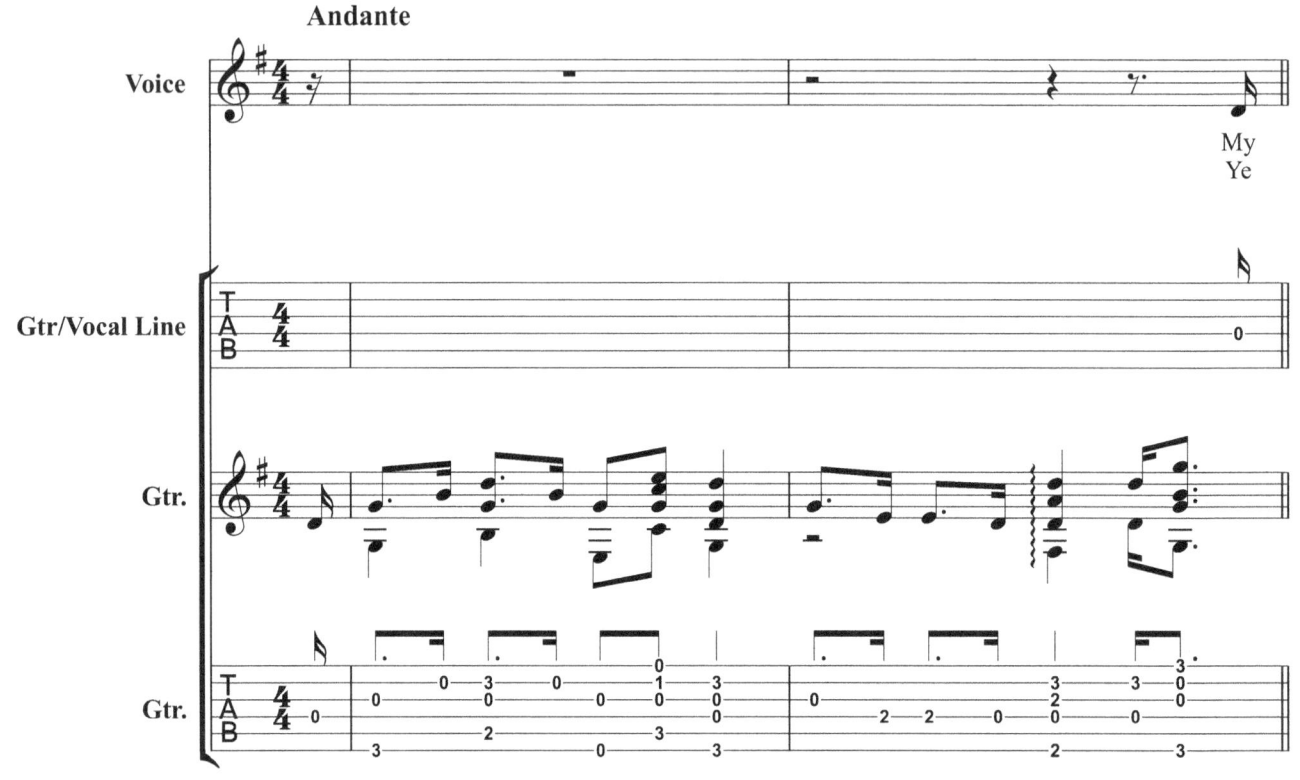

heart is sair, I daur—na tell, My heart is sair for some—bo—dy
pow'rs that smile on vir—tuous love, O sweet—ly smile on some—bo—dy Frae

45

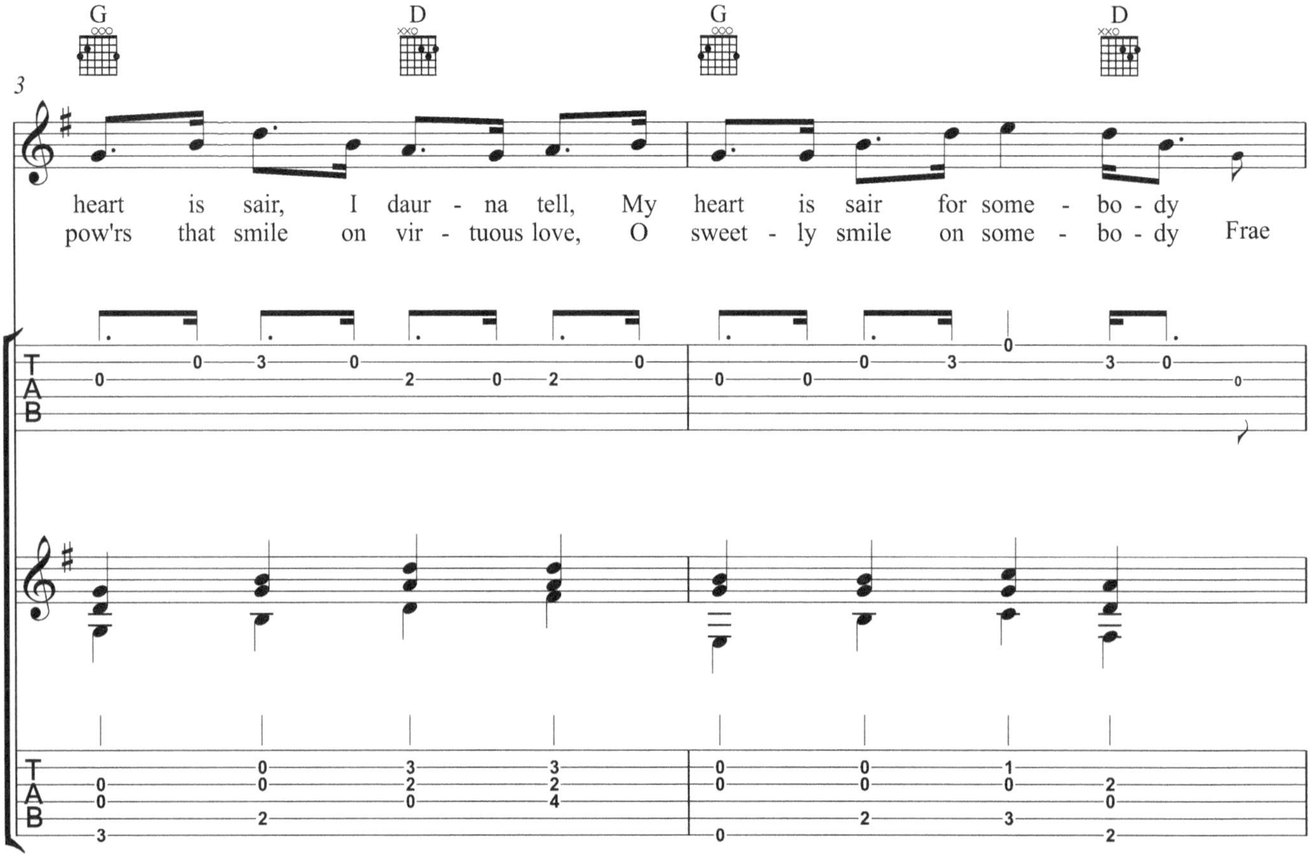

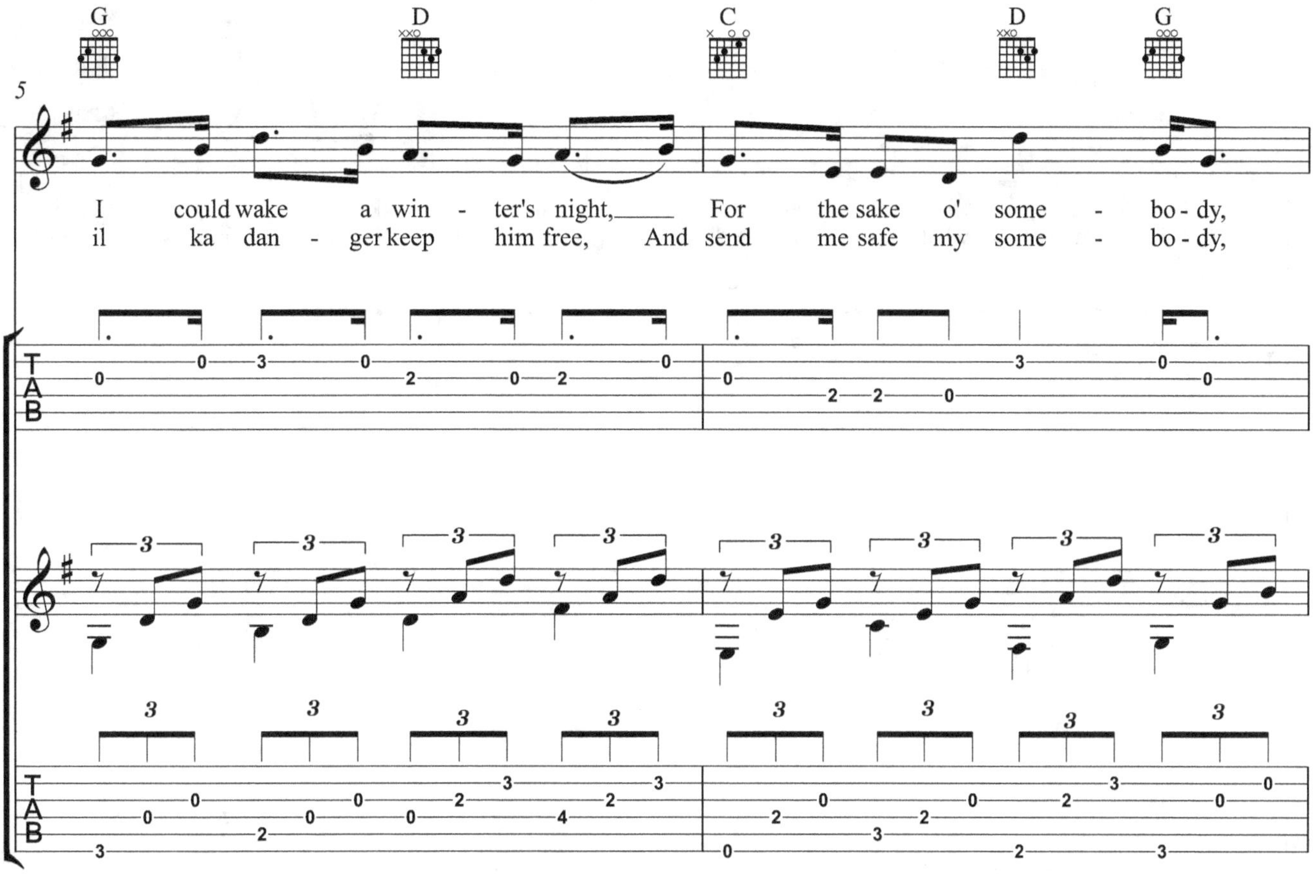
G D C D G
5
I could wake a win - ter's night, For the sake o' some - bo - dy,
il ka dan - ger keep him free, And send me safe my some - bo - dy,

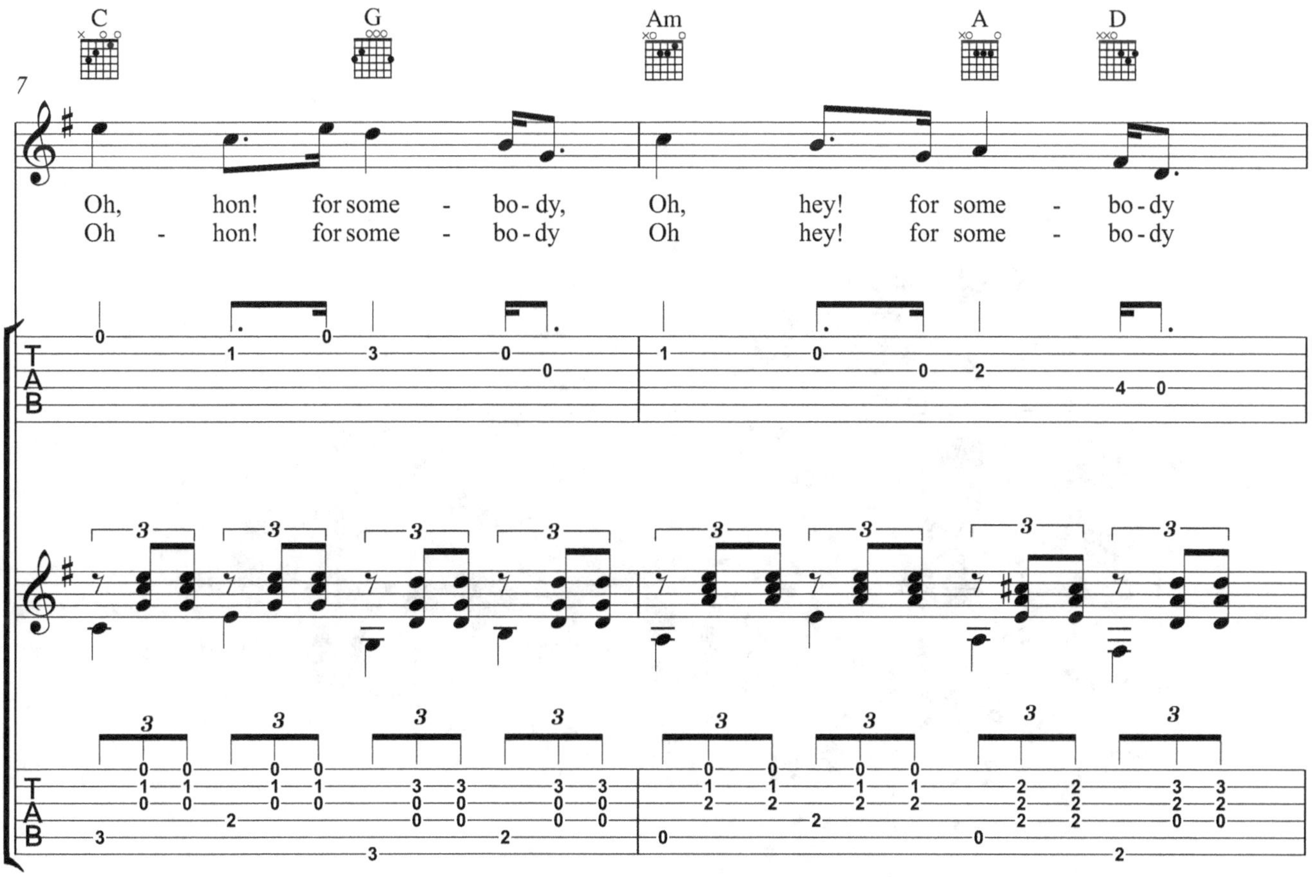
C G Am A D
7
Oh, hon! for some - bo - dy, Oh, hey! for some - bo - dy
Oh - hon! for some - bo - dy Oh hey! for some - bo - dy

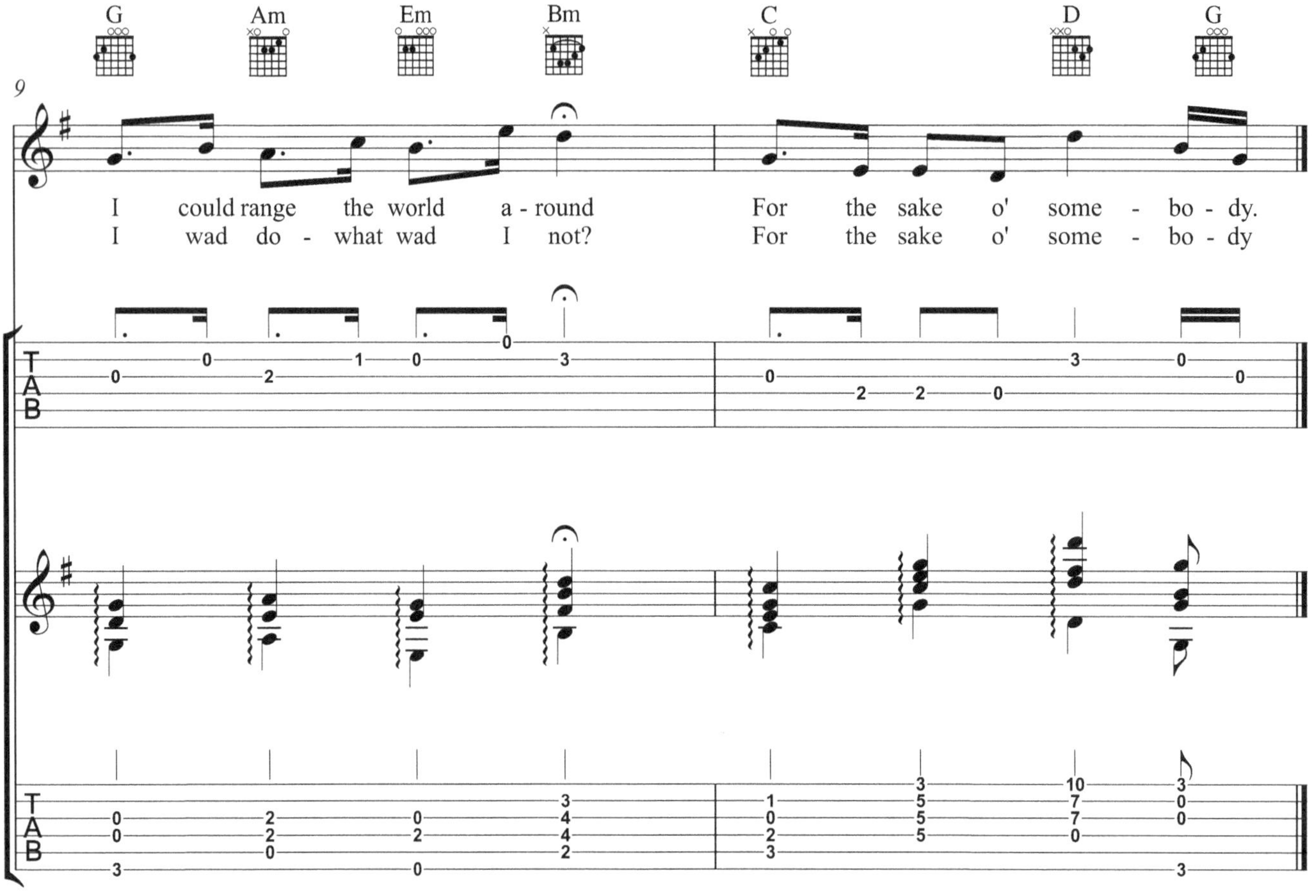

G   Am   Em   Bm   C   D   G

I   could range   the world   a - round   For   the sake   o'   some - bo - dy.
I   wad do - what wad   I   not?   For   the sake   o'   some - bo - dy

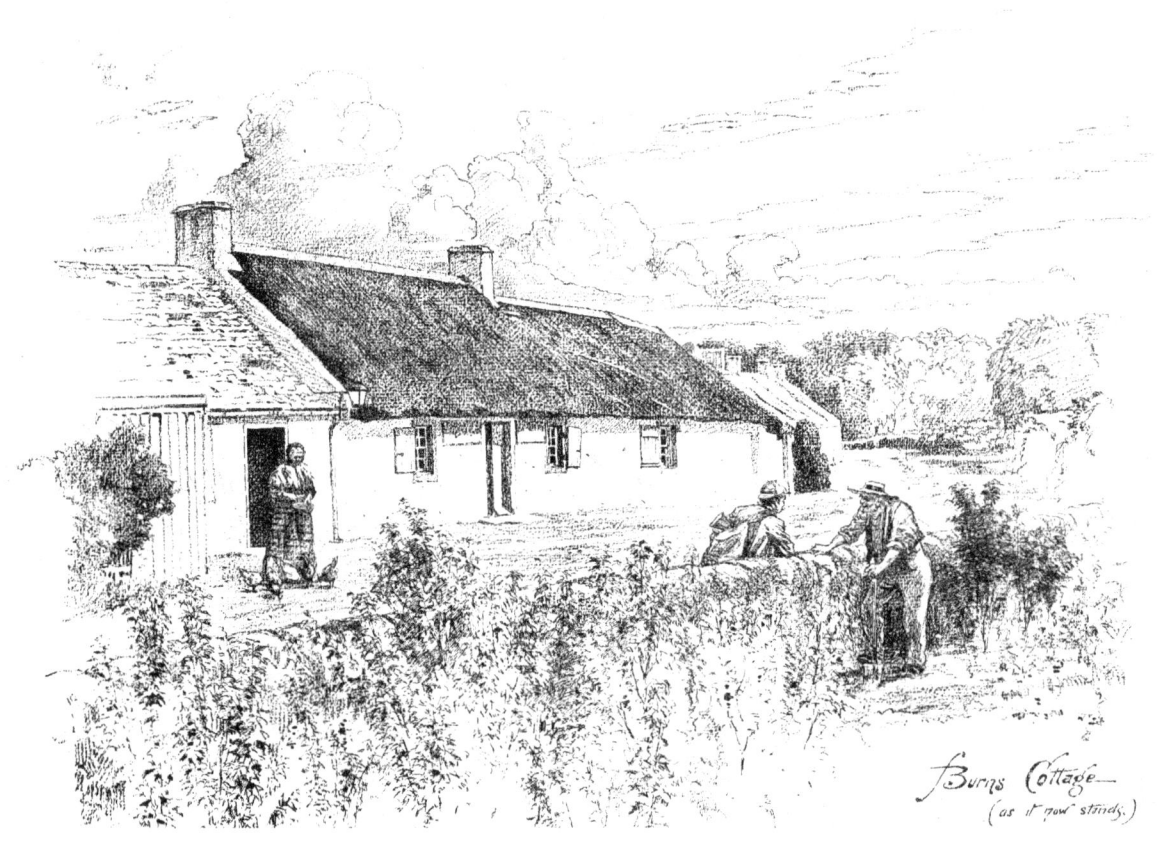

Burns Cottage
(as it now stands.)

47

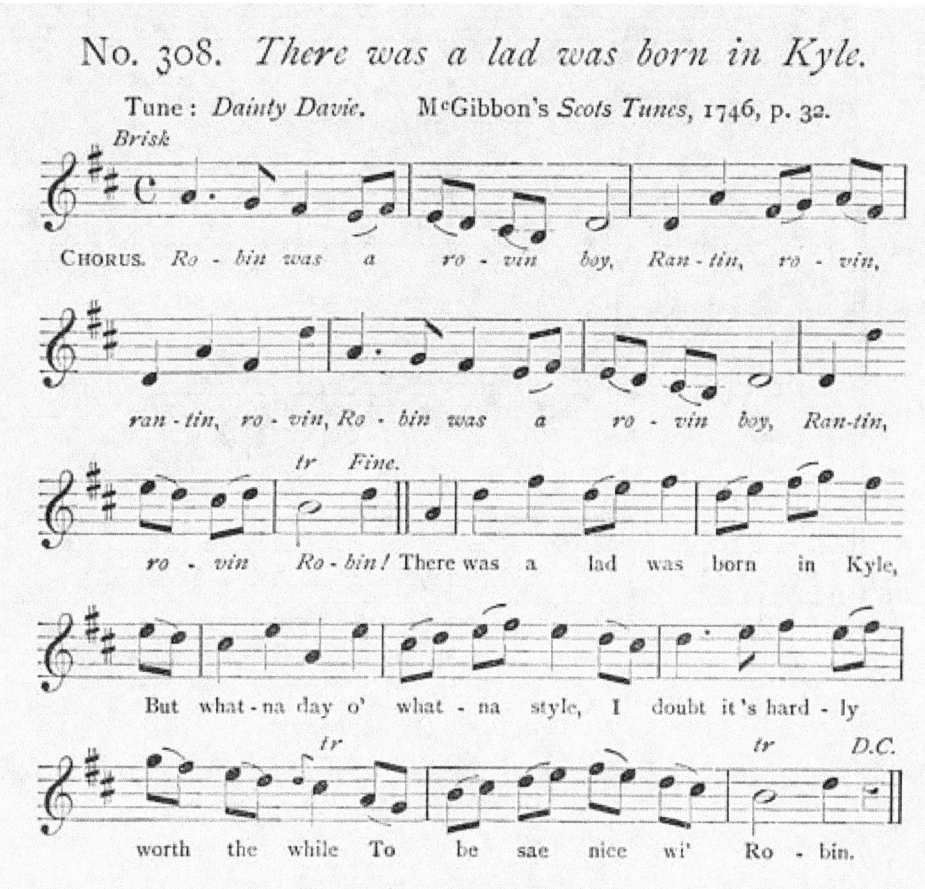

No. 308. *There was a lad was born in Kyle.*

Tune: *Dainty Davie.*   McGibbon's *Scots Tunes*, 1746, p. 32.

CHORUS. Ro - bin was a ro - vin boy, Ran - tin, ro - vin, ran - tin, ro - vin, Ro - bin was a ro - vin boy, Ran - tin, ro - vin Ro - bin! There was a lad was born in Kyle, But what - na day o' what - na style, I doubt it's hard - ly worth the while To be sae nice wi' Ro - bin.

CHORUS. *Robin was a rovin boy,*
Rantin, rovin, rantin, rovin,
Robin was a rovin boy,
Rantin, rovin Robin!

THERE was a lad was born in Kyle,
But whatna day o' whatna style,
I doubt it's hardly worth the while
   To be sae nice wi' Robin.

Our monarch's hindmost year but
      ane
Was five-and-twenty days begun,
'Twas then a blast o' Janwar win'
   Blew hansel in on Robin.

The gossip keekit in his loof,
Quo'scho 'wha lives will see the proof,
This waly boy will be nae coof;
   I think we'll ca' him Robin.

'He'll hae misfortunes great an'sma',
But ay a heart aboon them a';
He'll be a credit till us a';
   W'll a' be proud o' Robin.

'But sure as three times three mak
      nine,
I see by ilka score and line,
This chap will dearly like our kin',
   So leeze me on thee, Robin.'

Guid faith, quo' scho, I doubt you, sir,
Ye gar the lasses lie aspar,
But twenty fauts ye may hae waur, —
   So blessins on thee, Robin!

U

Reprint of the original version of There Was A Lad Was Born In Kyle

48

There Was A Lad Was Born In Kyle - Original Version

Robert Burns

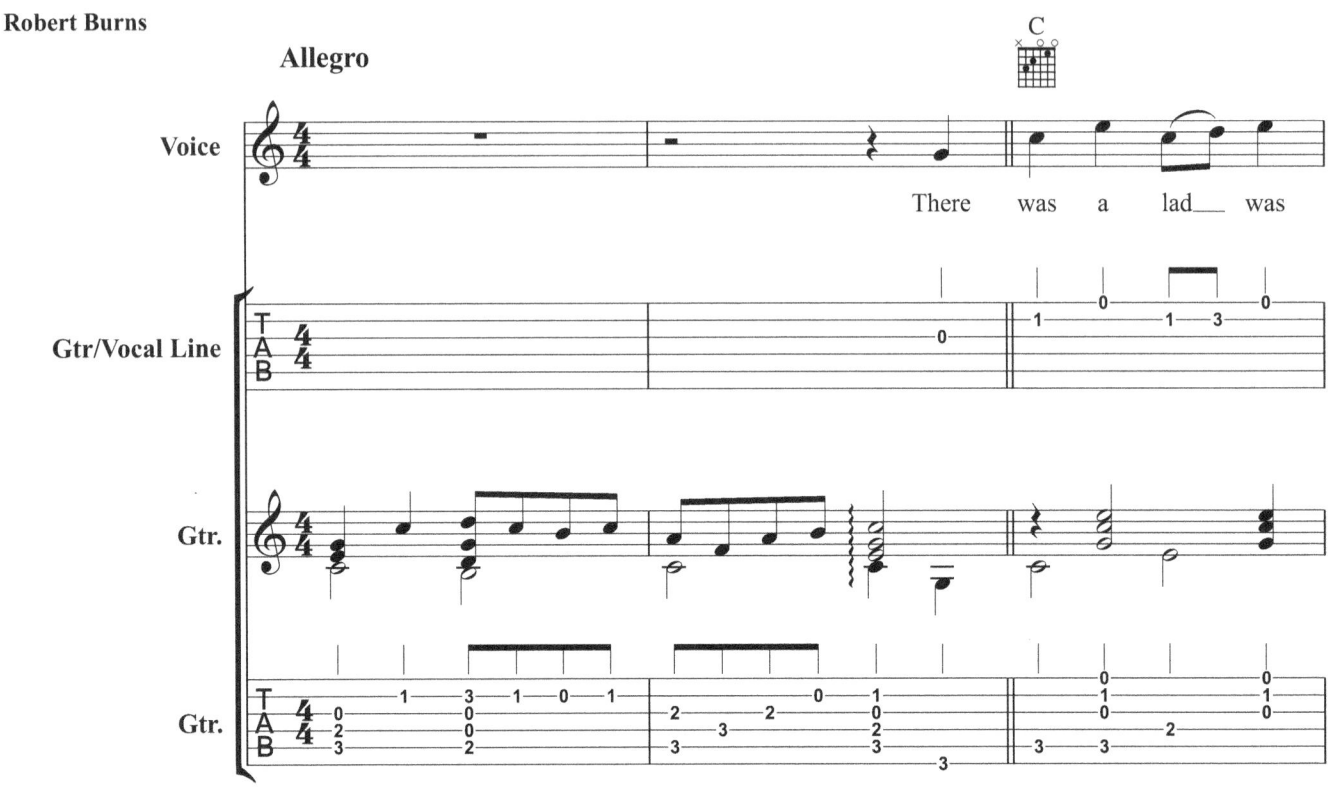

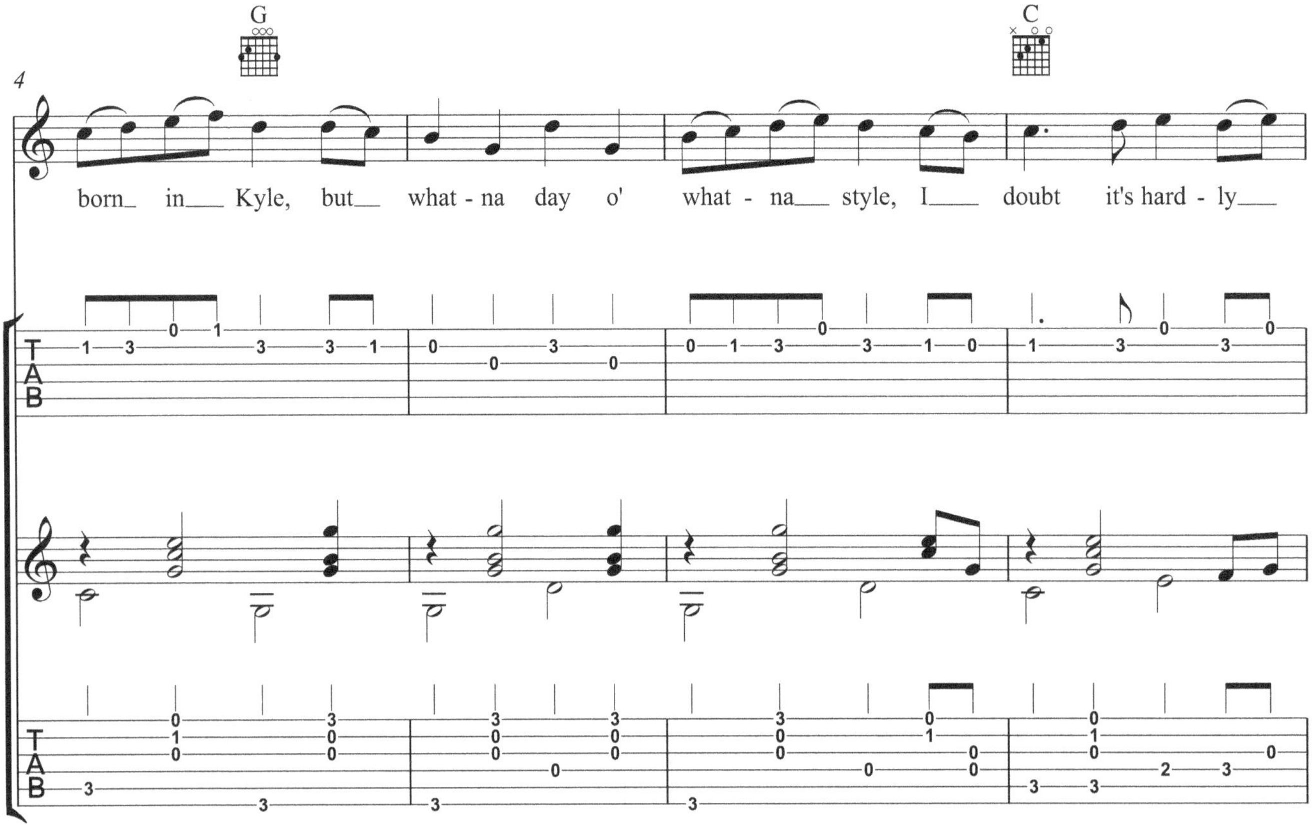

born__ in__ Kyle, but__ what-na day o' what-na__ style, I__ doubt it's hard-ly__

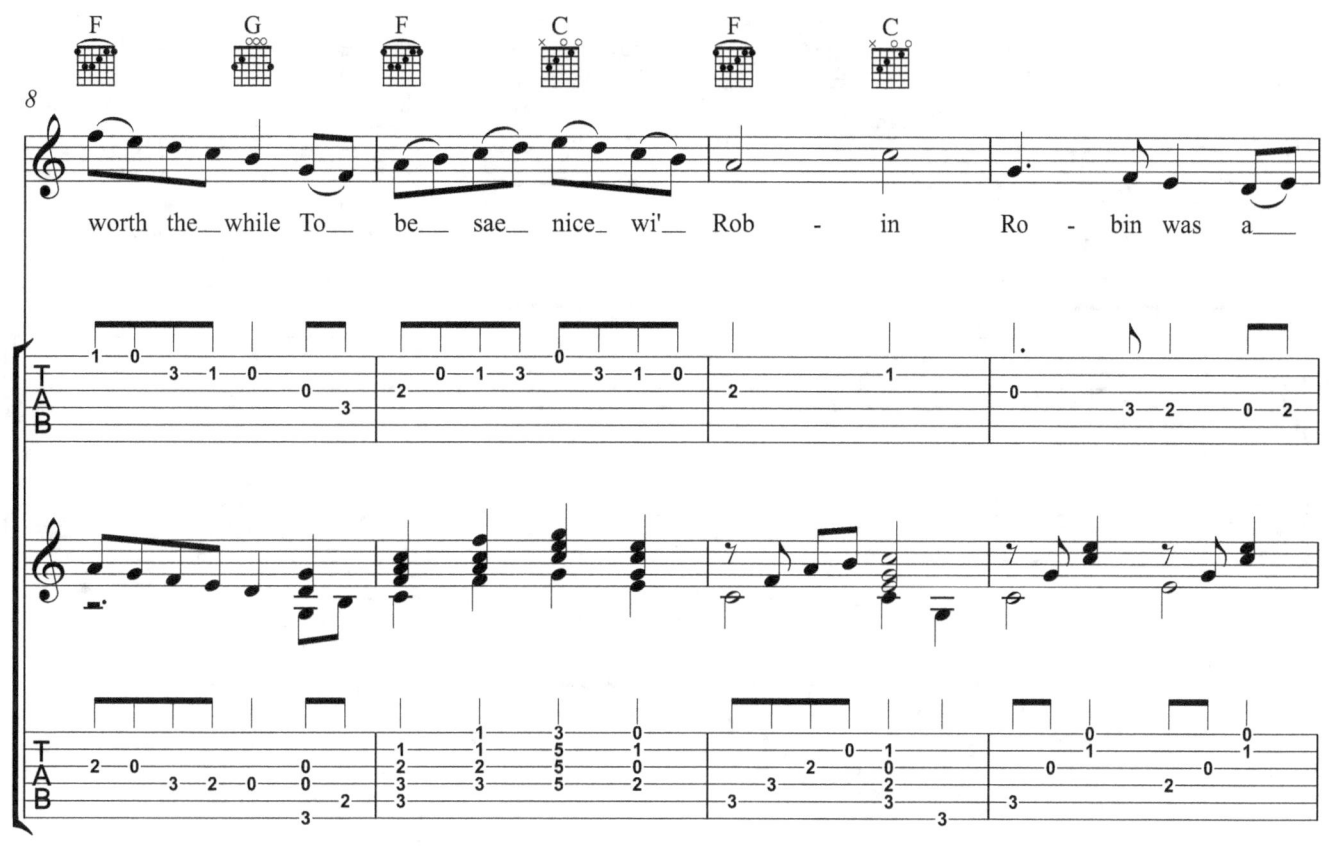

worth the__while To__ be__ sae__ nice_ wi'__ Rob - in   Ro - bin was a__

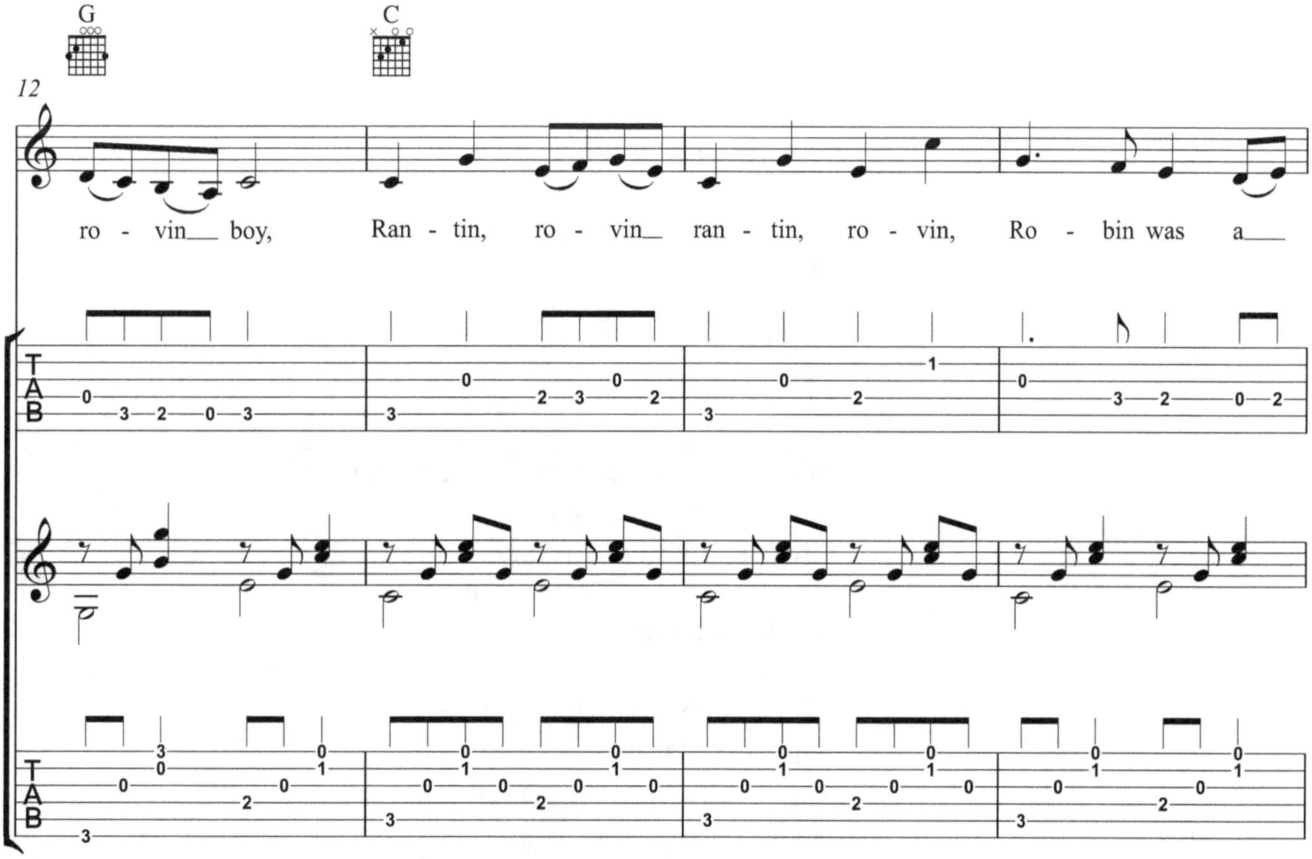

ro - vin__ boy,   Ran - tin, ro - vin__ ran - tin, ro - vin, Ro - bin was a__

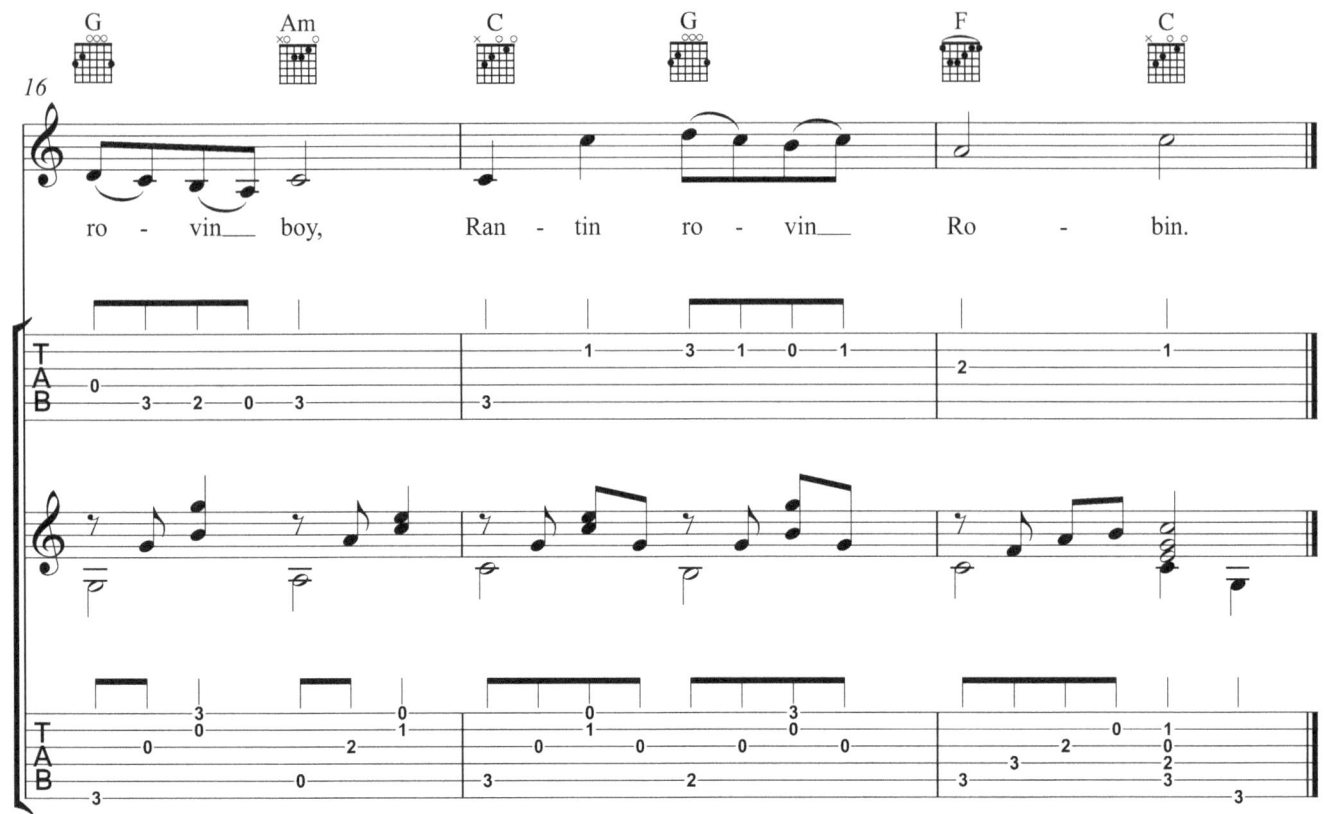

ro - vin__ boy, Ran - tin ro - vin__ Ro - bin.

Our monarch's hindmost year but ane
Was five-and-twenty days begun,
'Twas then a blast o' Janwar' win'
Blew hansel in on Robin.
For Robin was etc.

The gossip keekit in his loof,
Quo' scho:- ' Wha lives will see the proof,
This waly boy will be nae coof:
I think we'll ca' him Robin.
For Robin was etc.

'He'll hae misfortunes great an' sma',
But ay a heart aboon them a'.
He'll be a credit till us a':
We'll a' be proud o' Robin!
For Robin was etc.

' But sure as three times three mak nine,
I see by ilka score and line,
This chap will dearly like our kin',
So leeze me on thee, Robin!
For Robin was etc.

' Guid faith,' quo sho, ' I doubt you gar
The bonie lassies lie aspar;
But twenty fauts ye may hae waur -
So blessins on thee, Robin!'
For Robin was etc.

There Was A Lad Was Born In Kyle

Robert Burns

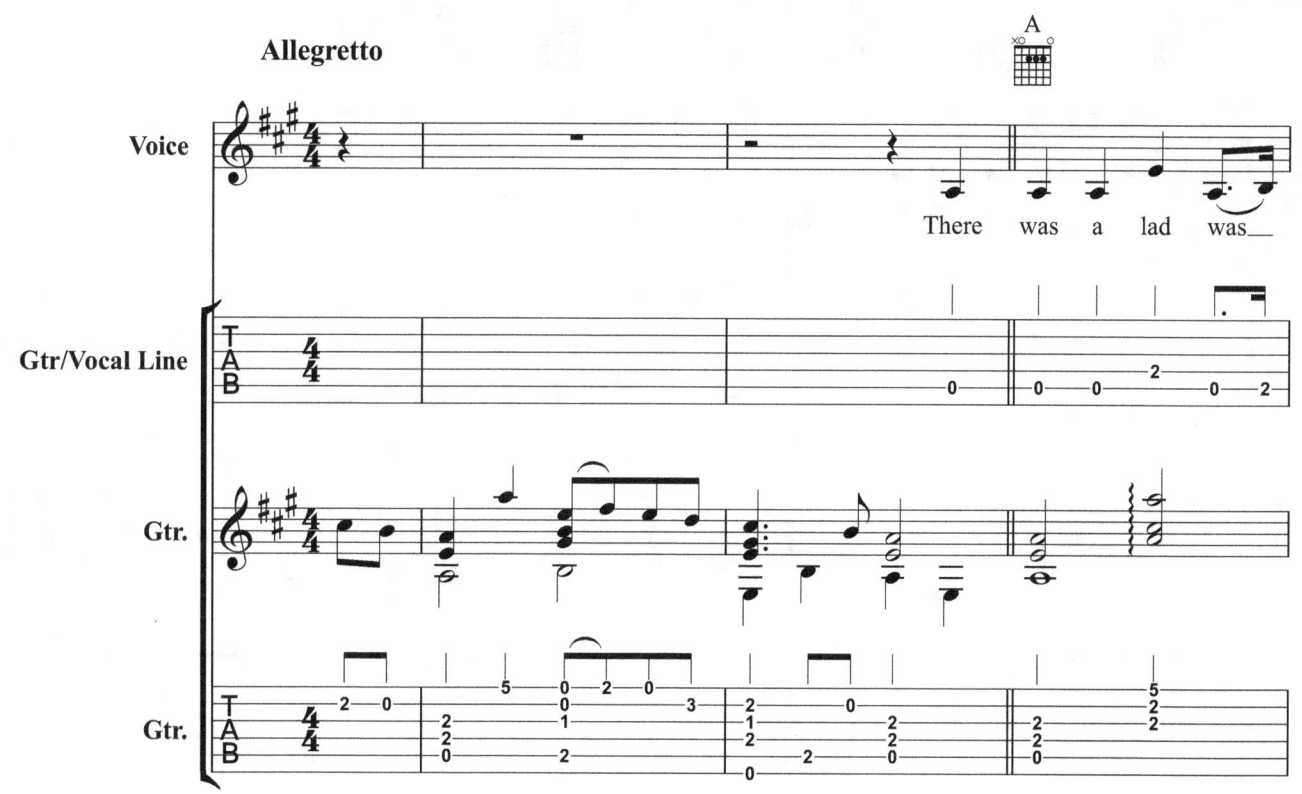

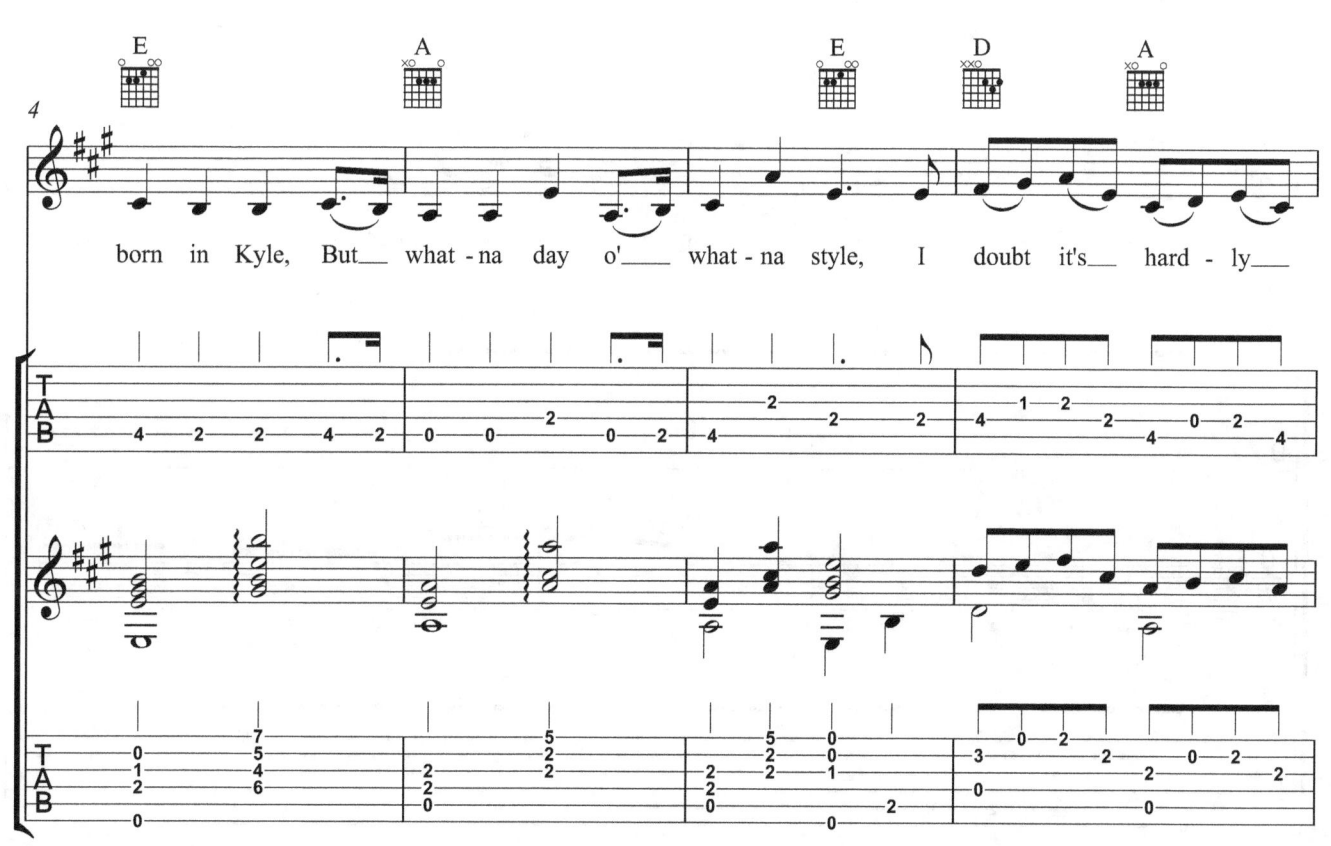

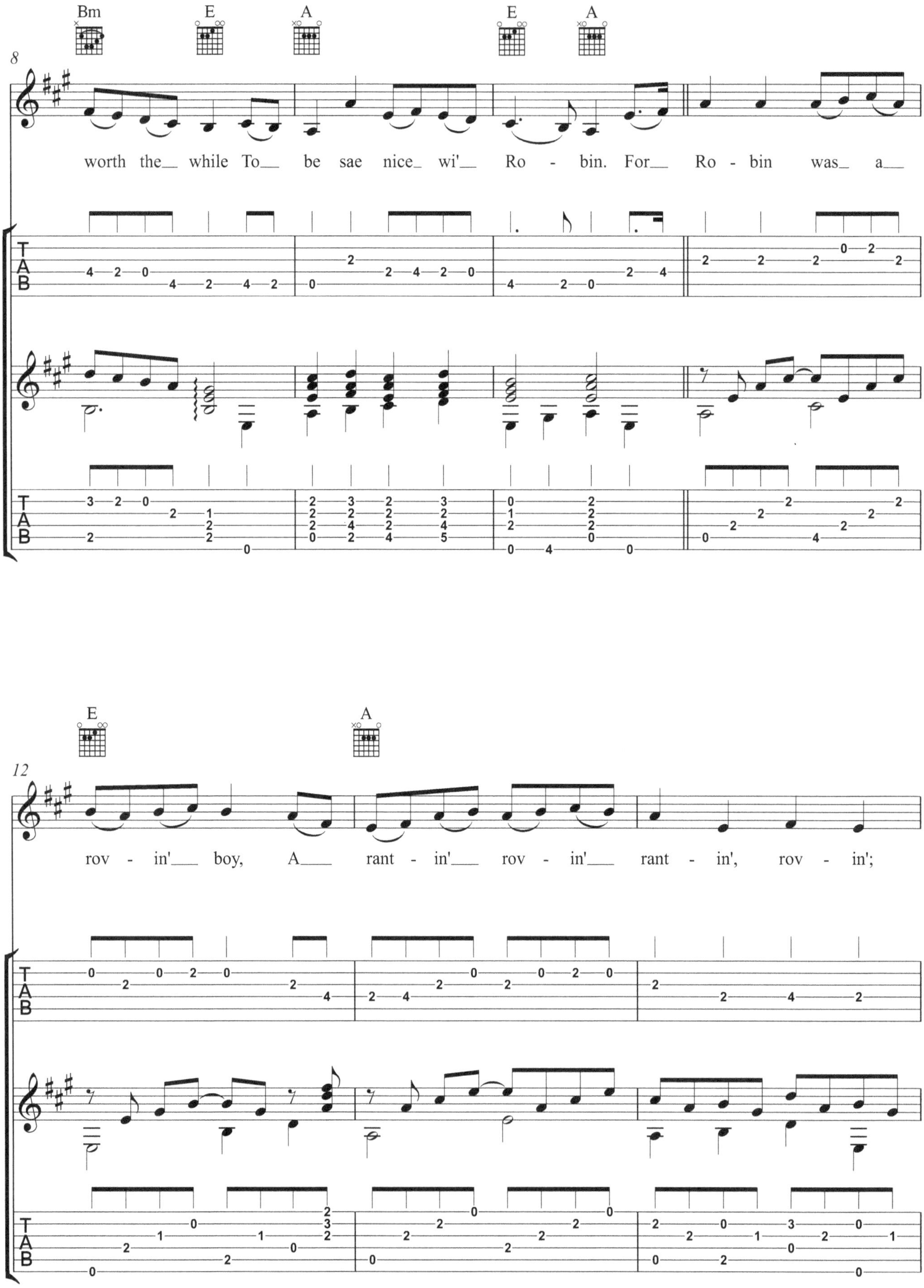

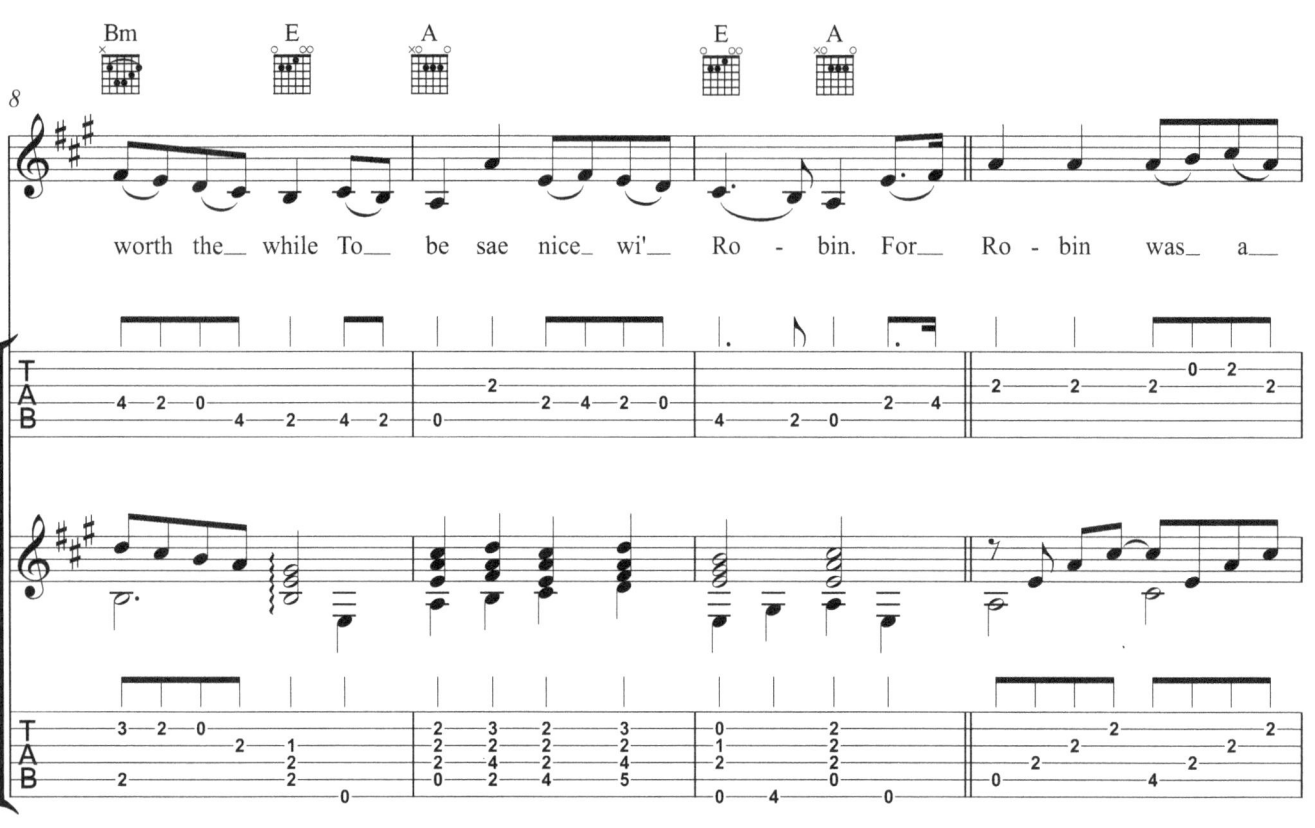

worth the__ while To__ be sae nice__ wi'__ Ro - bin. For__ Ro - bin was__ a__

rov - in'__ boy, A__ rant - in'__ rov - in'__ rant - in', rov - in';

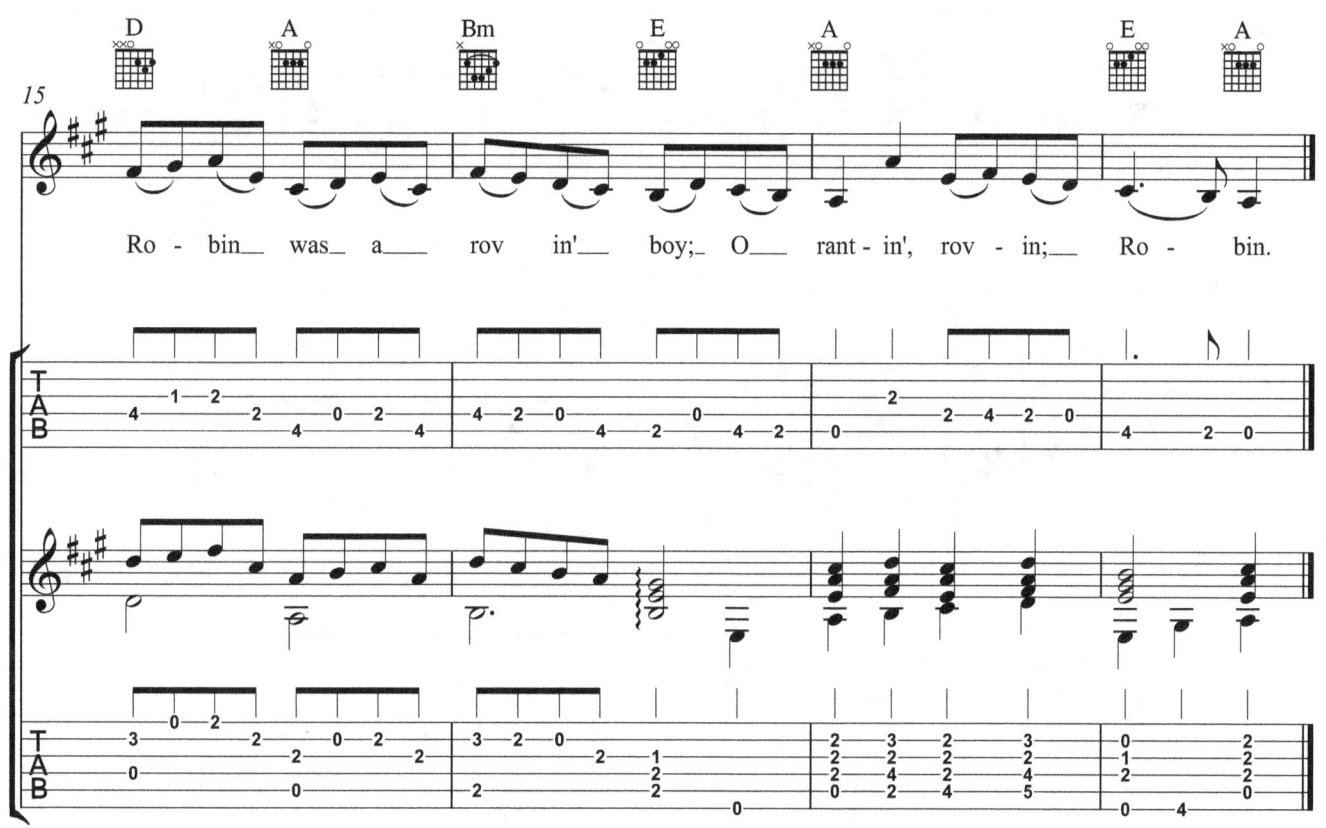

Ro - bin_ was_ a_ rov in'_ boy;_ O_ rant - in', rov - in;_ Ro - bin.

Our monarch's hindmost year but ane
Was five-and-twenty days begun,
'Twas then a blast o' Janwar' win'
Blew hansel in on Robin.
For Robin was etc.

The gossip keekit in his loof
Quo scho: "Wha lives will see the proof,
This waly boy will be nae coof:
I think we'll ca' him Robin.
For Robin was etc.

"He'll hae misfortunes great an' sma',
But ay a heart aboon them a',
He'll be a credit till us a':
We'll a' be proud o' Robin!
For Robin was etc.

"But sure as three times three mak nine,
I see by ilka score and line,
This chap will dearly like our kin',
So leeze me on thee Robin!
For Robin was etc.

Scots Wha Ha'e

Robert Burns

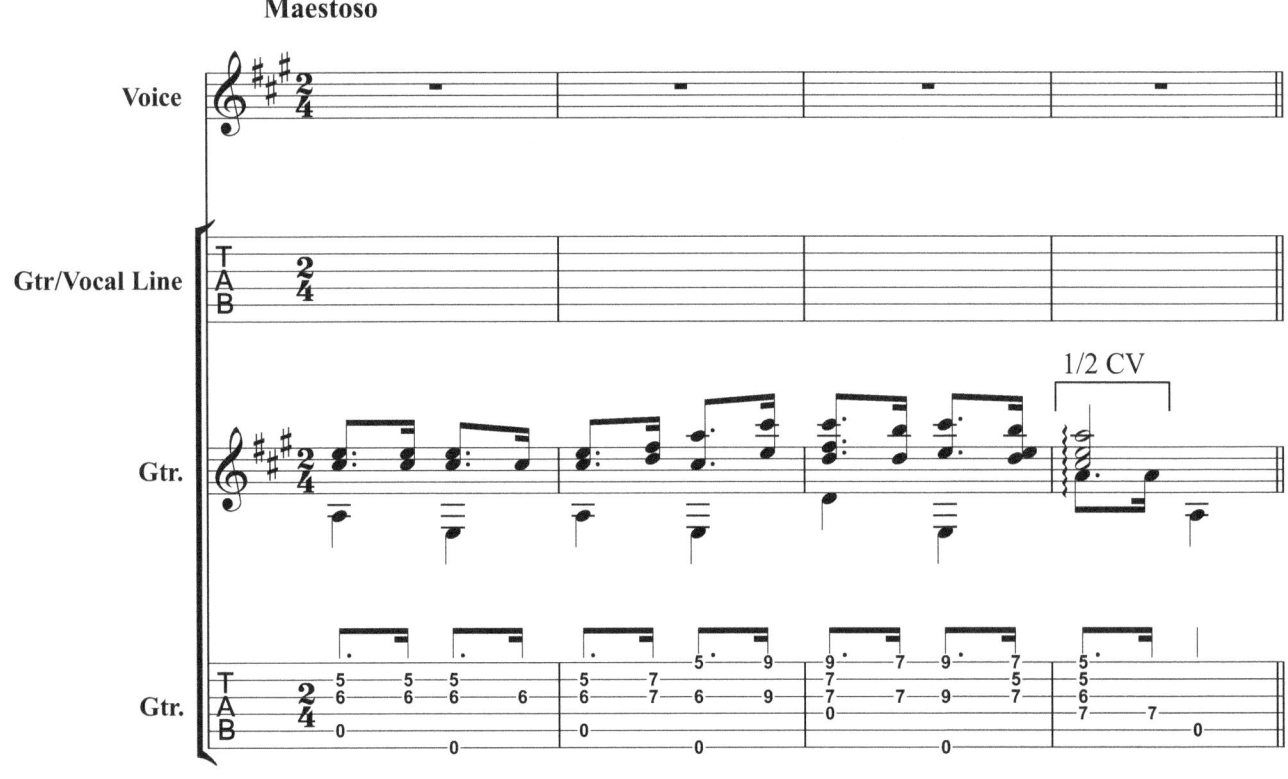

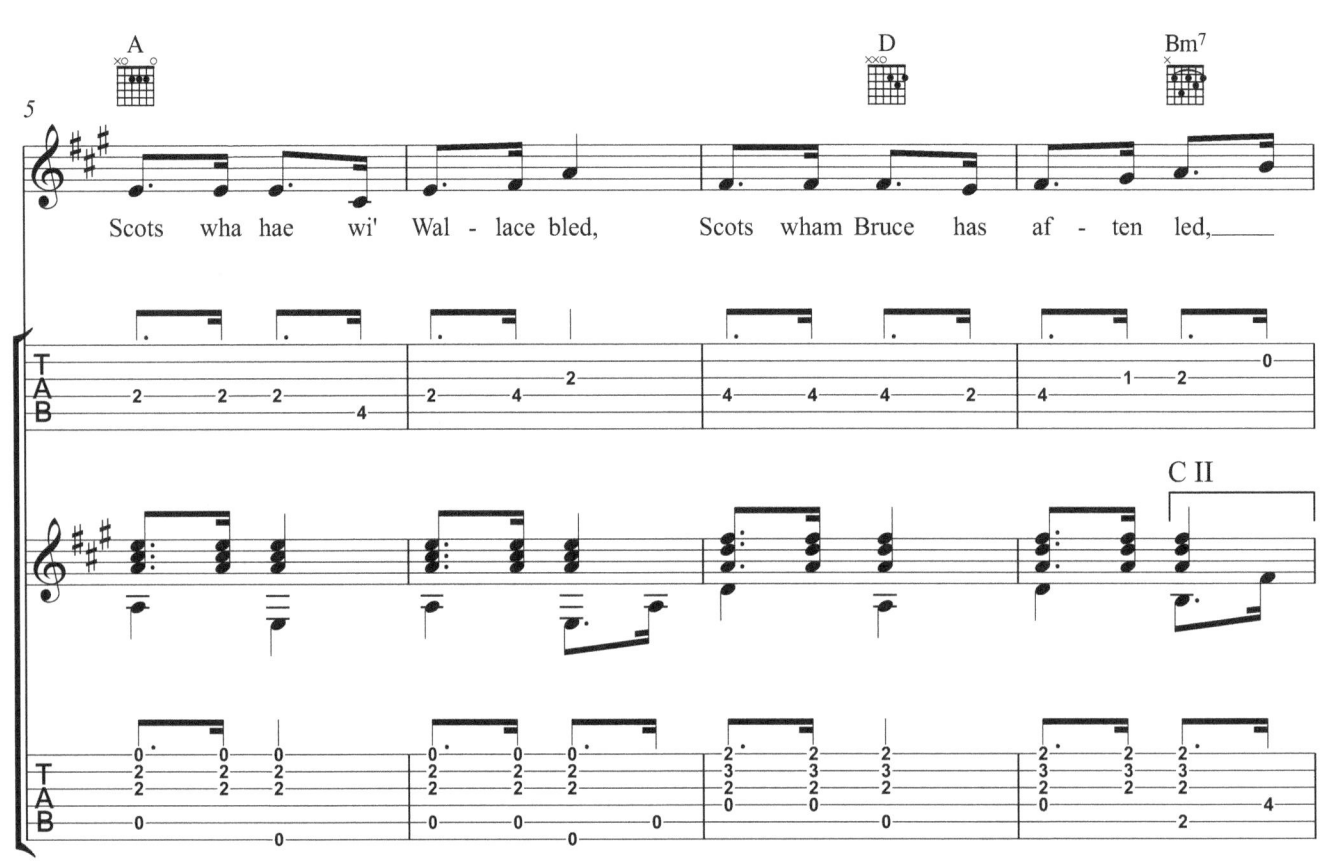

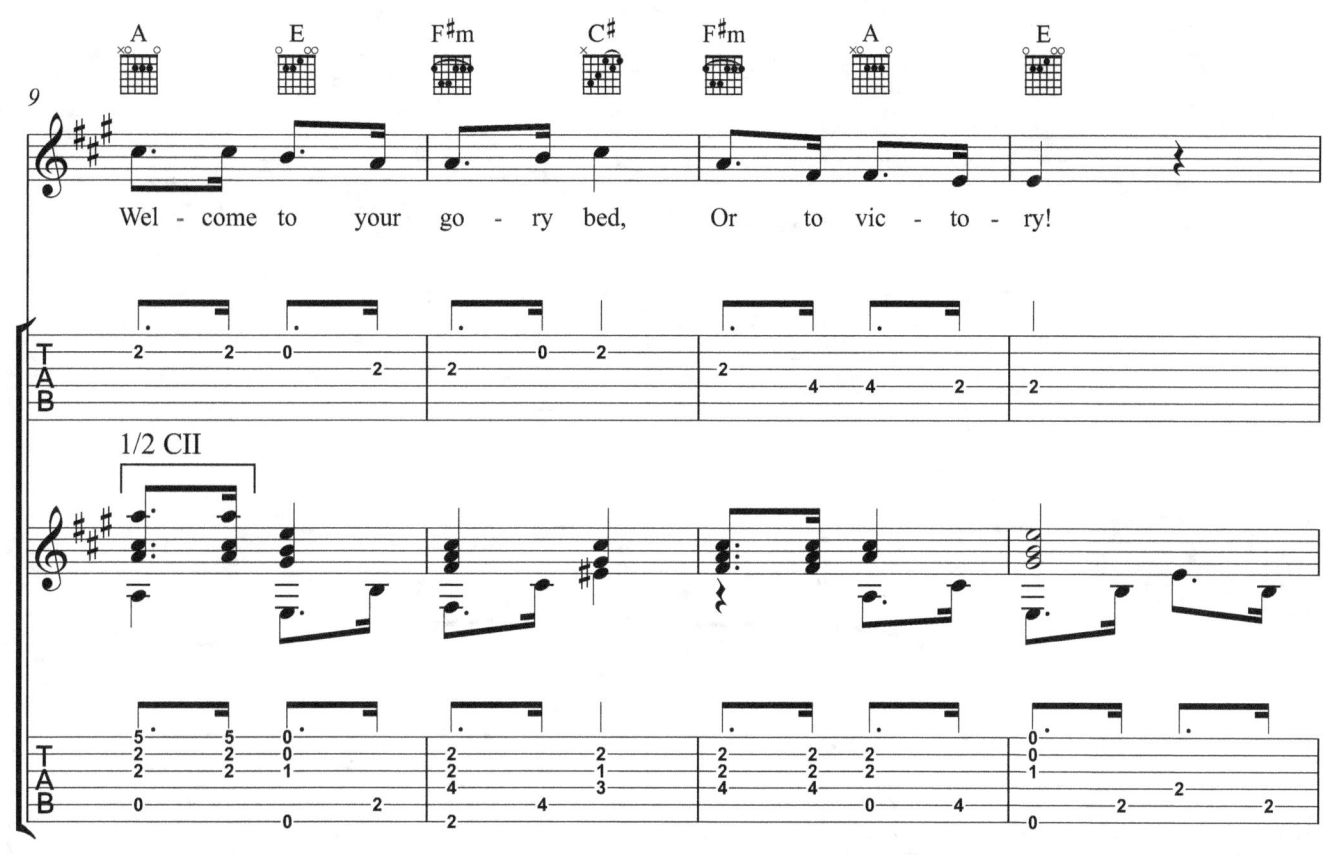

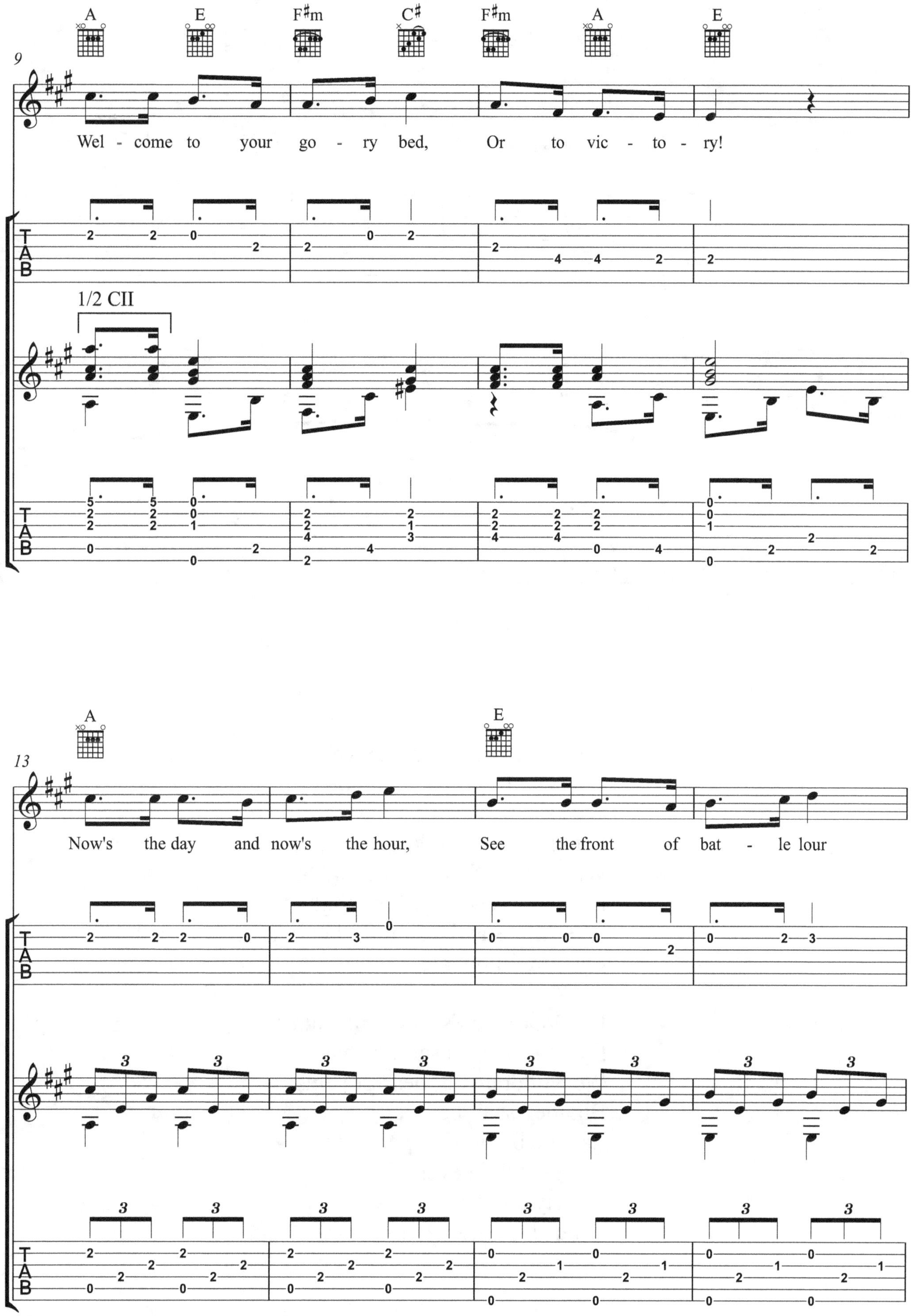

Wel - come to your go - ry bed, Or to vic - to - ry!

Now's the day and now's the hour, See the front of bat - le lour

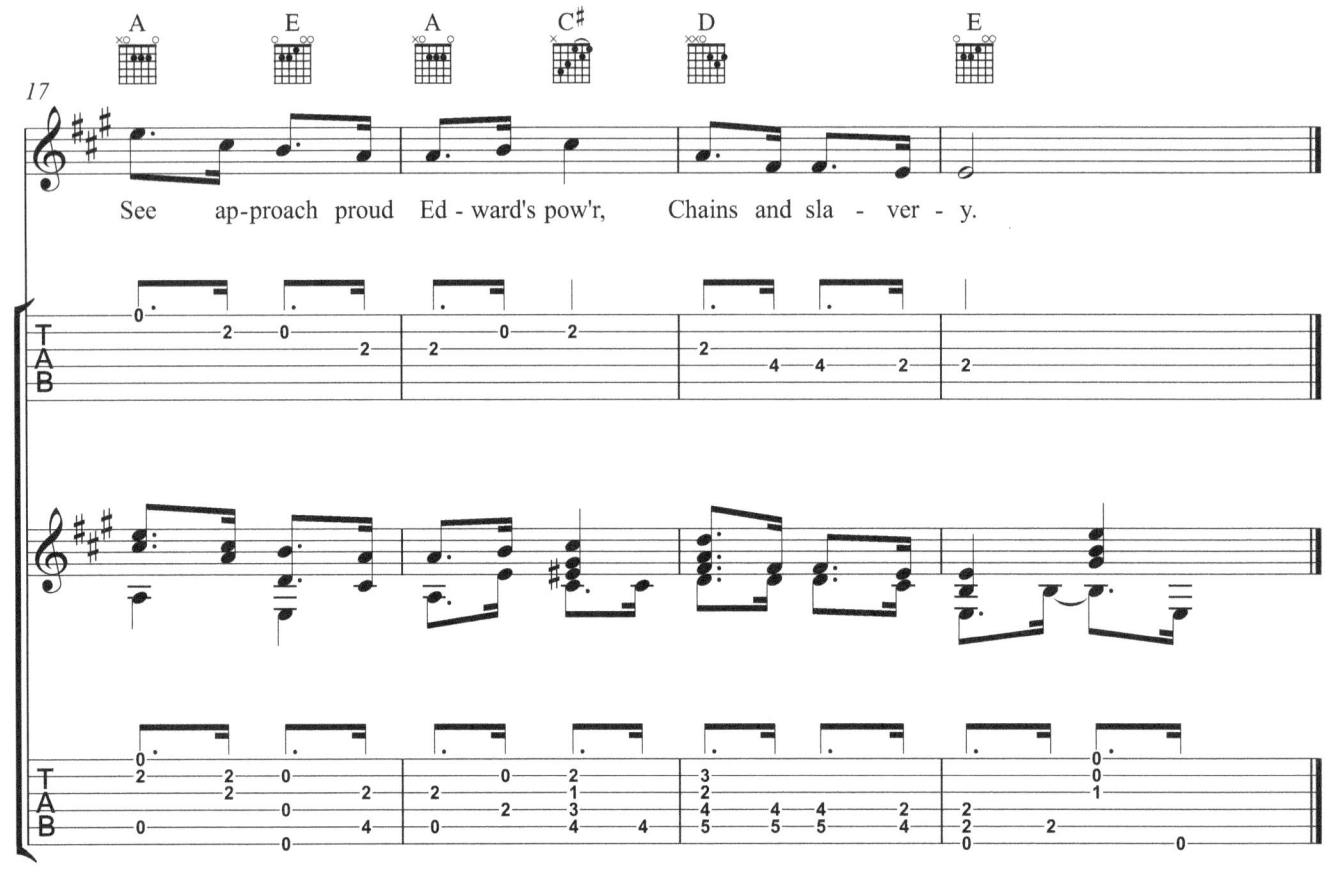

Wha will be a traitor-knave?
Wha can fill a cowards' grave?
Wha sae base as be a Slave?
Let him turn and flee.
Wha for Scotland's king and law,
Freedom's sword will strongly draw,
Free-Man stand, or Free-Man fa',
Let him follow me.—

By Oppression's woes and pains!
By your Sons in servile chains!
We will drain our dearest veins,
But they shall be free!
Lay the proud Usurpers low!
Tyrants fall in every foe!
Liberty's in every blow!
Let us Do — or Die!

Robt Burns was born at Alloway, in the parish of Ayr — Jan.ry 25th 1759 —

Jean Armour his wife was born at Mauchline Feb.ry 27th 1767 —

Sepr 3d 1786 were born to them twins, Robert, their eldest Son, at a quarter past Noon & Jean since dead at fourteen months old — March 3d 1788 were born to them twins again, two daughters who died within a few days after their birth. — August 18th 1789 was born to them, Francis Wallace; so named after Mrs Dunlop of Dunlop; he was born a quarter before seven, forenoon — April 9th 1791 between three & four in the morning, was born to them William Nicol; so named after Willm Nicol of the High School Edinr. — November 21st 1792 at a quarter past Noon, was born to them Elizabeth Riddel; so named after Mrs Robt Riddel of Glenriddel. —

Reproduction of Burns' Handwriting from His Family Bible

Ay Waukin O'

Robert Burns

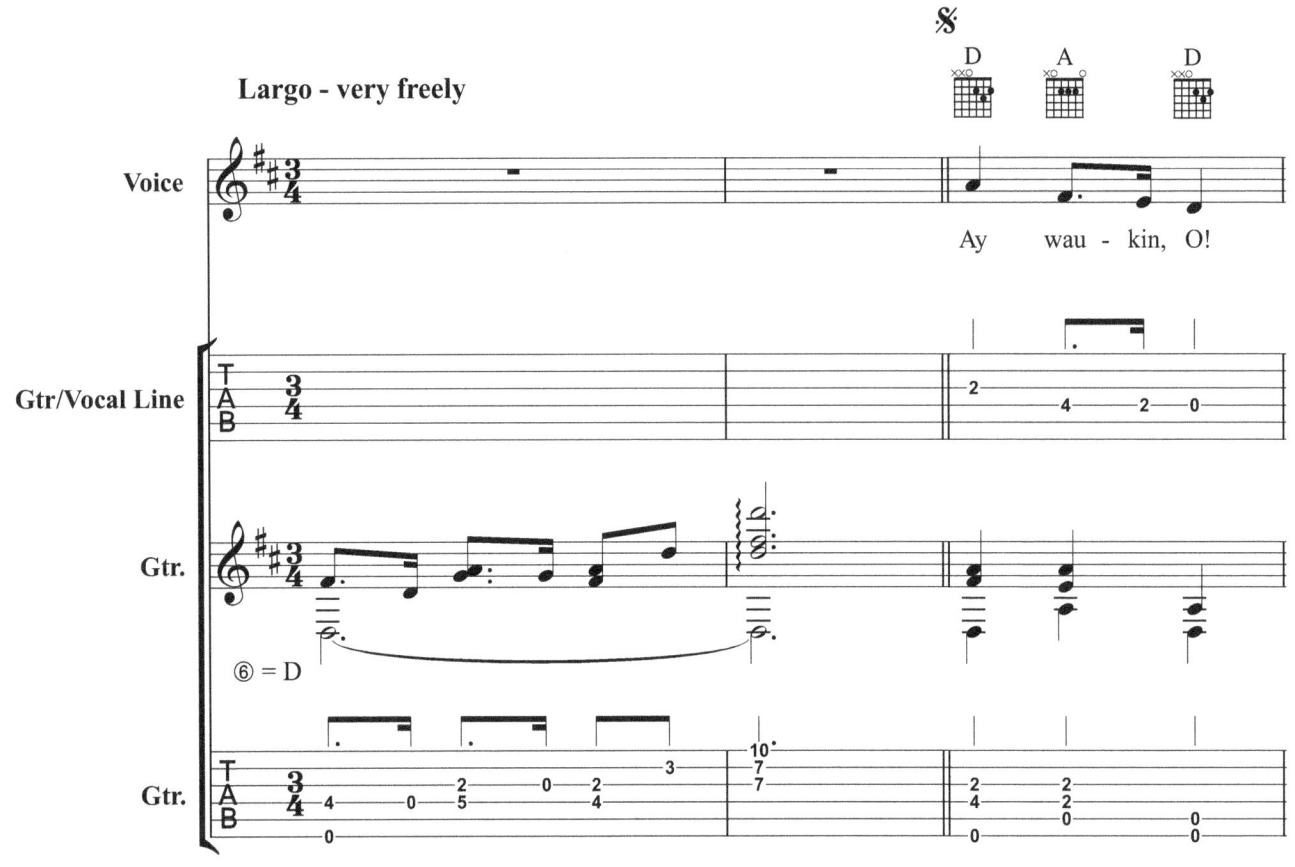

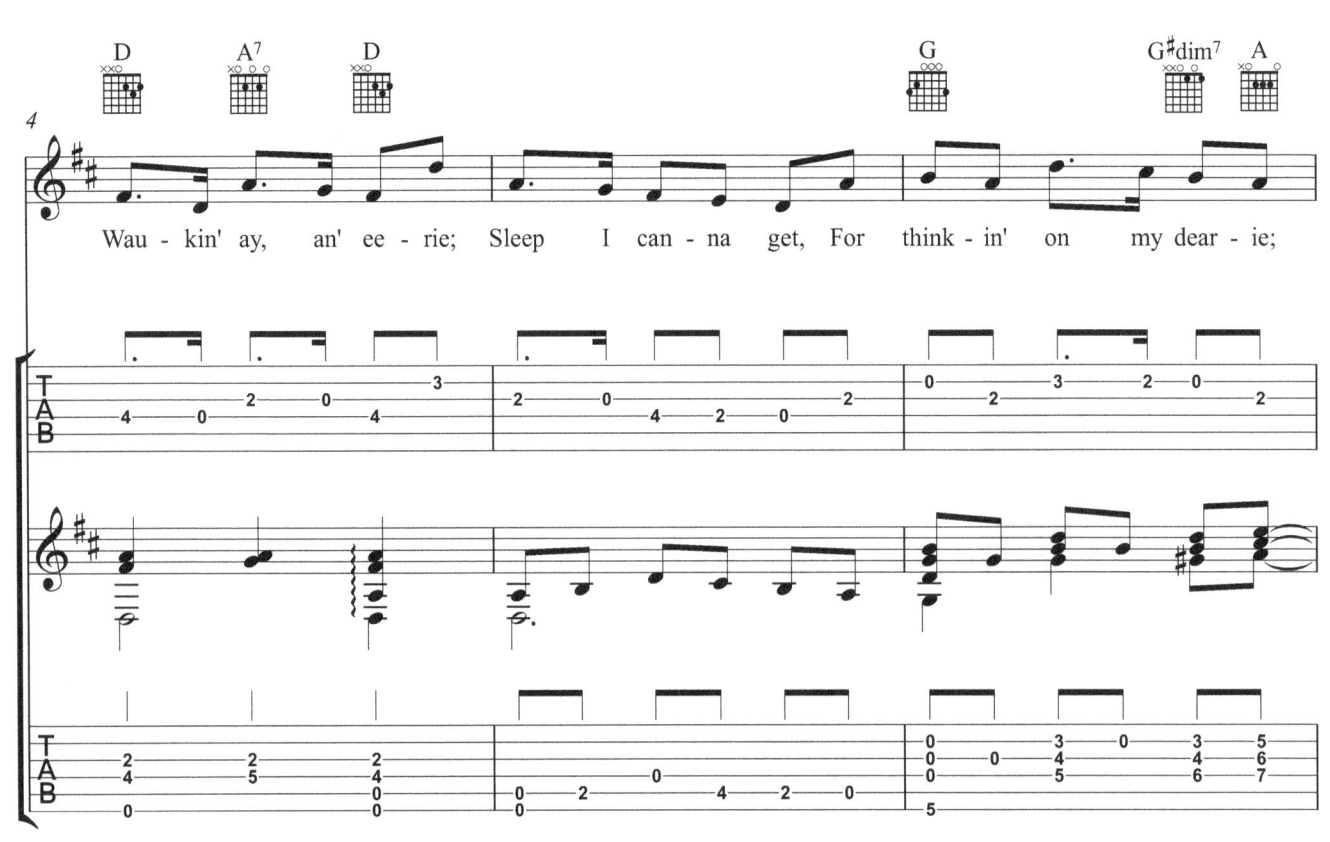

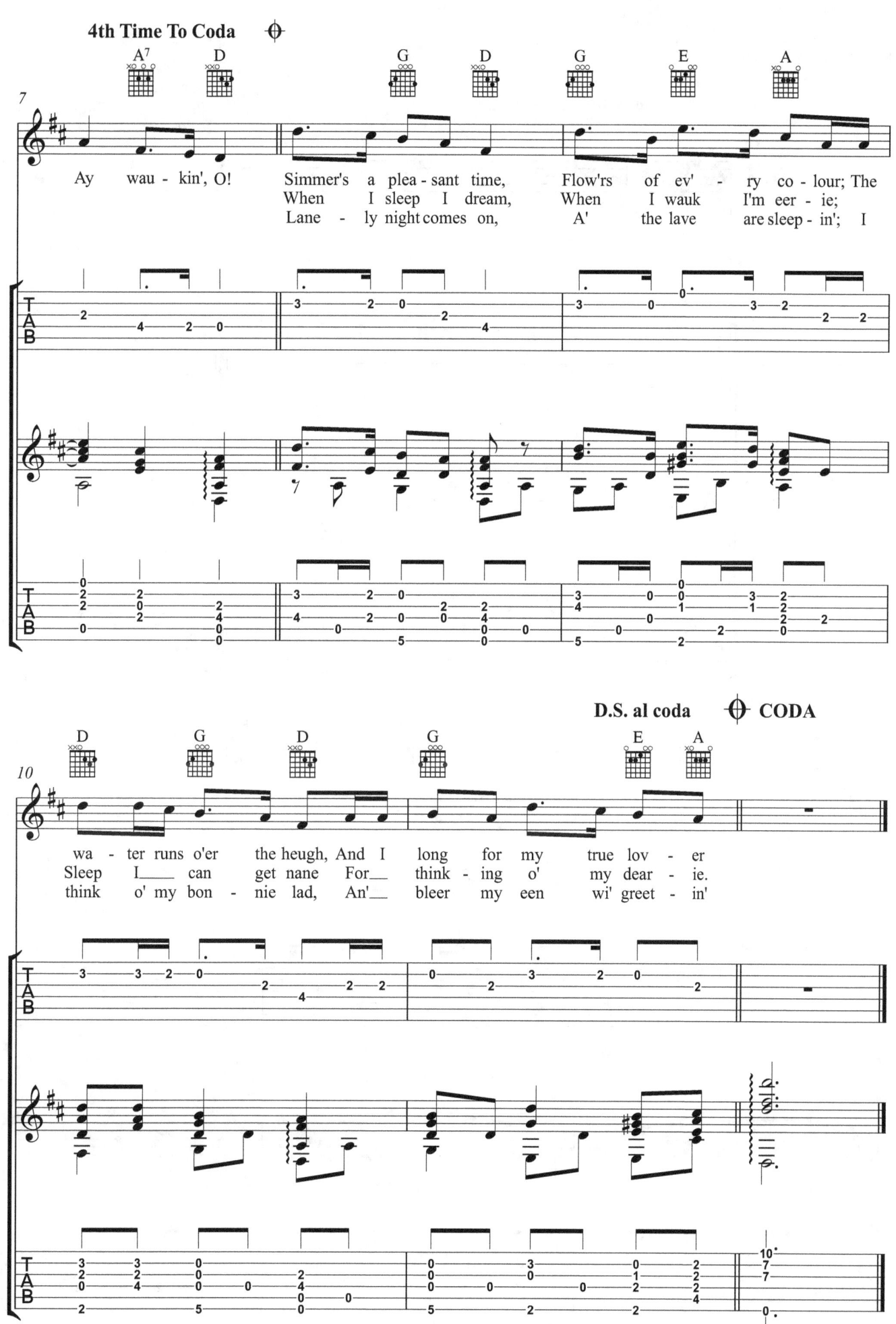

4th Time To Coda

Ay wau - kin', O! Simmer's a plea - sant time, Flow'rs of ev' - ry co - lour; The
When I sleep I dream, When I wauk I'm eer - ie;
Lane - ly night comes on, A' the lave are sleep - in'; I

D.S. al coda **CODA**

wa - ter runs o'er the heugh, And I long for my true lov - er
Sleep I can get nane For think - ing o' my dear - ie.
think o' my bon - nie lad, An' bleer my een wi' greet - in'

Up In The Early Morning

Robert Burns

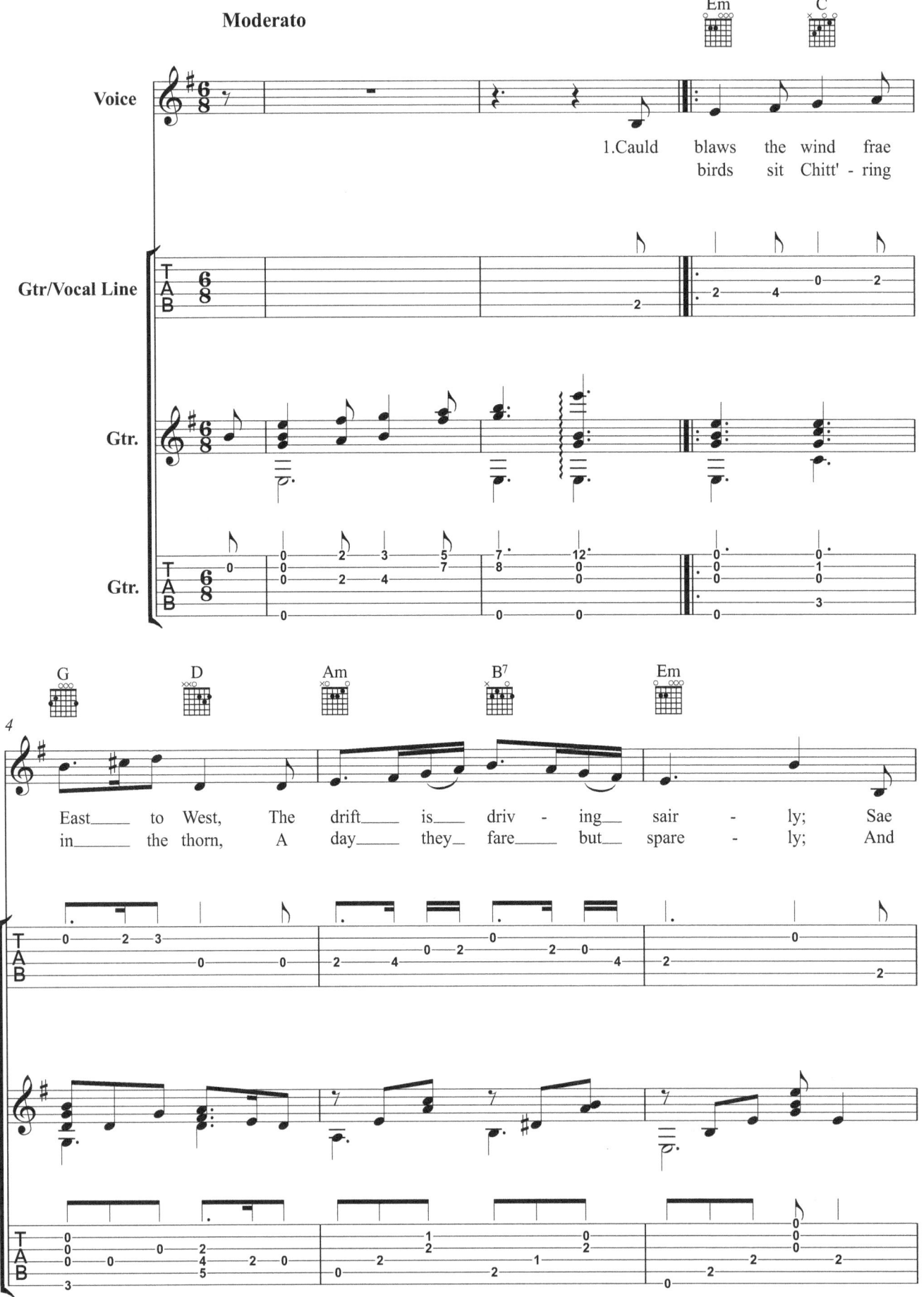

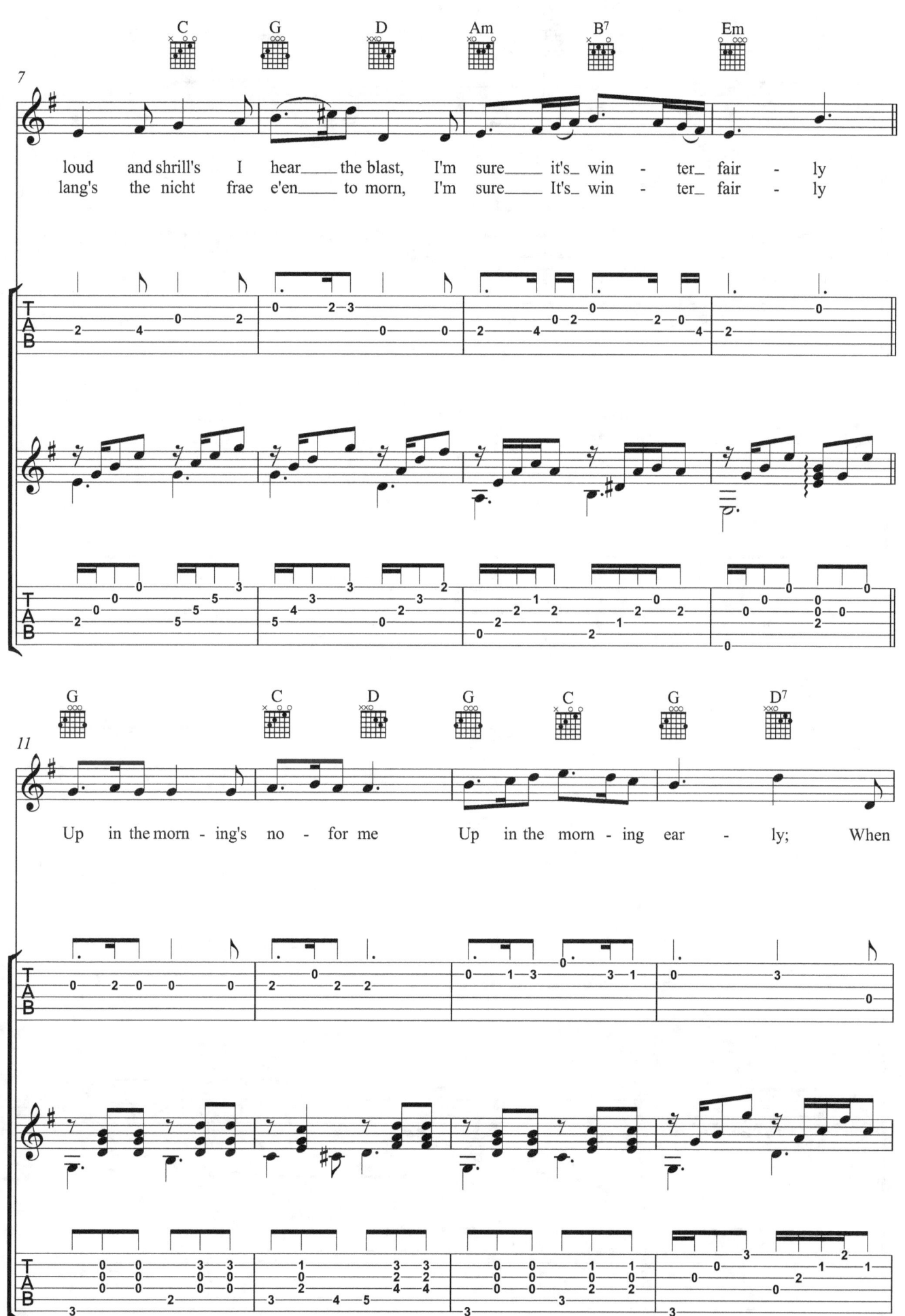

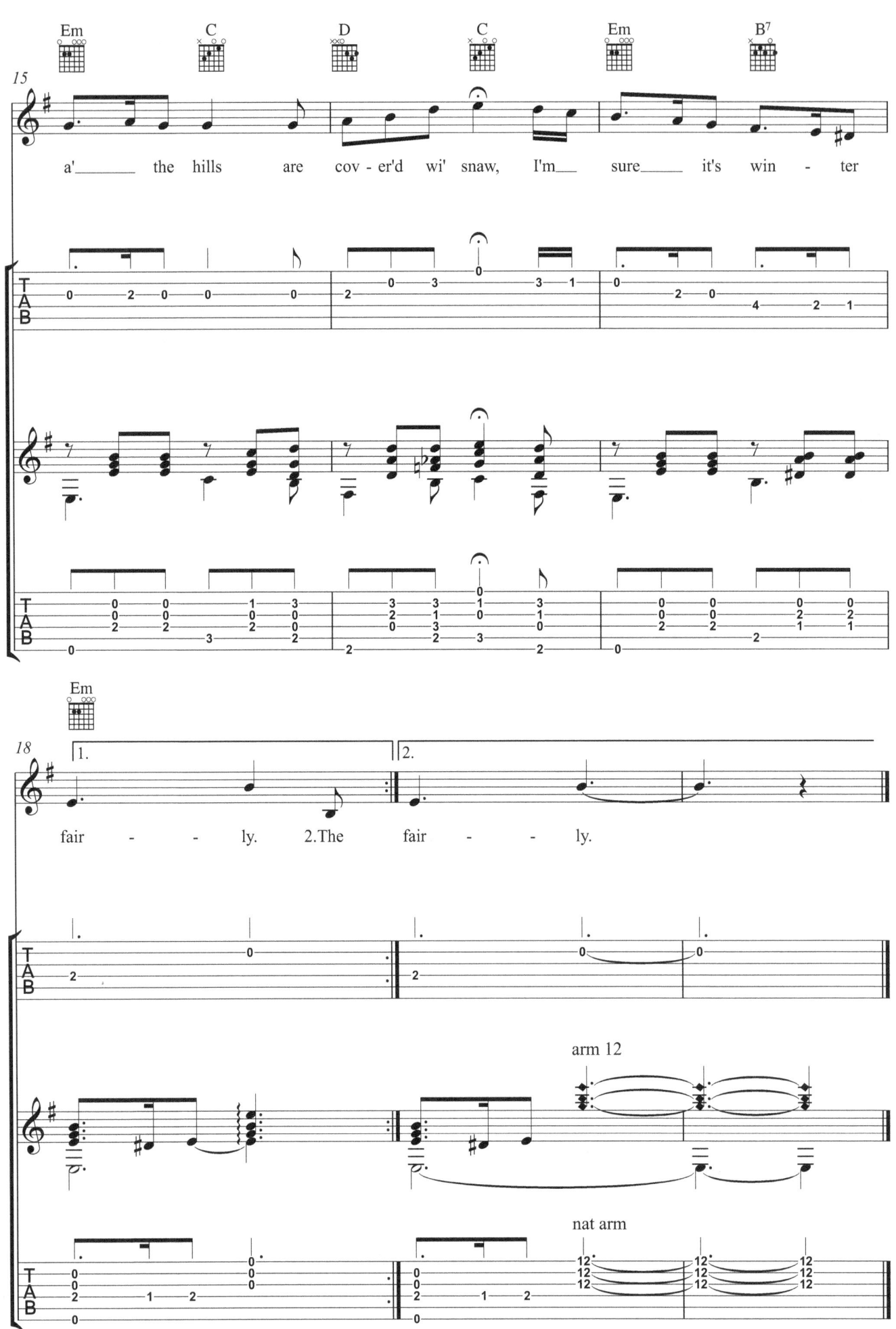

Glossary of Words Used in the Songs

A' – all

Aboon - above

Aft or Aften – oft/often

Amang – among

An – and

Ane - one

Ay – always

Bonie – handsome/pretty

Braw - handsome

Burnie – burn/small river

But - without

Bleer – blur

Blin' – blind

Bluidy - bloody

But – without

Brak - broke

Braw – handsome

Breeks - breeches

Cam - came

Cauf-leather – calf leather

Cauld – cold

Chittering - shivering

Daw – dawn

Deave – deafen

Droukit - wetted

Drumlie - muddy

Dwalt - dwelt

Eeen - eyes

Eye – before

Frae - from

Fu' - full

Gaed – went

Gang – to go

Gied – gave

Gif – if

Gin - if

Greet – weep

Gude - good

Hae - have

Heugh – hollow

Hunder – a hundred

I'se – I shall

Ken – know

Lee-Land – live long

Mae – more

Mak – make

Maun - must

Nae – not

Lave – rest/remainder

Lift – sky

Lo'ed – loved

Loun – a fellow

Maunna – must not

Minnie – mother

Mou' - mouth

Na - not

Naething – nothing

Nane – none

O' – of

Or – before

Poortith - poverty

Row - roll

Sae - so

Sair - strong

Sall - shall

Simmer – summer

Sin – since

Tint – lost

Quo - said

Wad – would

Wadna – would not

Weal - welfare

Waukin – waking

Weel – well

Wha – who

Wham – whom

Whatna - what

Wha's – who's

Wi' – with

Wimple – meander

Wrang - wrong

Ye'se – you shall

Yestreen – last night

Yon – yonder

Yowes - ewes

Ukulele Chord Diagrams for Songs in this Book

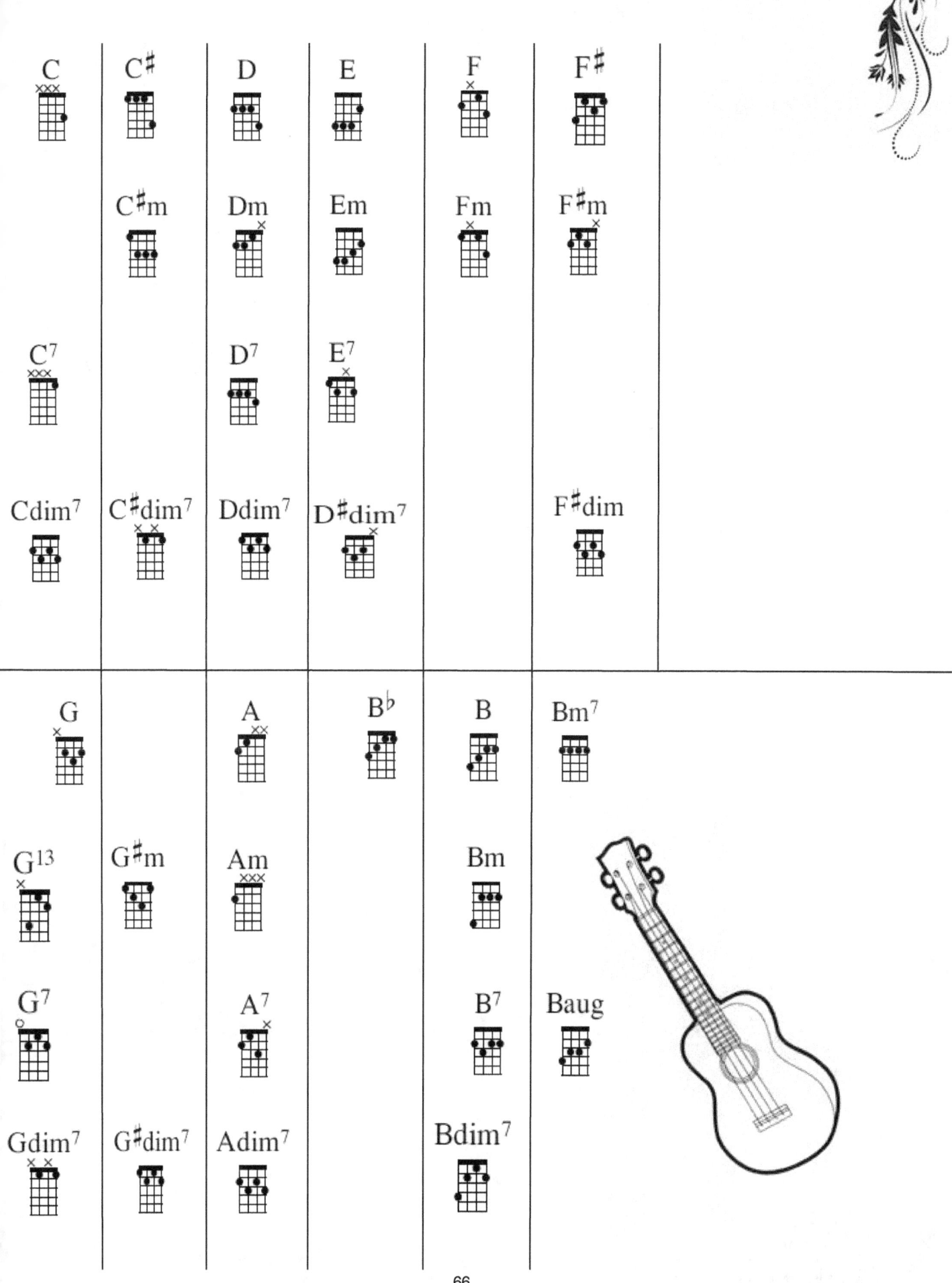

www.ingramcontent.com/pod-product-compliance
Lightning Source LLC
Chambersburg PA
CBHW081100180526
45170CB00005B/1833